MW01155919

With Malice Toward Some: ⸺ ⸺ ⸺
ments addresses an issue integral to democratic societies: how people faced with a complex variety of considerations decide whether or not to tolerate extremist groups. Relying on several survey-experiments, Marcus, Sullivan, Theiss-Morse, and Wood identify and compare the impact on decision making of contemporary information, long-standing predispositions, and enduring values and beliefs. The authors show that citizens have powerful predispositions and values that directly affect tolerance and how they respond to contemporary information, but that situational and contextual information directly influence their judgments in important ways as well. Citizens react most strongly to information about a group's violations of behavioral norms, and to information about the implications for democracy of the group's actions. The authors conclude that democratic citizens should have a strong baseline of tolerance, yet be attentive to and thoughtful about contemporary information.

With Malice Toward Some

This series has been established in recognition of the growing sophistication in the resurgence of interest in political psychology and the study of public opinion. Its focus ranges from the kinds of mental processes that people employ when they think about democratic processes and make political choices, to the nature and consequences of macro-level public opinion.

Some of the works will draw on developments in cognitive and social psychology, and on relevant areas of philosophy. Appropriate subjects include the use of heuristics, the roles of core values and moral principles in political reasoning, the effects of expertise and sophistication, the roles of affect and emotion, and the nature of cognition and information processing. The emphasis will be on systematic and rigorous empirical analysis, and a wide range of methodologies will be appropriate: traditional surveys, experimental surveys, laboratory experiments, focus groups, in-depth interviews, as well as others. These empirically oriented studies will also consider normative implications for democratic politics generally.

Politics, not psychology, will be the primary focus, and most works will deal with mass publics and democratic politics, although work on nondemocratic publics will not be excluded. Other works will examine traditional topics in public-opinion research and will contribute to the growing literature on aggregate opinion and its role in democratic societies.

With Malice Toward Some

Some

HOW PEOPLE MAKE CIVIL LIBERTIES JUDGMENTS

George E. Marcus
Williams College

John L. Sullivan
University of Minnesota

Elizabeth Theiss-Morse
University of Nebraska

Sandra L. Wood
University of North Texas

CAMBRIDGE
UNIVERSITY PRESS

Published by the Press Syndicate of the University of Cambridge
The Pitt Building, Trumpington Street, Cambridge CB2 1RP
40 West 20th Street, New York, NY 10011-4211, USA
10 Stamford Road, Oakleigh, Melbourne 3166, Australia

© Cambridge University Press 1995

First published 1995

Printed in the United States of America

Library of Congress Cataloging-in-Publication Data applied for.

A catalog record for this book is available from the British Library.

ISBN 0-521-43396-7 hardback
ISBN 0-521-43997-3 paperback

Contents

v

Figures and Tables

vii

TABLES

Preface
Political Tolerance and Democratic Life

The late twentieth century has witnessed astonishing technological advances that make information readily and widely available. In fact, people today are bombarded with information, to the point of what some have referred to as "information overload." Political events are covered twenty-four hours a day by Cable News Network (CNN). Newspapers like *USA Today* inform us of these events in easily digestible pieces; some newspapers, such as the *Washington Post*, have news available on Internet, the new "information superhighway." At any time of the day or night we can delve into the mass of political information at our fingertips and discover what is happening in the world. Making decisions when faced with this great quantity of information is daunting.

This book details how people come to make decisions, specifically concerning civil liberties issues, in light of new information. Almost every day we are confronted with stories about actual or potential infractions against a certain people's rights. Hate crimes, such as cross burnings or the vandalism of Jewish cemeteries, are not uncommon, and the passage of hate-crime laws to deter further actions by racist groups has become popular. Clashes between prolife and prochoice groups, and especially the recent murders of doctors who perform abortions, regularly make headline news. The influx of Haitian and Cuban refugees increases tensions in parts of the United States. Incidents of gay bashing and antihomosexual activities have gained particularly intensive news coverage, partly because of recent measures voted on in Oregon and Colorado. We also hear frequently about problems outside the borders of the United States, such as the increasing anti-Semitism in former Soviet-bloc countries or anti-immigrant sentiments and actions in Europe.

When faced with so much information, upon what factors are people's decisions about civil liberties based? What makes some people decide to be tolerant toward a noxious group and other people intolerant? Information available in a particular situation is likely to be important, but certainly not all information will have the same impact. What kinds of contemporary information significantly influence tolerance judgments? Answering such a question is not easy, but the complexity of the problem increases when we take into account that people differ and may well bring to bear in any decision-making situation different convictions and sensibilities. People do not confront new information about a noxious group with a completely open, unbiased mind. Instead, this new information meets with existing prejudices and opinions, and it is the combination of these factors that go into the making of tolerance judgments.

Our task, then, is to determine how people make civil liberties decisions, which raises a number of questions: Which of the many potential long-standing values and beliefs most affect people's current tolerance judgments? What kinds of contemporary information are especially potent? How do long-standing forces condition how people process the information that confronts them? We unravel the web of intertwining influences on tolerance judgments in stages. We begin by developing our theoretical framework in Part I and then test it empirically in Part II (at the aggregate level) and Part III (at the individual level). Ultimately, however, we must move away from examining tolerance judgments themselves and take a broader look at the implications of our model, which we do in Part IV.

As do many research projects, ours benefited greatly from the help and suggestions of several people. Special thanks go to Kelly-Kate Pease for her work as research assistant on the Nebraska experiments, and especially for her invaluable help in gathering the adult data. We also acknowledge the valuable contribution of Marcus Flathman for inspiring some of the Minnesota experiments. Also, we thank our many research assistants who have worked on various experiments: Jim Bates, Angela Bowman, Jenny Chanley, Tonja Holder, Beth Nelson, and Jessica Olson. Jeffrey Gray was very helpful in offering his comments on early drafts, as were Jenny Chanley, Tim Cook, John Hibbing, and Robert McCrae. Jim Kuklinski, series editor, and Alex Holzman, political science editor at Cambridge University Press, were very encouraging throughout the many stages of our work and offered many useful suggestions for improving the book. We thank Robert McCrae and Psychological Assessment Resources, Inc., for permission to use items from the NEO Five-Factor Inventory. We also acknowledge the financial support of the National Science Foundation (Grant SES-9224043).

We would also like to thank Prof. George ("Al") Goethals of the psychology department at Williams College for a timely suggestion after we had completed the first study. He said he would be more impressed if we could demonstrate that these findings held up in a replication. His gentle nudge led us to replicate the findings with a second sample of students. Then, after those results confirmed our initial findings, we decided to replicate those results with adults. By the time we completed the second replication, the benefit of researching yet more aspects of this project was obvious. While one may still disagree with our results and interpretation, our many replications clearly strengthen the overall argument.

Finally, we give special thanks to our spouses, Lois, Judy, Randy, and Robert, for their encouragement and hospitality, especially when we took over the host residence for days and nights of meetings on this project.

Lincoln, Nebraska
January 1994

PART I

Theoretical Background and Overview

OUR OPENING SECTION establishes the theoretical framework of the book. This first section provides background information, particularly in Chapter 1, and clarifies our model of decision making in Chapters 2 and 3.

Chapter 1 argues that political tolerance persists as a crucial dilemma in any democracy. As we mature, we identify with certain groups and may resist challenges by outgroups. Our partisan natures also leave us vulnerable to intolerant arguments. However, at least two factors moderate our intolerance. First, the individualism of American culture encourages us to separate our own identity from that of the group. Second, the diversity of our society requires us to interact with those who differ from us; in doing so, we are likely to learn that differences may be superficial. Chapter 1 introduces a major theme of our book, the centrality of emotions in how we understand the world.

In Chapter 2 we present our model of tolerance judgments. We posit that tolerance judgments (and perhaps other political decisions) result from three major influences: predispositions, such as personality; standing decisions, such as political attitudes about democratic principles; and contemporary information about the particular situation. Chapter 2 explores the roots of this theory in the symbolic politics literature before turning to a discussion of how previous research in political tolerance has informed our model of decision making.

Chapter 3 returns to emotion. We reject the presumption that tolerance judgments are essentially cognitive and suggest instead the importance of emotion. We explicitly use a theory

1

of emotionality articulated by Jeffrey Gray, a British neuro-
scientist. The two primary limbic systems are the behavioral
inhibition system, which mediates novelty and threat and so
may be particularly important for tolerance judgments that
may often focus on the threatening outgroups, and the behavioral approach system, which mediates action and suggests
when individuals will act on their political beliefs.

CHAPTER 1

Political Tolerance and Democratic Practice

I think, therefore I am.

Rene Descartes (1596–1650)

The heart has its reasons which reason knows nothing of.

Blaise Pascal (1623–62)

Tolerance is the pivotal dilemma of democracy in a pluralistic society. Political tolerance requires that democratic citizens and leaders secure the full political rights of expression and political participation of groups they find objectionable (Sullivan, Piereson, & Marcus, 1982). We maintain that the challenge of sustaining a politically tolerant society is enduring. However, while intolerance is an ever-present danger, it need not simply be accepted. To understand how to confront intolerance, we must understand how people react when faced with groups and ideas they find threatening. In this book, we will present an explanation for how people meet that challenge.

McClosky and Brill (1983) suggest that political intolerance may be more "natural" than tolerance:

The ubiquity of slavery and oppression throughout human history leads one to wonder whether intolerance rather than tolerance may be the easier and more natural posture for most people to assume. . . . If one has sufficient strength and cunning to repel the enemy, one is inclined to do so unless one has discovered that, for some reason, another type of response is legally or socially required, or preferred. (p. 13)

3

Some research suggests that intolerance may be cognitively easier for people than tolerance in part because of the ease with which people acquire stereotypes and prejudices about individuals and groups who differ from themselves (Aboud, 1988; Devine, 1989).

Against this backdrop of a naturally occurring intolerance, there is evidence that people can be convinced that tolerance is an important principle and that people can be taught to be tolerant (Avery, Bird, Johnstone, Sullivan, & Thalhammer, 1992; Brody, 1994). If people learn that all citizens should have the right to free speech, assembly, and so forth, then they can overcome the kind of intolerant prejudices discussed by McClosky and Brill.

In this book, we will examine the view that contemporary tolerance judgments reflect a complex mix of predispositions, previously established beliefs, and current information about the political context. All of these elements play a role, although not necessarily for all individuals at all times.

To develop this argument more fully, we need to identify the role preexisting influences and contemporary information play in pluralist democracies generally and in the United States more particularly. American society has a number of characteristics with important implications for the use of predispositions, established beliefs, and contemporary information in making tolerance judgments. American society is group oriented, highly mobile, and highly individualistic (Bellah, Madsen, Sullivan, Swidler, & Tipton, 1985; Tocqueville, 1974 [1835]). Additionally, among our most prominent values are economic individualism (Feldman & Zaller, 1992), support for capitalism (McClosky & Zaller, 1984), and the core democratic values of liberty and equality (Huntington, 1981; McClosky & Zaller, 1984).

Some of these characteristics, principally group loyalties and commitment to deeply held values and orientations, encourage sustained reliance on predispositions and established beliefs. Other characteristics, such as individuality, mobility, and diversity, encourage consideration of contemporary information. In the next section, we describe the relationship between these characteristics of our society and reliance on enduring predispositions, established beliefs, and contemporary information.

GROUP IDENTIFICATION, INDIVIDUALITY, AND DIVERSITY

American democracy exists within a society that is diverse, mobile, and dynamic. Each of us begins our journey during childhood within a specific setting. Depending on what personal circumstances shaped our family, neighborhood, and region, we find ourselves among groups defined by social categories of race, class, generation, and gender, among many others. For each of us certain categories may be prominent whereas others are less so.

The lessons learned from early group experiences shape enduring predispositions that guide future choices (Duckitt, 1989). Group identification is part of the normal developmental process and has enduring consequences. Volkan (1988) has argued that group identification is a natural and universal process that creates a sense of we/they (or in-group versus out-group). A similar assertion is put forward in the ethnocentrism literature (LeVine & Campbell, 1972). Research on stereotyping similarly finds that people naturally hold stereotypes of outgroup members. Devine (1989), for example, has shown that stereotyping is widespread and powerful. Thus, group loyalties and stereotypes, once acquired, remain lasting influences that are likely to have a powerful effect in shaping tolerance judgments (Allport, 1954).

In addition to experiencing the more parochial effects of group influences, people are influenced by cultural values and beliefs (Bellah et al., 1985; McClosky & Zaller, 1984). These values and beliefs help to define the established expectations we apply to judge the actions of those around us. While the cultural values of Americans are not completely uniform, some general consensus exists. Support for democracy and capitalism has a long history in our country (McClosky & Zaller, 1984). These two dimensions of political consensus are tied together by a strong belief in the individual and individual rights. Most Americans believe in equality of opportunity and individual rights of freedom of speech, religion, press, and assembly. Americans also support capitalist values to a far greater extent than citizens of other Western democracies. Of course, these values often conflict and then must be resolved in the political arena, but American commitment to these ideals remains strong.

Individual autonomy and diversity are two factors common in the American experience that may attenuate our reliance on predispositions and established beliefs. The development of liberal democracy depends on the emergence of the self-interested individual. Liberal democracy places a high value on individual worth, self-interest, citizenship, personal judgment, and the capacity for continual learning. American pluralism encourages, indeed demands, continued learning and the capacity to reexamine old lessons in light of new circumstances. The West has placed the idea of the autonomous self-enacting individual at the center of the value pantheon (Taylor, 1989).

More particularly, as people move freely in a diverse and pluralistic society, and as they engage in ongoing contemporary political debates, the hold of group loyalties and prejudices should recede somewhat to enable people to act individually (Marcus, 1988a). In our society, people develop as individuals and move from familiar settings to confront new individuals, groups, and ideas. Although citizens initially confront these novel challenges from partisan positions with expectations borne out of learned prejudices (Devine, 1989; Devine, Monteith, Zuwerink, & Elliot, 1991; Duckitt, 1989; Kinder & Sears, 1981; Linville & Jones, 1980), they are often able to move beyond the repertoire of learned prejudices and devote greater attention to and reliance on contemporary information.

How people confront new situations is of particular concern because American society has always been diverse. Of course, people may rely on the lessons they learned early in life, but diversity provides the impetus for at least some attention to contemporary information. Diversity in America has been shaped by the geographic mobility of its population (substantial population movements from one region to another, such as blacks going from the South to the North and West, whites going from the Northeast to the Southwest and South) and by waves of immigration into the society (German and Irish, followed by Cuban, Cambodian, Laotian, etc.). Many people experience a more local mobility, moving from rural society to urban, or from urban to suburban. In addition, many Americans experience upward and downward social and economic mobility.

As a result of all these sources of diversity and intermingling, Americans frequently come into contact with strangers. We interact daily with people with whom we have no prior or intimate history. However confident and secure we may be in our immediate social milieu, we expect to meet and be changed by contacts with new groups. Given these sources of diversity, and the frequency with which Americans meet and work with unfamiliar individuals and groups, they have a powerful incentive to learn about these novel people and circumstances. Thus, diversity provides an incentive to lessen complete reliance on established beliefs and predispositions.

It is clear that the research tradition that seeks to understand how people acquire the basic orientation to be tolerant or intolerant, while important and central, cannot provide a complete account. Democracy requires that citizens be open to challenging circumstances and take some of the responsibility they share with elected representatives for making political choices. While these decisions are informed by deeply held values and beliefs, they are also influenced by contemporary information about current situations. Indeed, pluralist democracy demands no less.

THE ENDURING PROBLEM OF TOLERANCE

The characteristics of American society and pluralist democracy that influence the effects of predispositions and contemporary information create the very conditions that make tolerance a central problem of democratic life. If society successfully enables its members to become self-aware and self-enacting individuals, the society will be peopled with diverse and, at least on occasion, contentious actors. Citizens will differ not only in social background characteristics but also in belief and vocation, avocation, and personality. These differences will create the domain within which political disputes emerge; some to be addressed and resolved, some to be transformed, and some to be ignored (Mansbridge, 1980).

People approach these disputes from partisan positions. This partisanship is exacerbated when citizens are faced with groups espousing extreme ideologies. The majority tends to react strongly against abhorrent outgroups whenever they challenge the fundamental consensus of the American pluralist system. Because we are partisan, we often react poorly to such attacks on our values, refusing to allow these groups to have full political and civil rights. Examples of such partisanship may include attacks on civil liberties for communists in the 1950s and 1960s, and on gays and lesbians, or neo-Nazi groups, in the 1980s and 1990s. Tolerance remains an enduring problem because diversity and partisanship make it necessary to continually renew civil libertarian principles.

How do Americans apply principles of tolerance when they are confronted with people who hold extremely different political beliefs or espouse unpopular causes? The discrepancy between abstract and concrete judgments of tolerance will be used to illustrate the more general issue of the relative role of contemporary information and long-standing considerations in making current tolerance judgments.

Numerous studies show that when Americans are asked about their support for the principles of democracy they consistently give almost unanimous endorsement of these principles (see, e. g., Jackman, 1978; McClosky, 1964; Prothro & Grigg, 1960). People agree that all are entitled to their rights, such as free speech. For example, McClosky (1964) reports that more than 94 percent of the American electorate agreed with the statement, "No matter what a person's political beliefs are, he is entitled to the same legal rights and protections as anyone else." However, when these same principles are applied to specific circumstances, support drops precipitously. Fully 36 percent agreed with the statement, "When the country is in great danger we may have to force people to testify against themselves even if it violates their rights" (McClosky, 1964).

More recent studies have found comparable results (McClosky & Brill, 1983). Thus, the public continues to express strong endorsement of the general principles of free expression *and* great reluctance to sustain these principles when asked to apply them to noxious groups. Five general explanations may account for this slippage, three of which focus on the role of predispositions and pre-established beliefs.

The dominant explanation is simply that this inconsistency results from the public's failure to understand properly that the application of general principles demands compliance in concrete circumstances (McClosky & Brill, 1983).[1] A second explanation for this slippage is that many people acquire deeply held malice against some groups, often racial or ethnic in nature. The stronger the malice, the greater the likelihood that it will overwhelm any commitment to democratic values. Thus, people may rely on deeply held partisan feelings that run counter to a commitment to tolerance (Brady & Sniderman, 1985; Kinder & Sears, 1981).

Previous research on tolerance suggests third and fourth explanations. When people were asked to explain the reasons for their decision to tolerate or not tolerate their "least liked" political group, some of them gave democratic principles themselves as the basis for denying political rights to this group (Sullivan et al., 1982). The third explanation is that some citizens believe that unless a political group itself supports democratic principles and would apply them to others, that group forfeits its own rights. In other words, if democratic principles are supreme, then we must support these principles by not allowing undemocratic groups the opportunity to destroy democracy. Fourth, in the minds of these people, groups exercising their political rights have the obligation to behave according to the rules of the game. Thus, a different set of deeply held principles, based on the values of order and stability, might conflict with the principle of tolerance. For example, people who believe that all citizens have an obligation to be patriotic may limit the reach of tolerance when considering those who appear to be unpatriotic. When the principles of patriotism and tolerance clash, tolerance gives way.

All of these explanations rely on the presumption that people make tolerance judgments largely guided by predispositions and previously established beliefs. The first explanation suggests that unless people have the cognitive ability to connect abstract principles to concrete situations, they will rely on their more natural predisposition to be intolerant. The second explanation accounts for the slippage by pointing to continuing malice against the target group. The third explanation, in a sense, questions whether the slippage is real by adopting a particular interpretation of democratic principles and how they are best sustained. The fourth explanation raises the possibility of a countervailing value conflict between different interpretations of how to apply democratic principles.

None of these explanations considers a fifth possibility, that people are mindful of contemporary information – that they pay careful attention to the threat posed by the group in question and to the particular context in which the issue arises. To the extent that people feel threatened, they are less inclined toward political tolerance. They use contemporary information about the group and context to overrule any long-standing beliefs in applying democratic values directly.

GUT REACTIONS, THINKING, AND JUDGING

Thus far, we have argued that political tolerance judgments result from both established convictions and contemporary influences. It appears that deeply entrenched beliefs ordinarily will be most influential. One of the tasks of this book is to identify the circumstances under which new information plays a substantial role. One key to such an approach may be found in the provocative role of threat and the attention-grabbing role of emotion, experienced as increas-

ing anxiety. The specific circumstances in which established beliefs
are set aside may depend on increases or decreases in perceptions
of threat, a precursor to anxiety.

As evidenced in our epigraph to this chapter, Descartes highlights
a dominant theme in Western thought: the preeminence of thinking
and reason. In Western culture reason is believed to be the crowning
achievement of the human race and the predominant faculty on
which we should rely to make judgments, especially judgments of
justice. Democratic theorists have nearly unanimously assumed that
democratic choices must be the result of thoughtful and deliberate
judgments (Galston, 1988; Gutmann, 1987). Until recently most
Western philosophers have taken the strong position that decisions
are best made by excluding the influence of emotions (Kant, 1977;
Rawls, 1971).

However, in the realm of politics, reason does not rule alone.
Pascal's rejoinder to Descartes reminds us that we cannot ignore the
role of emotions. More particularly, we suggest that emotions appear
to play a central role in the apprehension of threat. If political tolerance judgments are influenced by enduring predispositions and
beliefs, as well as by contemporary information, then the specific
feelings provoked by the appearance of threat play a role in drawing
our attention to changes in circumstances and the need to supplement our long standing convictions in light of new, contemporary
information. And, if emotions do play this role, then understanding
how and when shifts in mood take place, as well as the consequences
that follow, becomes central to understanding tolerance judgments.
Because the dominant view denigrating emotionality is so deeply
ingrained, we need to excavate this perspective before we present a
different view.[2]

It is a long-standing presumption that people in the grip of high
emotion are more likely to make impulsive and pernicious decisions.
To the extent that people are emotional, they succumb to the appeals of intolerance. If we give in to anger and hate, then intolerance results. So, the standard guide is to be rational rather than
emotional. By focusing on reason, eschewing emotional reactions,
citizens avoid the deleterious effects of passion.

When we think about the connection between emotion and politics several themes emerge. First, emotions are closely linked to
instincts. However we define instincts, we generally think of them
as fixed forces, not subject to timely adaptation to changing circumstances. Instinctive forces impose themselves without regard to con-

temporary circumstances. Therefore, instincts encourage us to make decisions automatically.

Second, being emotional prevents us from seeing clearly. Emotions distort perception. As Robinson (1937) said, "Political campaigns are designedly made into emotional orgies which endeavor to distract attention from the real issues involved, and they actually paralyze what slight powers of cerebration man can normally muster." Particularly in the political realm, emotions will detract from cool, reasoned judgments.

Third, we generally hold that being emotional is normatively inferior to being rational. As Alexander Hamilton (1961) put it, "Why has government been instituted at all? Because the passions of men will not conform to the dictates of reason and justice, without constraint." We should "think with the head not the heart." Notice that this conception so deeply divides feeling and thinking that it locates each in different sites in the body. Reason is given the favored placement.

Finally, being emotional is often taken to be a childish state, a condition to be outgrown and left behind. Reason, thinking clearly, provides the sure path to our true interests and to justice. Therefore, emotions are antagonistic to thinking clearly and making good decisions. Being emotional is incompatible with being rational (Janis, 1982; Janis & Mann, 1977).

The most crucial presumption underlying this conception is that humans can rely solely on their ability to reason and can, at the same time, prevent emotions from distracting them. It is not surprising, therefore, that the most common remedy for ending intolerance, as it is for ending racial prejudice, is to encourage deliberation (Devine, 1989; Devine et al., 1991; Stouffer, 1955).

Recent studies complicate this view. People make different decisions when encouraged to think about the choices before them than they do if encouraged to rely on their feelings (Millar & Tesser, 1986; Wilson, Dunn, Kraft, & Lisle, 1989). However, one should not thereby conclude that decisions made by relying on feelings are necessarily inferior to those made by thoughtful deliberation.

Wilson (1991) found that most people make objectively poorer decisions when instructed to think about a decision than when they are left uninstructed. For example, college students were asked to rate samples of jam for a taste test. Students were randomly assigned to one of two groups. One group was told, before they tasted the jam, that they would be asked to list their reasons for liking or dis-

liking each jam. The control group was given no such instruction.
Those given the "reasons" instruction made different choices from
those given no instruction. The latter made ratings significantly
closer to those made by *Consumer Reports* experts than did the "reasons" group. A study of college-student course evaluations, also by
Wilson, found similar results. Students were instructed to "stop and
think" about each piece of information about nine college course
descriptions. When asked to write down their reasons for rating each
course, students were less able to match the expert ratings of faculty
than students in the control group, who were not asked to "stop
and think" and were not asked to write down their reasons. The
principal conclusion Wilson drew was that inviting people to engage
in introspection and deliberation left them *less* able to make decisions comparable to those of experts than when they made a gut
decision.

   In the context of political tolerance this suggests that the position
that democratic judgments must be made through thoughtful deliberation may be too simplistic. As Wilson shows, reason alone may
not result in the desired outcome. If reason is not the entire story,
perhaps emotion can play a constructive role in people's tolerance
decisions. Emotional responses are complex and could serve to decrease *or* increase levels of tolerance, depending on the nature of
contemporary information. If emotional responses control when
and how we pay attention to contemporary information, then understanding the role of threat perceptions and changing levels of
anxiety may yield a more complete view of tolerance judgments, a
view that combines predispositions and attention to contemporary
information.

   How do feelings influence thinking? And how might they influence political tolerance judgments? We examine these questions
throughout this book. Since affect plays a critical role in our broader
model of tolerance judgments, it requires careful exposition. We
therefore lay out our theoretical model of tolerance judgments in
Chapter 2 and then discuss Gray's explicit model of emotions, and
how emotions interact with cognition and behavior, in Chapter 3.

THE PLAN OF THE BOOK

Our concern is to understand how people make political tolerance
judgments. The end result of that goal is a model that accounts for
how people make political judgments. We argue that members of a

democratic public make use of established values and beliefs when they make political tolerance judgments *and* that they take into account observations of the immediate circumstances. An empirical demonstration of those dual capacities has implications beyond our principal concern of understanding how people make civil liberties decisions.

We will hold in abeyance a full discussion of these broader concerns until the concluding chapter. However, we can outline the principal questions that guide our work:

- Which established convictions do people rely upon, and how do they utilize them when they make tolerance judgments?
- Do people attend to the contemporary environment, and if so, which features are influential when they make political tolerance judgments?
- Finally, do people make judgments in the same way, or are there important individual differences in how they go about making civil liberties decisions?

These three questions form the principal framework that structures this study. To answer the questions, the model we propose incorporates theoretical advances from a wide variety of research programs, most importantly Gray's theory of emotionality; the traditional tolerance literature; social-psychological studies of attitudes and behavior; personality theory; and political science research on expertise and public opinion. We believe that, at a very general level, this model could be applied to any number of political judgments people make, although we focus specifically on tolerance judgments.

This book reports on a variety of survey-experiments designed to explore how people make these tolerance judgments. The next two chapters in Part I develop the theoretical framework that guides our empirical analysis. Chapter 2 lays out our broad theoretical model and includes an application of the model to the existing tolerance literature. In Chapter 3, we draw upon recent work on emotions to develop a theoretical basis for explaining the prominent role of threat when people make tolerance judgments. Here our focus is on the particular role that emotions play in directing attention toward threatening stimuli.

In Part II, we begin the process of empirically testing our model. Chapter 4 presents the basic studies in which we test the extent to which people draw upon contemporary information to supplement their long-standing values and beliefs when they make contemporary tolerance judgments. In particular, we begin to address the impact that threatening information in the current environment has on citizens' tolerance judgments.

Part III moves beyond the overall results discussed in Part II to a consideration of individual differences in how people respond to contemporary information. In Chapter 5 we examine the role of threat in greater depth, focusing on threat as a predisposition and as an enduring belief. Here, we also examine whether certain types of individuals are more likely than others to be affected by threatening information. Chapter 6 focuses on democratic principles. Democratic principles may be deeply held and enduring beliefs that influence some individuals more than others. Democratic norms can also be part of the contemporary information environment when political actors make appeals to democratic principles. Some individuals may respond to these appeals by moving away from their established beliefs. Chapter 7 explores how robust our findings are across time, and examines the role of source credibility, expertise, and malice toward certain groups. Finally, Chapter 8 investigates individual differences in personality and how they shape tolerance judgments. Some personality types may give greater attention to the present while others may rely more strongly on deeply held values and beliefs.

Part IV concludes the book by drawing out the broader implications of our model for understanding tolerance, behavior, and the role of emotions in politics. Chapter 9 focuses on the behavioral implications of tolerant and intolerant judgments, exploring their likely impact on the political process. Chapter 10 summarizes the overall findings and develops the more general implications of this work.

CHAPTER 2

Antecedent Considerations and Contemporary Information

> The historical processes and events that have shaped a
> person's complex make-up can never be fully unraveled.
> Nevertheless, our task is not hopeless. A person's current
> behavior must be determined by factors that exert their
> effects right here and now. Past events are important only
> to the extent that they have left an enduring mark on the
> person, a mark that continues to wield its impact.
>
> Icek Ajzen, *Attitudes, Personality, and Behavior*

In this chapter, we introduce the conceptual framework that guides
our analysis of tolerance judgments. At the most general level, we
attempt to distinguish between long-term and short-term influences
on these judgments. We will review briefly some theoretical approaches that have emphasized long-term influences and others that
emphasized short-term influences. We then introduce the concepts
we use to analyze the role of established convictions and more immediate environmental influences. Finally, we apply these conceptual distinctions to the existing literature on political tolerance.

For years scholars have studied long-term and short-term influences on political attitudes and behavior. Yet there is little agreement about the relative importance of these two sets of influences
in shaping citizens' opinions and behaviors. On the one hand, the
symbolic politics literature and personality studies emphasize the
effects of early socialization. On the other hand, the rational choice
and social cognition literatures pay greater attention to the role of
information stemming from people's more immediate circumstances.

*Look for
examples
of such thing*

The central idea of the symbolic politics approach is that people respond automatically and affectively to abstract political symbols based on predispositions, such as party identification, political ideology, and racial prejudice. Symbols that evoke basic and fundamental responses include such stimuli as "communists," "the KKK," "drug kingpins," "Woodstock," "homeboys," and "Saddam." These symbols are powerful, so much so that when linked to less emotionally charged political stimuli, they can extend their reach quite broadly. Highly emotionally laden symbols play an integral role in shaping public opinion and political behavior. Citizens' responses to such political symbols are conditioned by values and beliefs acquired during early socialization that endure relatively unchanged throughout the life cycle (Sears, 1993: p. 121).

The symbolic politics approach would be extremely static unless some mechanism allowed for adaptive responses to a changing environment. According to Sears (1993), change is introduced into the system through shifts in the meaning of symbols. A changing political environment can lead to an alteration in the meaning of a symbol. When this happens different predispositions are elicited by the symbol. For example, "liberalism" in the 1960s held positive connotations for many people, whereas in the 1980s it evoked more negative connotations. This change in meaning did not reflect a change in people's basic predispositions, but rather a change in the connotation that a symbol provoked, evoking of a different set of predispositions. As a result, public opinion changed and the political climate shifted in such a way that public policy was altered. Another possible source of political change is that symbols may be emphasized to varying degrees over time, evoking different predispositions that in turn lead people to express different opinions and evaluations.

A wide variety of personality theories also emphasize the importance of predispositions. Approaches as diverse as psychoanalysis and dispositional theories assume that personality characteristics developed early in life shape adult behavior. For example, in political psychology, the theory of the authoritarian personality attributes right-wing political ideology to early disturbances in child-rearing patterns. Another example is Barber's (1985) analysis of twentieth-century presidents. He emphasized the role of early childhood experiences in developing presidential character, which in turn played a central role in determining whether or not a president became enmeshed in a failing line of policy.[1]

Other approaches pay relatively greater attention to the perception and use of information available in the current environment. Rational choice theory assumes that, to be rational, individuals must adjust to a changing environment in order to enact their preferences effectively (Downs, 1957). If people are creatures of their distant past, then they will be unable to incorporate new information about costs and benefits into their calculations and will likely make self-defeating and ineffective choices. Rational choice models place a premium on acquiring and using current information, full or partial, in making informed decisions.

Much research in social cognition and information processing similarly highlights the influence of available information on evaluations and judgments, and assigns a secondary role to long-standing predispositions (Sears, 1993: p. 137). This research emphasizes how people react to a package of contemporary information, that is, how information is processed, stored, and retrieved for use in making judgments. Studies in this tradition do occasionally examine individual differences in how people process information, such as expert–novice differences. They seldom, however, examine the relative role of individual predispositions and contemporary information on current decisions and judgments.

As applied to public opinion and survey research, some scholarship has assumed that predispositions play a relatively minor role. In the 1960s, for example, Converse (1964) argued that many people did not have established political attitudes, and their responses to many political stimuli were essentially random. More recent work in political cognition has emphasized the impact of question wording and order on survey responses (Achen, 1975; Piazza, Sniderman, & Tetlock, 1989; Zaller & Feldman, 1992). Small differences in wording and order are seen to have a strong impact on expressions of opinion because predispositions are assumed to be relatively weak.

In updating Converse's argument, Zaller (1992) asserted that people responded to survey questions based on whatever considerations came immediately to mind. These considerations were strongly affected by the flow of information from the immediate political environment. Zaller contended, for example, that "the probability that a person will support or oppose a given policy depends on the mix of positive and negative considerations available in the person's mind *at the moment* of answering a question about it" (1992: p. 51, emphasis added).

Heterogeneity

Zaller's work does provide a role for predispositions such as political knowledge, partisanship, and ideology. His model provided a stronger role for predispositions among the politically astute because they were more likely to perceive a relationship between incoming information and their existing predispositions, and because they had a deeper knowledge base with which to counterargue new information. Among the less astute, his model emphasized that people store a vast assortment of conflicting attitudes in their long-term memory, which means that they do not generally have a single, true attitude on most political topics. Rather, the attitude they express depended on a complex combination of short-term memory and how current information was encoded, perceived, or interpreted (Zaller, 1992: p. 38).

Other recent research emphasizes the important role played by information conveyed by the current political context. Sniderman and his colleagues, for example, examined how the structure of information shapes public opinion on issues of racial and political tolerance (1991a, 1993). Contemporary information and how it is conveyed plays a strong role in affecting the attitudes expressed by citizens. Other recent work by Brody (1991), Fan (1988), Page and Shapiro (1992), and Zaller (1992) has emphasized the important role of elite and media cues in affecting public opinion. Contrary to the image presented by research in the 1950s and 1960s, which concluded that citizens' predispositions rendered them largely unresponsive, this recent work has portrayed citizens as more malleable and responsive to elite discourse presented through the mass media.

A broad overview of the development of the field of political psychology suggests that the dominant approach in the 1940s and 1950s emphasized the study of political personality; in the 1960s and 1970s, the emphasis shifted somewhat toward the study of political attitudes and ideology; and in the 1980s and 1990s, studies of information processing, including media effects, have become more prominent (McGuire, 1993). The first era seems to focus more heavily on predispositions, the second on long-term beliefs and attitudes, and the most recent era on the effects of contemporary information. This is merely a broad characterization because scholars in all three eras have paid attention to multiple sets of influences; nevertheless, the relative emphases have differed.

ANTECEDENT CONSIDERATIONS AND
CONTEMPORARY INFORMATION

Scholars have used a variety of terms to distinguish between long-term predispositions and short-term environmental influences. For example, Sears (1993) referred to "symbolic predispositions" that shape how citizens interpret and respond to contemporary information. Zaller (1992, ch. 2) distinguished between predispositions and the use of information, arguing that opinions are a "marriage" of the two. He argued that predispositions distill a person's lifetime experiences, including childhood socialization and social and economic status. The focus of his analysis was on the term "consideration" defined as "any reason that might induce an individual to decide a political issue one way or the other" (p. 40).

Although Sears and Zaller differentiated between two primary influences on people's judgments, we want to make a further distinction in our analysis. We will use the term *antecedent consideration* to refer to the entire class of long-term influences that have long-lived effects (as against the contemporary influence of new or concurrent information) on the judgments people make.

We will examine two types of antecedent considerations, both of which reflect the premise that earlier beliefs, values, attitudes, prejudices, and stereotypes help shape current attitudes and behavior. We will use the term *predisposition* to refer to the subclass of antecedent considerations that are deeply rooted and stable individual characteristics, and that result in generalized predilections to think, feel, and behave in certain ways.

We focus in our research primarily on three predispositions: personality, global sense of threat, and political expertise. Personality characteristics are perhaps the most obvious example of what we mean by predispositions. They tend to be stable and enduring over time and have a generalized effect on attitudes and behavior. Based on the research of Gray, as well as Petty and Cacioppo, we examine four personality traits that are likely to be related to tolerance judgments: extraversion, openness to experience, neuroticism, and need for cognition. We also examine threat as a predisposition – a global, generalized view that the world is a dangerous and threatening place. Certain people might feel that threat and danger are pervasive, whereas others might generally feel that the world is a pretty safe place. Finally, political expertise refers to having a strong knowl-

edge base about politics in general, not just civil liberties. The more
people know about politics generally, the more they can draw on
that knowledge when faced with a specific situation that demands a
tolerance judgment.

Predispositions are just one type of antecedent consideration.
Standing decisions refer to the antecedent considerations that are established attitudes and beliefs applied to a specific domain, in this
instance civil liberties and political tolerance. We do not conceptu-
alize standing decisions as fixed and clearly bounded positions.
Rather, standing decisions reflect a general stance that provides for
a range of potential responses to any concrete situation. The latitude, of course, differs from individual to individual, with some
having wide margins within which their opinions may vary, and others having narrow margins. All individuals, however, have some potential range – not a singular position – that allows them to respond
differently under varying circumstances.[2] Standing decisions, although they are relatively stable, are not as deeply rooted as predispositions.

A major distinction between predispositions and standing decisions is that the former refer to a generalized effect while the latter
are more specific and circumscribed. For example, someone who is
generally rigid and dogmatic may be predisposed to be intolerant.
Political intolerance, although a consequence of that predisposition,
is only one of many consequences. A tolerant standing decision to
support democratic values, however, applies to civil liberties issues
but not necessarily more broadly to other aspects of life. For example, those who believe in democratic principles apply them to
politics, but not to the social realm (Sullivan et al., 1982: pp. 237–
239).

Another distinction between predispositions and standing decisions is their malleability. It is very difficult to change an adult's
personality structure. For example, people who are rigid and dogmatic are not easily transformed into flexible, open people (Altemeyer, 1994). On the other hand, although still difficult, it is
relatively easier to teach people to adopt a standing decision supportive of democratic norms (Avery et al., 1992; Brody, 1994).[3]

We examine three standing decisions that are important to the
study of tolerance. First, some people strongly support abstract democratic principles concerning civil liberties, whereas others are less
supportive. The more strongly people hold these principles, the
more likely they are to apply them in concrete situations involving

noxious groups (Sullivan et al., 1982). Commitment to democratic principles is therefore a standing decision that people bring into any particular situation requiring them to make a tolerance decision.

Second, we also include as a standing decision people's prior decisions about whether to tolerate a group they especially dislike. What makes this a standing decision? We argue that over time, people will tend to make similar tolerance judgments when faced with a highly disliked group within a particular context. In essence, this standing tolerance decision is something of a habit that people can fall back on when a new but similar situation demands a judgment concerning civil liberties. Of course, for some people, any given decision about a particular type of group will be their first and therefore cannot be considered a habit. Even for these people, however, a tolerance decision is not made completely de novo but instead is influenced by long-standing biases and prejudices.

Finally, a third standing decision important to our study is one particular form of perceived threat. Unlike the global feeling of threat described as a predisposition, people may feel particularly threatened by a specific group, say religious fundamentalists, or type of group, say racists, and base their tolerance decision in part on this type of threat as a standing decision. For example, some people may have decided that racist groups – of various hues – are too dangerous or vile and ought not to be tolerated. Others may have decided that certain types of groups that challenge mainstream social norms, such as radical feminists and gay-rights groups, are objectionable but deserve to be tolerated. When we ask respondents questions about their least-liked group, then, many of them may rely on a decision they have already made not just about that particular group, but about a generic type of group of which their least-liked is only one example.

Our conceptualization of the relationship between predispositions and standing decisions has important implications for the arguments we make later in this book. We argue that the effect of predispositions on current attitudes is felt indirectly through standing decisions. Standing decisions are then directly related to current attitudes. That is, once standing decisions have been taken into account, predispositions should add little or no additional predictive power. This conceptualization is similar to that proposed by Fishbein in his discussion of the impact that "external variables" (what we call predispositions) have in predicting behavior. According to Fishbein (1980: p. 103), although the theory of reasoned action "does not deny the importance of . . . 'external' variables, it does question the assumption that variables of this type are *directly* related to behavior and can thus be used as explanatory constructs . . . external variables influence behavior only *indirectly*, by influencing the attitudinal and normative considerations that ultimately determine behavior." Although we are primarily interested in what explains current attitudes rather than behavior, we agree with Fishbein that the effects of predispositions are primarily encapsulated in attitudes, or what we refer to as standing decisions.

By *contemporary information* we refer to new stimuli available from the current environment. Contemporary information can be direct or mediated, symbolic or literal, normative or descriptive. It can be obtained through a number of sensory modalities and further processed by a variety of affective and cognitive faculties. These processes can be conscious, nonconscious, or both. The important point to emphasize is that this information is available in the present and therefore must be gained from the current environment. For example, while watching television, a person might see a story on a gay-rights march. The contemporary information gathered from the story includes who was in the march, what they said and did, and the general context of the political action. This information is then used to make a subsequent decision.

What contemporary information is likely to influence tolerance judgments? We consider five types of information. First, information about an unpopular group's actions is likely to have an impact. We have already discussed threat as a predisposition and as a standing decision, but people can also obtain threatening information about the group from the current environment. Drawing on the work of Jeffrey Gray, which we discuss in much greater detail in Chapter 3, we expect that information portraying a group as belligerent and treacherous will affect people's willingness to tolerate the group. A second type of substantive information that potentially could be important concerns the probability that a group will gain power. The more information people obtain that leads them to perceive a group to be powerful, the less tolerant they might be. Third, certain cues in the environment may lead people to approach a tolerance decision in a more thoughtful or a more affective state of mind. People who focus on their thoughts may differ in their tolerance judgments from people who focus on their feelings at the time they make a decision. Fourth, we referred to people's commitment to democratic principles as a standing decision, but commentators or activists involved in a particular situation may evoke specific interpretations of democratic principles. A person interviewed on television, for example, might argue on behalf of freedom of speech. Or someone might highlight the fact that the group would undermine civil liberties if it obtained power. These evocations of democratic principles are pieces of contemporary information. Finally, tolerance decisions may be affected simply by the credibility of the source providing relevant information. In this sense, source credibility becomes a piece of contemporary information itself.

Since our conception of standing decisions is that people have a range of acceptable opinions, then the role for contemporary information is to influence which of these acceptable options are actually incorporated into people's judgments. The point selected within this range in any particular circumstance is influenced by the specific information obtained from the political context.

We do not assume, however, that people always make tolerance decisions in the same way. We use the term *individual differences* to denote the idea that people may differ in how they make tolerance judgments and in how they process contemporary information. People differ in the predispositions and standing decisions they hold, and these individual differences may then affect the extent to which they are tolerant or intolerant. For example, people vary in their level of political expertise, and people with greater political knowledge are likely to be more tolerant than the less knowledgeable (McClosky & Brill, 1983; McClosky & Zaller, 1984). Individual differences are also likely to affect how people process contemporary information. Some people may simply be more influenced by certain types of contemporary information than other people, depending on their predispositions or standing decisions. If this is so, then some people may be impervious to information available in the current environment, relying instead on their antecedent considerations when making tolerance judgments. Other people, however, may be open to contemporary information, paying less heed to their predispositions and standing decisions.

A few examples may help clarify what we mean by individual differences. In each case, the predispositions or standing decisions a person brings into a situation involving civil liberties condition how he or she processes contemporary information. Some people may be predisposed to be more open to certain kinds of information, thereby basing their tolerance decision on that information. For example, Gray's work suggests that people who feel highly threatened by the world will be especially attentive to threatening information about an unpopular group. The world seems to be a dangerous place, and sure enough, here is a group acting in a threatening manner. Other people may clutch more strongly to their antecedent considerations, thereby remaining unaffected by contemporary information. For example, Zaller's (1992) work leads us to expect that people who are very knowledgeable about politics will counterargue the information prevalent in the environment. Or people who are strongly committed to democratic principles are likely to remain unaffected by appeals to democratic norms because of their motivation to counterargue these appeals. They already know what their principles are – contemporary evocations of norms cannot sway them.

In addition to predispositions, standing decisions, contemporary information, and individual differences, a central concept in our analysis will be *contemporary judgments*. By this term, we refer to specific decisions that individuals make in the present. Contemporary judgments can be automatic applications of predispositions or standing decisions, but they can also respond to contemporary information about the specific subject matter of the judgment in question. For example, with regard to civil liberties, individuals may make judgments about a current controversy such as whether gay-rights activists should be allowed to hold a rally in their community. If they oppose gay rights, have a personality predisposition that tends to be dogmatic, and have arrived at a standing decision that gay-rights activists are bad and ought to be stopped wherever possible, then their contemporary judgment might reflect their predisposition and their standing decision. Such a contemporary judgment, however, is made within a specific political and social context, and information provided by that context may often play a role in helping people arrive at a particular tolerance judgment (Sniderman & Piazza, 1993). Contemporary information could therefore lead individuals to move one direction or the other within their range of acceptable standing decisions.

Table 2.1 summarizes the distinctions we have introduced and suggests the central empirical issues we consider in this research. How much influence do antecedent considerations have? Does contemporary information influence contemporary judgments? If so, what kind of contemporary information makes an impact, and under what conditions?

To summarize, our analysis of tolerance judgments examines pre-

Table 2.1. *Antecedent considerations, contemporary information, and contemporary tolerance judgments*

Antecedent Considerations		Contemporary information	Contemporary judgments
Predispositions	Standing decisions		
such as personality gender other demographic factors	such as belief in democratic principles	such as news about the current activities of an objectionable group	such as a current decision, or judgment, to support or oppose the rights of an objectionable group

dispositions, standing decisions, contemporary information, and individual differences to produce a richer view of how citizens make political choices. We expect that most people make judgments that are influenced by long standing prejudices and principles, beliefs and values. To the extent that people rely on these antecedent considerations, they have made what can be described as a range of prejudgments. Rather than providing a newly formulated choice, people may recall their established position and apply it in order to make a decision. But people will, under certain circumstances, augment their standing decisions with current information. This book seeks to identify the role of both antecedent considerations and contemporary information in contemporary tolerance judgments.

The task before us, then, is to develop our framework for analyzing tolerance judgments so that it both identifies antecedent considerations and the circumstances under which they are dominant, and specifies the circumstances under which people pay attention to and are affected by contemporary information. The first stage is to turn to past research for a more detailed discussion of the relative importance of predispositions, standing decisions, and contemporary information in making tolerance judgments.

AN APPLICATION OF OUR MODEL TO THE POLITICAL TOLERANCE LITERATURE

Antecedent Considerations

Beginning with Stouffer's (1955) seminal study of tolerance, analysts have emphasized the importance of predispositions, particularly personality. Stouffer, for example, found that rigidity, authoritarianism, and optimism were related to tolerance: "Intolerance may be a systematic factor in personality, whatever its object, and distrust of political deviants may be only one phase of a larger social and psychological problem – distrust of one's fellow man" (p. 107). Sullivan, Piereson, and Marcus (1982) also found that personality was an important determinant of political tolerance. Specifically, psychological security, composed of dogmatism, a lack of trust in people, and a focus on lower-order psychological needs such as safety and security, was strongly associated with political intolerance. Others have measured this construct differently, but often with similar results: authoritarian, closed-minded people generally tend to adopt an intolerant standing decision when faced with racial, ethnic or political groups that differ significantly from them (Altemeyer, 1988; McClosky & Brill, 1983).

Education is a second predisposition that is strongly linked to political tolerance and has been much more widely studied than the related concept of political expertise. Prothro and Grigg (1960) argued that adherence to democratic principles in specific situations (what we would call contemporary tolerance judgments) is strongly influenced by education. Those who have a "greater acquaintance with the logical implications of the broad democratic principles" will be most likely to make tolerant contemporary judgments, although they will not always do so. Prothro and Grigg assumed that people can logically connect abstract principles about freedom of speech to real situations, or they cannot. They learn this through formal education, and once formal education ceases, people's decision to be tolerant or intolerant functions as a standing decision.

McClosky (1964) agreed with Prothro and Grigg. He contended that people must learn about democratic beliefs and habits because those beliefs are unlikely to exist in any "state of nature." It is a heavy burden to ask people to submit unconditionally to democratic values and procedures. Compliance with the democratic rules of the game demands extraordinary forbearance, self-discipline and a willingness to suffer opinions, actions, and groups regarded as repugnant. McClosky argued that the need for self-restraint is intrinsically difficult to comprehend and even more difficult to honor. Only "articulates" or political elites have the requisite experience, knowledge, or temperament to exhibit forbearance toward those they dislike and to exhibit strong support for both democratic values and their application to unpopular groups and ideas. The predispositions of education and participation were seen as central prerequisites to tolerance.

Education was also the primary reason given for the stunning increase in political tolerance that Nunn, Crockett, and Williams (1978) found when they replicated Stouffer's study in the 1970s. Americans had become significantly more tolerant of the rights of communists. In 1954 and 1973, respondents were asked whether it was more important to find out all the communists "even if some innocent people should be hurt" or "to protect the rights of innocent people, even if some Communists are not found out." A dramatic shift in responses occurred, with 32 percent choosing to protect the innocent in 1954 and 70 percent opting to protect the innocent in 1973. While Nunn and his colleagues suggested that the changes were due to higher levels of education that create more tolerant standing decisions, it is possible that this change could have resulted from contemporary information that discredited the communist witch hunts of the 1950s, or from some combination of new information and a more educated public that made more tolerant standing decisions.

While Sullivan, Piereson, and Marcus (1982), using their least-liked group strategy,[4] questioned the direct effects of education on political tolerance, they did not completely dismiss the possibility that education has an effect as a predisposition, particularly when the link between education and support for democratic principles is considered.

Standing decisions on issues such as support for democratic values and civil liberties are strongly influenced by predispositions such as education and personality. As we noted earlier, we expect standing decisions to encapsulate many of the effects of predispositions. However, it is useful to consider standing decisions separately from predispositions because they are more malleable and fluid. Political attitudes, for example, are more likely to change than one's personality.

Scholars have agreed that support for general principles of democracy is both widespread among Americans and important for political tolerance judgments (McClosky & Brill, 1983; Prothro & Grigg, 1960; Sullivan, Piereson, & Marcus, 1982; Sullivan, Shamir, Walsh, & Roberts, 1985). When applied to specific situations however, this consensus breaks down. For example, although more than 90 percent of Prothro and Grigg's respondents agreed with the principle of minority rights, when the principle was applied to unpopular groups such as communists, the consensus disappeared.

McClosky and Brill (1983) suggested that relying on standing decisions rather than making continuous reassessments is generally desirable for most people:

> For psychological and sociological reasons too complex to be considered fully here, human beings exhibit a powerful tendency to discover or settle upon social norms ... to which one can refer without having to debate every issue as though for the first time. Through such standards people avoid the psychological pain of continuous conflict and disagreement. Norms supply, in effect, settled opinions and therefore provide conditions for stability and predictability in everyday life as well as in public affairs. (p. 14)

Not only does this argument explain why most citizens prefer standing decisions to continuous reassessments; McClosky and Brill embellished it to explain why, in concrete situations, so many citizens opt for intolerance. It is because they "distrust what they do not understand or cannot control" and they do so to "feel safe against the terrors of the unknown" (pp. 13–14). The standing decision, then, for many ordinary citizens, is one of general support for democratic norms coupled with a more specific intolerance. Absent extraordinary effort to adopt a contrary standing decision, intolerance often prevails.[5]

McClosky's arguments support the presumption that citizens – articulates and inarticulates alike – respond to particular civil liberties challenges on the basis of predispositions and long-standing decisions. However, quite different forces regulate these two groups' contemporary decisions. The former's decisions may reflect a stable *principled* commitment born of experience and expertise. The latter's decisions may reflect a predisposition that relies on instinct and emotion, lacking in forbearance.

More recently, Gibson (1992b) also weighed in on the side of standing decisions when examining the impact of tolerance on people's perceptions of political freedom, including perceived government repression and self censorship. Gibson (1992b) speculated that

> while one can imagine that there are [contextual] effects on [political] attitudes and actions, politics is rarely salient enough for people to engage in continuous reality testing. The stronger effects are likely to be in terms of more basic political orientations that change over longer periods of time.

In no area of political life are these social interactions more important than in the area of conformity and political tolerance. (p. 339)

Standing decisions provide the least difficult means for making decisions, and people are likely to rely on them rather than to continually reassess their not-very-salient political beliefs.

Our brief review of the tolerance literature in terms of our model clearly shows that very little systematic discussion exists concerning the role of predispositions, standing decisions, and the use of current information in citizens' tolerance judgments. Most studies of political tolerance have not addressed how citizens process information about the groups and contexts involved when they have to make political judgments about civil liberties. A preponderant, but implicit, assumption exists that most citizens have a definite bias to be either tolerant or intolerant when and if extremist groups challenge their core values. That assumption follows from the methodological individualism underlying most research on political tolerance and from its focus on individual differences in standing decisions.

For example, based on the empirical literature summarized in Table 2.2, one might imagine two ideal types of citizens. One type might include ordinary citizens who are relatively uneducated, isolated, uninvolved in politics, show only a lip-service commitment to democratic norms and have dogmatic, closed personalities and authoritarian attitude structures. Another type might include citizens who are highly educated, centrally located with regard to the networks of normative communication in society, highly politically sophisticated, strongly committed to democratic norms and their legal applications, and have open personalities and flexible attitude structures.

Each of these two types of citizens may indeed have very strong predispositions and firm standing decisions – the former toward political intolerance and the latter toward political tolerance. Both types may also pay attention to contemporary information. They respond to the nature of the unpopular group involved in the situation, the political context within which the group seeks to exercise its political and civil rights, and whether the context involves political unrest and instability or relative political calm.

Consider these two ideal types and the 1978 case of the American Nazis (National Socialist Party of America, the NSPA). This group wanted to hold a public rally in Skokie, Illinois, a Chicago suburb

Table 2.2. *Summary of selected studies of political tolerance*

Author	Nature of data	Descriptive findings	The "more tolerant" are:
Stouffer, 1955	Community elites and two national mass samples	Tolerance low toward communists and related groups	Demographic: Younger; more educated; northerners, westerners; city dwellers; men; non-churchgoers Personality: Less rigid, less authoritarian, and more optimistic Perceptions of threat: Less threatened Political sophistication: Elites more tolerant than masses
Prothro & Grigg, 1960	Two local mass samples	Consensual support for democratic principles; dissensus on specific applications	Demographic: More educated and higher income
McClosky, 1964	Elite sample of national convention delegates and national mass sample	Consensual support for democratic principles; dissensus on specific applications	Political sophistication: Elite consensus on principles and application; mass dissensus on application; elites more tolerant than masses
Davis, 1975	National mass sample	Tolerance toward communists and atheists increased about 23% between 1954 and 1972–73	Demographic: Increase in tolerance of these groups due in part to education and cohort replacement; most due to across the board increase
Lawrence, 1976	National mass sample	Tolerant majority on most demonstrations and petitions studied; consensual support for most democratic principles, usually applied to specific applications	Demographic: More educated Issue orientation: Nature of issue and of group matters; more sympathetic toward demonstrators' goals Democratic norms: More supportive of abstract norms, strongest variable
Nunn et al., 1978	Community elites and national mass sample	Tolerance of communists and related groups greater than in 1950s; tolerant majority	Same findings as Stouffer; increased tolerance mainly due to education
Sullivan et al., 1982	National mass sample	Tolerance low toward individuals' least-liked political groups	Demographic: More educated, have higher income; younger, nonrural residence Democratic norms: Stronger in their support of democratic norms Personality: Less dogmatic, more secure Perceived threat: Less threatened

Study	Sample	Finding	Correlates of tolerance
Gibson & Bingham, 1983	Members and leaders of ACLU and members of Common Cause	ACLU more tolerant of Nazis than Common Cause	Democratic norms: Stronger in support of libertarian beliefs
McClosky & Brill, 1983 and McClosky & Zaller, 1984	National sample of community leaders and activists, and two national mass samples; and National convention delegates; several national mass samples	Disjuncture between abstract norms and concrete applications; mass public generally intolerant	Demographic: More educated, higher occupations, larger cities and the non-South, less religious, women; Political sophistication: Elites more tolerant than masses; more knowledgeable and interested; Personality: Lower on misanthropy, conformity, and anomie; higher on tolerance of ambiguity, flexibility, self-esteem; Democratic norms: Stronger support for abstract democratic norms; Political: Liberal, more participatory
Sullivan, Shamir, Walsh, & Roberts, 1985	National mass samples in three countries	Same as Sullivan, Piereson, and Marcus, 1982	Similar to Sullivan, Piereson, and Marcus
Gibson, 1987	Gay political caucus in Houston	Gays tolerant of rights of the Ku Klux Klan; the intolerant are often ill-prepared to act on their intolerance	Demographic: More educated; Personality: Less dogmatic, more trusting; Democratic norms: Higher support in general, especially for freedom of assembly; Perceived threat: Less threatened, have less expectation of violence; Political: More activist, participatory
Sniderman, Tetlock, Glaser, Green, & Hout, 1989	National mass sample	Much of the public exhibits consistent, principled tolerance	Demographic: More educated; Political: Liberal
Peffley & Sigelman, 1990	Stouffer's 1954 data	Intolerance of Communists historically grounded	Perceptions of threat: Less threatened but threat not as strong as in least-liked group model; Political sophistication: More knowledgeable about Communism

Table 2.2. (*cont.*)

Author	Nature of data	Descriptive findings	The "more tolerant" are:
Gibson, 1992a	National mass sample	Tolerance low toward most disliked group, through 4th most disliked group	Demographic: More educated, less religious
Gibson, 1992b	National mass sample	Correlates of tolerance insensitive to measurement strategy	Demographic: More educated, men Personality: More secure, more open-minded Democratic norms: More supportive of both general and procedural norms Perceptions of threat: Not a strong relationship
Sullivan, Shamir, Walsh, Barnum & Gibson, 1993	National mass and elite samples in four countries	Elites tend to be tolerant, citizens intolerant	Personality: Less dogmatic Democratic norms: More supportive of abstract norms and procedural norms Perceptions of threat: Public, less threatened; elites, less true

with a substantial Jewish population. Based on information from the media, some people who were predisposed toward intolerance might have concluded that the NSPA was a powerless and marginal group, which had agreed to abide by significant restrictions on the kinds of signs and logos they would display. To them, the NSPA did not represent any significant threat. As a result, some of these citizens might have been willing to tolerate this action despite a general antagonism to public rallies by extremist groups.

Conversely, some of the individuals of the second type who were predisposed toward tolerance might have concluded that the NSPA was itself intolerant, that its message was hurtful, and that the threat posed to Jews in Skokie was real. As a result, they might have been willing to impose sufficiently severe time, place, and manner restrictions on the NSPA to ensure that it was unable to hold its rally. Thus contemporary information can play an important role even among people who are already strongly predisposed.

If contemporary information can influence people who have very strong predispositions and standing decisions, then it can influence those with moderate predispositions even more. Most ordinary citizens probably have moderate predispositions; they have a decent but not extraordinary education; they have some interest and involvement in politics but are not strikingly sophisticated; they can be somewhat dogmatic but can also be open-minded, and so forth. In other words, contemporary information likely affects most citizens, even those with a predisposition to support or oppose the civil liberties of unpopular groups in society. The following section will explore how contemporary information has been addressed in the tolerance literature, particularly information pertaining to threat.

Contemporary Information

Although the tolerance literature emphasizes the importance of antecedent considerations, contemporary information may play an important role in people's contemporary tolerance judgments. A few studies have occasionally strayed into that realm. For example, Stouffer (1955) recognized that his study of tolerance reflected heightened concern about Communist infiltration in the United States during the McCarthy era. As Stouffer pointed out, "For the purposes of this study, the tolerance of nonconformity is *solely* within the broad context of the communist threat" (p. 54). His results depended on the nature of the times and on the information in-

dividuals were receiving about the communist threat, and he recognized that their attitudes might change when confronted with
different information. Later research conducted by Davis (1975)
analyzed increases in tolerance toward communists and atheists between 1954 and the early 1970s. He found that cohort replacement
and increases in education (both predispositions) explained most
of the increases that *could* be explained. However, most of the ob-
served changes were uniform across all education and age groups,
and Davis could not explain them statistically using the variables
available. These results raise the possibility that changes in contemporary information – the nature of the times and a different political
climate toward these groups – led citizens to be less threatened and
more tolerant.

Lawrence's research (1976) on political tolerance also touched
on the role of contemporary information, although that is not how
he conceived his work. He explained tolerance by focusing on three
variables: education, general norms, and issue orientation. He measured general norms as general evaluations of particular activities,
ranging from the easiest (petitioning) to the most difficult (tem-
porarily blocking the entrance of a government building). Issue
orientation reflected attitudes toward soft issues (pollution, crime)
and hard issues (legalization of marijuana, discrimination in hous-
ing). He also considered attitudes toward "soft" groups, such as
neighbors, and "hard" groups, such as black militants. Lawrence
found that education, issue orientation and general norms had independent effects on tolerance. General norms had the strongest
effect, but Lawrence also concluded that "tolerance is highly issue-
related. Respondents who are more sympathetic to the goals of demonstrators are considerably more likely than those neutral or hostile
to permit the demonstration to take place" (p. 99). This issue information is often available in the immediate environment.
Therefore, antecedent considerations had an impact on tolerance,
as did contemporary information about the nature of the issues involved.

McClosky and his colleagues also acknowledged the role of shifting, contextual contemporary information. McClosky and Zaller
(1984) left space for the impact of contemporaneous influences.
For example, they argued that "the degree of freedom an open
society permits is bound to vary somewhat from one group or occasion to another, and from one period to another, depending on
the estimates made by the authorities, the elites and the general

public about the degree of danger they face" (p. 39). Similarly, eruptions of intolerance may be the response of "some Americans and their leaders to perceived threats to order or national security" (p. 46). Finally, McClosky and Brill (1983: pp. 23–24) noted, for example, that conduct tolerated in peacetime may be considered unacceptable in wartime. They also suggested that tolerance decisions are affected by who commits the act, their purposes, and under what conditions the act is committed. They provide clear examples of individuals modifying standing decisions based on current circumstances and information.

Gibson's (1987) analysis of Houston homosexuals' tolerance of the KKK may provide the most explicit discussion of the role of standing decisions and current, contextual information in influencing tolerance judgments:

Opinion is to a large degree a function of more general attitudes toward democratic freedoms. But it also is affected by perceptions of the context of the dispute. Those who expected violence to take place in the event of the Klan demonstration – even those expecting violence not from the Klan, but directed toward the Klan – were less likely to support the right of the Klansmen to demonstrate. Many people with different opinions on the controversy had the same level of general support for freedom of assembly. Their opinions differed because of their perceptions of the context – the contextual cost – of the demonstration. The particular context, and how it is perceived, seems to play a significant role in opinion formation in civil liberties disputes. (pp. 445–446)

The type of information that seemed to affect most of the Gay Political Caucus activists pertained to the threatening nature of the group. While most (71 percent) would allow the group to march, 29 percent of the gay activists would not allow the KKK to demonstrate. Of those who were opposed to the demonstration, the justification given by two-thirds was the fear of violence associated with the KKK, both historically and in this particular demonstration. Here, we see the role of contemporaneous information as the respondents focused on the particular events surrounding the proposed Houston march. About a third of the intolerant respondents said the location of the march was critical to their decision. They thought that the march might be appropriate outside the gay quarter of Houston. Finally, about one-eighth of those who wanted to restrict the Klan's rights suggested that the Klan could demonstrate only if it paid the costs associated with the demonstration (estimated at about $60,000) to the city of Houston. These results show how important the role of contemporary information was to many gay-rights activists when they decided whether to allow the Klan to march.[6] Contemporary information played a central role in assessing the degree of threat posed by the group and its planned activities.

Gibson (1987) concluded that the KKK's association with violence triggered the gay activists' intolerance. Of those who expected nothing to happen at the march, 79 percent would allow the march to take place. Among those who expected some confrontations, 58 percent would allow the march. Among those who expected violence to occur, a mere 28 percent would allow the march. Even among those who were willing to tolerate that particular demonstration in Houston, about half would not tolerate a demonstration if they expected violence to occur. Gibson also found a strong relationship between support for freedom of assembly and a lower expectation that violence would occur. Those who supported free assembly were more likely to expect a peaceful Klan demonstration. Gibson suggested that this was due to selective perception that minimized the threat posed by unpopular political groups. Alternatively, the contemporary information may not have been strong enough to cause these individuals to feel sufficiently threatened to overcome their tolerant standing decision.

Threat Perceptions as Contemporary Information

Theoretically, then, threat perceptions could function as a predisposition, standing decision, or contemporaneous information about the particular groups, situations, and immediate contexts. Heightened threat perceptions could reflect a personal disposition to believe the world is generally a threatening place. Perceptions of threat toward a particular group may also reflect some enduring antipathy toward and beliefs about that group. Alternatively, threat perceptions might be formed from contemporaneous information about a group, its activities, and the political context of those actions.

Stouffer (1955) suggested, in fact, that threat operates as a "predisposing" tendency that affects tolerance judgments. But he discovered that community leaders who perceived a high level of threat from communists remained more tolerant than members of the public who perceived a lesser degree of threat; this led him to conclude that there is a relationship between perception of internal Communist danger and tolerance, but not high enough to suggest that changes in perception of danger alone would automatically and simultaneously result in changes in tolerance. The two variables do have something in common. But tolerance or intolerance may be a disposition too deeply rooted in a man's or woman's personality structure to be responsive to a merely negative information program which minimizes the internal Communist risk, even if the facts should justify such an interpretation of the risk. (p. 193)

Yet threat perceptions might function as predisposing tendencies. Stouffer did not think they were as rooted in personality as tolerance judgments themselves, and so they might be more susceptible to change.

However, if threat perceptions reflect a standing decision, as Stouffer suggested, then perceptions of threat should be affected by other relevant variables such as personality. For example, suppose some individuals have a personality structure that fosters a predisposition to perceive threats from the environment and that also affects how they respond to threat perceptions. Individuals who have more dogmatic, authoritarian personalities should more quickly perceive threats from nonconformist political groups. If so, then threat perceptions ought to correlate with measures of personality. They should also more swiftly translate this threat into intolerance. However, the data in Figure 2.1 do not support this proposition. Those who are dogmatic, insecure, and unsociable are no more, and no less, likely to perceive their least-liked group as threatening. Threat perceptions in the survey data are in fact exogenous to measures of social background, personality, ideology, and support for the general norms of democracy (Kinder & Sears, 1981; Sullivan et al., 1982, 1985).

Given that threat perceptions in these survey data are exogenous, it seems likely that threat perceptions may be, at least in part, products of the contemporary information environment. They are not merely a by-product or residue of social learning or personality development. We suspect that threat perceptions do incorporate some elements of a standing decision about the danger presented by a particular group (see Chapter 5). However, contemporary information also strongly influences perceptions of the group's current nature, activities, and ideas.

These findings led us to develop a series of survey-experiments designed to explore if, when, and how people react to different types of information relevant to tolerance judgments. These stud-

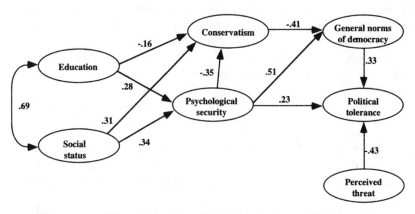

Figure 2.1. *Abbreviated path model of political tolerance (NORC 1978)*

ies focus particularly on information about the potential threat posed by the unpopular group. Chapter 4 reports several survey-experiments that examine how people form threat perceptions and feelings about these groups. It also discusses how such impressions and feelings can inhibit or enhance attention, deliberation, and levels of political tolerance.

Before describing these survey-experiments, however, we will review the recent theory and research on emotions conducted by British psychologist Jeffrey Gray. Gray's work is particularly suited to the study of threat perceptions because it focuses on how emotions guide ongoing assessments of contemporary information. His central concern is how people perceive and react to threatening information in the current environment. After providing this theoretical backdrop, it should be much clearer how the survey-experiments described in Chapter 4 allow us to draw conclusions about the influence of particular types of contemporary information on threat perceptions, which in turn influence the nature of tolerance judgments.

CHAPTER 3

Thinking and Mood

When people are feeling friendly and placable, they think
one sort of thing; when they are feeling angry or hostile,
they think either something totally different or the same
thing with a different intensity: when they feel friendly to
the man who comes before them for judgment, they regard him as having done little wrong, if any; when they
feel hostile, they take the opposite view.

Aristotle, *The Rhetoric*

If, as we argued in Chapter 1, emotions influence political tolerance
judgments, in spite of the long-standing hope that reason would
prevail, we must take account of emotional factors. Our study must
include an empirical investigation of affect if for no other reason
than to better understand how reason and emotion collectively
shape political judgments. But to accomplish that goal we need to
have a theory that can identify which emotions matter, identify when
and why they matter, and show how emotion and reason interact.

The work of a British psychologist, Jeffrey Gray, has been very
influential in guiding our understanding of the functions that emotions serve (Gray, 1981,1984, 1985, 1987a, c, 1990). According to
Gray's theory and research, emotions provide ongoing assessments,
much as the reading provided by a thermometer tells us the tem-
perature, or as the movement of numbers in a digital clock tells us
the time. So too, Gray suggests, changes in mood report changes in
ourselves and in our immediate environment.[1]

Gray is a neuropsychologist and his theory of mood rests on the
functioning of specific brain systems. Since we do not study these

systems, our results cannot provide a direct test of Gray's theory. His theory, however, provides a useful framework to direct our thinking about threat perceptions and to suggest hypotheses about how these perceptions might affect political tolerance judgments. We rely on Gray's model to guide our analysis of threat, to gain insights into how threat can function as contemporary information, and to generate ideas and hypotheses that we can actually test. We therefore provide in this chapter a fairly detailed account of Gray's model to show clearly how our hypotheses concerning tolerance evolved and to clarify the ideas upon which they are based.

Gray's model of emotionality describes three systems that collectively form the limbic system. The three systems are: (1) the fight/flight system; (2) the behavioral inhibition system; and, (3) the behavioral approach system. These systems underlie emotion both in its aspect of mood (i.e., state reactions to contemporary stimuli) and in its aspect of personality (i.e., stable or "trait" patterns of response). In this chapter we will restrict our attention to the application of Gray's theory to mood. This discussion sets the theoretical basis for explaining how contemporary information can come to influence political tolerance judgments. In Chapter 8, we will explicate how Gray's three systems underlie personality theory.

The limbic systems process and manage positive and negative "reinforcers."[2] Positive reinforcers strengthen existing linkages between actions undertaken and reactions to that experience. They also are essential to learning new behavioral routines. Negative reinforcers weaken existing relationships and interrupt normal ongoing actions. By assigning emotional significance to sensory information, identifying some stimuli as positive reinforcers and others as negative reinforcers, the limbic systems play an essential interpretative function. Thus, the limbic systems are fully involved with learning and memory, and with the implementation of behavioral routines.

The first system, fight/flight, differs from the other two systems in that it deals with controlling innate responses to unconditioned punishment and nonreward. Because most politically relevant circumstances in most democracies deal with mediated and symbolically meaningful stimuli, this system is not directly relevant in the domain of everyday politics. Most, if not all, political tolerance judgments are made in response to mediated information, so we do not need to discuss the fight/flight system further.[3]

The two remaining systems, the behavioral approach system (BAS) and the behavioral inhibition system (BIS), deal primarily with conditioned or secondary reinforcers – that is, stimuli that are not in themselves informative, but which the subject has learned to associate with either good or bad consequences. Learning is a central feature of both the behavioral approach and behavioral inhibition systems; they both influence primarily motivated, not reflexive, behavior, which distinguishes these systems from the fight/flight system. The most important point to make about these two systems is that they are fully engaged in the learning process. They are sensory (i.e., information) processing systems that yield mood changes as the product of their contemporary evaluations.

Because these two systems deal with mediated stimuli, that is, secondary reinforcers, they are relevant to politics and to everyday experience. Secondary reinforcers are stimuli that have acquired the status of reinforcers by their association with the experience of reward, nonreward, or punishment. Most of our experience relies on such associations, rather than on direct responses to unmediated experiences of reward and punishment. Therefore, it is important to understand how the behavioral inhibition system is centrally involved with perceptions of threat, and how the behavioral approach system is centrally concerned with executing ongoing learned action.

THE BEHAVIORAL INHIBITION SYSTEM

The BIS scans the environment for novelty and intrusion of threat. It warns us that some situations and some people are unpredictable and dangerous. The BIS generates this warning by making us more anxious and wary.[4] These moods constitute one of two dimensions of emotional response and are most relevant to understanding the relationship between perceptions of threat and political tolerance.

Gray's theory suggests that we recognize the appearance of a threatening group or individual by an increase in anxiety, and that the onset of increased anxiety stops ongoing activity and redirects attention to the threatening display.[5] Strangers generally provoke anxiety because feeling anxious is how humans distinguish the novel and the threatening from the familiar. While we can judge the feelings of others, even strangers, with a measure of accuracy (Ekman et al., 1987; Mauro, Sato, & Tucker, 1992; Stinson & Ickes, 1992), we have a harder time accurately assessing strangers than friends (Stinson & Ickes, 1992). Emotional reactions enable us to make assessments (Forgas, 1992; Kling, 1986).

The BIS produces behavioral and affective responses, not conscious thoughts. Because this system is linked to "higher" cognitive systems, it provokes conscious thinking in specified circumstances. This system cycles rapidly and continually. The BIS compares sensory information about the world with expectations obtained from the BAS. That is, the BIS compares expectations of what is normal for the enaction of a specific plan with incoming sensory information about the surrounding environment. As long as the comparison shows no discrepancy between expectation and reality, the BIS does not interrupt ongoing attention and action, and it generates feelings of reassurance. However, when the BIS detects unexpected and/or threatening stimuli, it generates moods of increasing anxiety. When such moods are generated, the BIS interrupts ongoing activity and shifts conscious attention toward the intrusive stimuli (MacLeod & Mathews, 1988; Pratto & John, 1991). The ability of the system to recycle swiftly enables subtle and swift changes in the environment to register in mood changes.

Figure 3.1 presents a schematic representation of the BIS. This limbic system compares plans, the unfolding of learned behavior, to signals from the environment with a special strategic concern for evidence of novelty, intrusion, and threat. The ability of this system to work without requiring conscious attention enables people to engage in introspection and deliberation when signals of threat or novelty are absent. Because the necessary checking of the safety of the environment is handled outside the realm of consciousness, we can comfortably and safely become fully enaged in such imaginative tasks as pondering deeply about some problem, daydreaming, or idle speculation. We need not break away from our deep involvement to look up or look around. Yet when the BIS notices something out of the ordinary, we are quickly brought back to the here and now. We have probably all had the experience of being deeply engaged in a really good book so that we are, in essence, "in the book." We are also likely to have been startled when someone entered the room and our attention was swiftly shifted from the imaginative world of the story to the surprise appearance of a friend or family member suddenly standing just next to us.

In most normal instances shifts in the moods of anxiety–reassurance do not persist very long, unless, of course, the presence of the

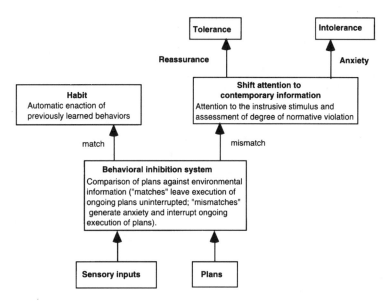

Figure 3.1. *Schematic representation of the behavioral inhibition system*

disturbing event is unabating.[6] This would suggest that the system is not biased, that is, that each cycle is to a large degree unaffected by the prior cycle (MacLeod & Mathews, 1988; Usala & Hertzog, 1991). The system is constantly ready to increase anxiety and shift attention to any new appearance of a threat, to increase anxiety if the normative violation mismatch becomes more serious, or to decrease anxiety to enable attention to shift to other matters if the normative violation becomes less serious or if the intrusion disappears.

Understanding the BIS suggests insights and hypotheses central to the relationship between threat and political tolerance. We can describe contemporary circumstances that seem most likely to increase tolerance and those that seem most likely to increase intolerance. Gray's theory suggests that when things are going well and no threat is apprehended, people rely on their standing decisions. However, when people are confronted by noxious groups, they are likely to feel threatened and might either reaffirm their previously adopted commitments or adjust them. His theory also suggests that whether any adjustment is made will depend upon the kind of information people have available at the moment of decision. More specifically, it suggests that contemporary information about the intrusive group that reassures people about its behavior will strengthen tolerant attitudes. On the other hand, contemporary information that indicates greater belligerence or treachery will increase anxiety and encourage more intolerant attitudes.

Anxiety signals the increased relevance of contemporary information; when we become more anxious we rely less on habits, customs, and antecedent considerations. When current information makes us more anxious or more reassured, we may move away from our standing decisions to be less or more tolerant. In the absence of changing moods of anxiety–reassurance, we pay less attention to contemporary information and rely on preestablished habits of response.

Since political tolerance occurs in a context of noxious groups or individuals, Gray's theory suggests that an increase in anxiety is one means by which humans identify threat. This theory provides the mechanism to explain when contemporary information is influential; that is, when novel or threatening circumstances arise. We should also draw attention to the obverse implication that when novel or threatening circumstances are not apparent, we will not pay as much attention to contemporary information.

THE BEHAVIORAL APPROACH SYSTEM

The BAS is directly involved with task execution. The moods generated by this system, most commonly called positive affect, vary along the mastery or trust dimension. This is the second of the two dimensions of emotional response. Changes in mood, from gloomy to enthusiastic, tell us that we are bursting with confidence, energy, and eagerness. Alternatively, when our mood changes from enthusiastic to gloomy, we conclude that we are exhausted and beaten. According to Gray, this assessment provides crucial ongoing information about how well we are conducting ourselves and how well our previously learned behaviors are functioning. Gray suggests that people will engage in those actions that they feel enthusiastic about and draw back from those that cause them despair. The BAS therefore gauges the success or failure of recalled actions, contemporary experience, and anticipated activities that fall within the category of previously learned behaviors.

The ability to undertake strategic actions requires swift feedback on the success of intermediate steps in the sequence of actions. The shifting moods generated by the BAS provide precisely this information. When this feedback is not present, as when a person is in a state of deep depression, emotional responses are disconnected from either the success or failure of subject-initiated action. A depressed person does not emotionally respond to good events or news. Instead of feeling hopeful or elated, a depressed person continues to feel gloomy and remains passive. So, it is not surprising that variations in this dimension are powerful predictors of the willingness to engage in previously learned actions (Sacks & Bugental, 1987; Seligman, 1975). Positive moods have been found to predict helping behavior (Carlson, Charlin, & Miller, 1988), and they are the best single predictor of which candidate a citizen will support (Marcus, 1988b; Rahn, Aldrich, Borgida, & Sullivan, 1990).

Psychologists have coined the term "information processing paradigm" to describe the large number of studies that focus on how people gather and use information (Hastie, 1986). Psychologists engaged in the information processing research paradigm frequently observe that gathering information is costly. This cost assessment offers a sensible explanation for why people are not widely and fully informed on many matters even of general public importance. A more useful insight, perhaps, is that all physical effort, including thinking, is costly and leads to exhaustion. The willingness to undertake a course of action must be based on the continual gauging of the prospects of success, the anticipated effort, and the current stock of physical and psychic resources. The BAS provides this assessment, the results of which occur as shifts in the moods that define the positive affect dimension. Experiencing increased elation strengthens the motivation to expend effort and strengthens expectations of a successful outcome, whereas feeling depressed weakens the motivation to expend effort and undermines expectations that the outcome will prove successful.

The principle of political tolerance directs how we should react to the actions of others. The behavioral approach system has a parochial focus. It is concerned with our own actions and the actions of those with whom we identify. This focus includes the learned behaviors we rely on to manage tolerance. Some people may join marches to support the rights of others, while other people may join marches to oppose a group they dislike. Whether for or against, those who are politically active engage in complex learned behaviors that have become integrated into their behavioral repertoire. Whether we engage in a behavior depends on many different external circumstances. The BAS provides insight into the internal, or motivational, dynamics that are also important in understanding when and whether someone is moved to action. Having learned how to do something does not, of course, mean that someone will readily engage in the behavior, but the BAS provides emotional support for such behavior.

Gray's theory therefore suggests that modulations of moods in this dimension should be related to politically tolerant or intolerant behaviors. While we do not analyze direct behavioral measures, we do consider people's intention to engage in tolerant and intolerant behaviors. Recall that the BAS modulates the moods that range between depression and elation. The moods that denote the depression end of this dimension (a lack of arousal of the BAS) mark weakened motivation to engage in the associated behavior. The moods of elation and enthusiasm (the arousal state of the BAS) mark heightened motivation to act. The principal insight that we draw from this account is that the greater the intensity of feeling associated with a behavioral act that is already a part of the learned repertoire, the greater the motivation to enact the behavior. This suggests that among people who have learned to support the general norms and principles of democracy, those whose support is more intensely felt are most likely to act in support of their beliefs. Thus, when we turn to predicting the likelihood that people will act on their tolerance judgments, our understanding of Gray's depiction of the BAS will serve to guide our theoretical expectations.

Figure 3.2 presents a schematic representation of the BAS.[7] Here, we use the term *plans* to emphasize that learned behavior is generally a sequence of coordinated and choreographed actions that, to be effective, must flow smoothly and often interact with the actions of others in a similarly dynamic fashion. Thus, though we need not detail how the brain stores and recalls such plans, we do note that the limbic system requires such information in order to monitor the unfolding of learned behaviors so as to evaluate their success or failure, and to recruit more physical and psychic resources as circumstances warrant. It is precisely because the BAS works unobtrusively to monitor ongoing action that we can enact learned behaviors "automatically" without conscious intervention at the level of specific motor actions.

GRAY'S SYSTEMS AND CHANGES IN MOOD

Gray's model explains changes in mood as a function of these two systems.[8] Let us consider what changes in mood mean. When people

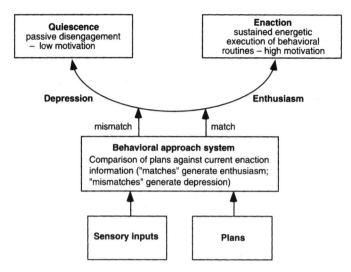

Figure 3.2. *Schematic representation of the behavioral approach system*

report that something or someone makes them feel *anxious*, as opposed to *relaxed*, then we can infer that an unexpected event or a novel or threatening person or group has been apprehended.[9] These moods identify the presence or absence of threat, and it is the change in these moods that people rely upon to assess whether a person or group is threatening. These changes should be central to whether people react to threats with tolerance or intolerance.

On the other hand, when people feel *elated* as opposed to *depressed*, these moods are linked to anticipated self-initiated actions either by oneself or as part of an established group. These moods, and their changes, are not related to novelty and threat and so we might suggest that they have little to do with tolerance. This would be true if we ignored the question of the linkage between tolerant attitudes and tolerant behaviors. Because what people do in regard to their tolerance has such important ramifications, perhaps even more than what they believe, these moods and their changes are centrally important for better understanding of the attitude–behavior linkage.

Just as the experience of color is generated by three specific types of cells in the eye that then produce an amalgam that we experience as an array of colors, so too the limbic systems interpret sensory data to produce mood. Just as we cannot experience a pure color generated by just one type of cell, we cannot experience a single mood generated by only one of these systems. Emotional experience is a composite generated by these dynamic systems.

However, while overall emotional experience at any given moment is a composite formed by differing degrees of arousal, we should not ignore the specific focus of each emotional system. Each emotional system controls particular relationships among emotional, behavioral, and cognitive outcomes. We often assume that characterizing someone as "emotional" describes in some meaningful way how we understand what he or she is saying or doing. From what we have said, it follows that being "emotional" is too broad a term. Using the term "emotional" ignores some important distinctions. Human beings experience different emotions for different reasons and, having experienced these emotions, are likely to feel, behave, and think in systematically and predictably different ways.

Table 3.1 summarizes the workings of the two major limbic systems.[10] It identifies the specific emotional, behavioral, and cognitive attributes of each system. It also contrasts the kind of information that each limbic system targets for attention and appraisal as well as the emotional, behavioral, and cognitive reactions that occur when each system is engaged.

Table 3.1 shows that only the BIS has the strategic function and ability to identify when the familiar and secure are invaded by something or someone novel and threatening. In a familiar environment, we can safely enact already learned behaviors. But in an unfamiliar world, we need to be more guarded and hesitant about enacting previously acquired habits. The specific emotional response of increased anxiety informs us when we are moving into an unsettled and uncertain situation or when something or someone unexpectedly intrudes upon us. Moreover, the BIS, when aroused, increases attention to the here and now and shifts attention to novel and intrusive stimuli. Finally, and most important, when the BIS is aroused, it weakens our reliance on habit and dispositions and encourages attention to contemporary information (Marcus & MacKuen, 1993).

The BIS is a dedicated threat-recognition system. The identification of "we" and "they" is a central part of our feelings about the world. Emotional responses to events, groups, proposals, and individuals will depend primarily upon whether they fall within our familiar circle or represent the strange, the unfamiliar, or the threatening. If we subscribe to universal principles, it follows that

Table 3.1. *The dual systems of emotional arousal and their consequences*

Events associated with limbic system arousal	Behavioral inhibition system	Behavioral approach system
Stimuli that provoke system specific arousal	1. Signals of novelty 2. Signals of threat	1. Signals of subject's plans or behavior resulting in success 2. Signals of success of group(s) that subject identifies with
Characteristic moods of arousal	Feelings of anxiety	Feelings of enthusiasm
Behavioral consequences of system arousal	1. Inhibition of ongoing behavior 2. Weaken current attitude–behavior linkage	1. Increased motivation for the behavior at hand 2. Strengthen attitude–behavior linkage
Cognitive consequences of system arousal	1. Attention shifts away from ongoing behavior and toward the intrusive event or circumstance 2. Learning new routines of response	1. Inattention to contemporary information 2. Disinclination to evaluate habitual responses
Political consequences for understanding tolerance	1. Intensity of relevant emotional arousal (e.g., anxiety) controls whether or not information is sought about the threatening group 2. Contemporary consideration of the extent of normative violation by the threatening group	Intensity of relevant emotional arousal (enthusiasm, not anxiety) controls whether or not actions are likely to be taken against the threatening group

we should apply them uniformly. However, since our feelings are influenced by whether actions or people appear to be familiar or strange (Forgas, 1992; Lanzetta & Englis, 1989), we will adjust our judgments to the extent that we experience the changing moods of anxiety or reassurance.

More important, the moods of the BIS can encourage or discourage learning. Anxiety can be a powerful stimulus for increased attention, whereas feelings of reassurance can encourage inattention. Studies have shown that increased anxiety can cause greater disinclination to proceed according to habits and predispositions, and to engage in learning (Marcus & MacKuen, 1993). Increased anxiety may be a crucial step that controls when we think and what we think about, when we pay attention to our contemporary environment, and when we blithely proceed as if all is normal.

On the other hand, the BAS controls behavior. Thus, when people enact their attitudes, the moods of the BAS are centrally relevant. Motivation is often absent from cognitive accounts of how people think (Hastie, 1986). By incorporating emotion into the study of political tolerance, we obtain theoretical purchase on the attitude–behavior linkage. Understanding how the BAS works provides an explanation for when and how motivation ebbs and flows. Feelings of elation are markers of success, whereas feelings of depression mark failure. Thus, as moods shift toward feelings of success, motivation to engage in or sustain the behavior is strengthened. On the other hand, when failure is experienced or anticipated, moods shift toward gloomy or depressed and weaken the motivation to commence or continue the action. Thus, the behavioral implications of tolerance judgments depend on feelings about the actions that have been learned and linked to tolerance (or intolerance). The crucial feelings that mediate the linkage between tolerant attitudes and actions are those of elation or depression.

Gray's model suggests a reassessment of a problem identified in Chapter 2. A puzzling element of the model of tolerance discussed there was that threat is an exogenous variable, unrelated to personality and other demographic variables. We suggested that threat perceptions may be part of the current information context. As individuals receive new information about a group or event, they use it to make tolerance judgments. Gray's model indicates how that might occur through the BIS.

Consider how individuals approach a tolerance dilemma. They bring to their decision making certain antecedent considerations such as personality, gender, and various political beliefs and attitudes. All of these factors may weigh in their civil liberties decisions. Yet contemporary decisions are not made in a vacuum, but within a real political context, one that provides information about the political groups involved and the circumstances within which they propose to act. Gray's model suggests that the most relevant information drawn from this environment activates or mutes perceptions of threat. The BIS allows people to monitor the contemporary environment, to determine whether the threat posed by the group is real or not, and to evaluate how severe it might be. If they feel reassured, the BIS may prompt them to be more tolerant. On the other hand, if the threat seems imminent and real, then the BIS may push them toward intolerance.

This theoretical account informs the studies we designed to examine the role of contemporary threat information about unpopular political groups. Our experimental manipulation of contemporary information focuses on perceptions of threat for two reasons. First, the survey research described earlier shows that threat perceptions are central to tolerance judgments. Second, Gray's theory suggests that contemporary information as monitored by the BIS is central to threat perceptions.

As we emphasized earlier, our studies do not directly measure limbic system arousal. Gray's work provides a working metaphor to help us understand threat stimuli and their role in tolerance judgments. Drawing on Gray's conception of the BIS and BAS furnishes theoretical guidance in the form of working hypotheses that examine the connection between threat and tolerance. We also gain an interpretative framework for understanding and communicating the results of our studies. We turn to a discussion of our survey-experiments in Chapter 4.

PART II

Contemporary Information and Political Tolerance Judgments

IN THIS PART, we begin the process of empirically testing the theoretical model of tolerance judgments we laid out in Part I. Since past research has focused almost exclusively on the effects of antecedent considerations on tolerance, we must first establish that contemporary information makes a difference. If tolerance judgments are based solely on the predispositions and standing decisions people hold, then a major part of our theoretical argument – especially the role of threat as contemporary information – would be fallacious. On the other hand, if contemporary information influences tolerance judgments even when we take antecedent considerations into account, then we have taken the first step toward substantiating our theory.

We empirically test our basic model in two ways. First, in Chapter 4 we conduct survey-experiments that allow us both to measure the crucial antecedent considerations found to be important in past research and to manipulate the information subjects receive to determine if certain kinds of contemporary information affect tolerance more than others. If our theoretical model is correct, we should find that antecedent considerations play a major role in determining contemporary tolerance judgments, but that contemporary information matters as well. Specifically, as we argued in Chapter 3, it is threatening information, especially about a group's behavior, that should significantly influence people's tolerance judgments. Second, in Appendix 4A we lay out, for interested readers, our checks to validate the studies. Certain assumptions that we make in Chapter 4, for example that people are reacting to the contemporary information the way we assume they are, need to be tested to make sure that our theoretical explanation is on target.

CHAPTER 4

Tolerance Judgments and Contemporary Information — The Basic Studies

> People react with their guts instead of their head and then justify intellectually what their gut reactions are. Guts have nothing to do with this. . . . If guts decided what kind of Bill of Rights we were going to have, . . . we'd have a very different country. We'd probably have something closer to a dictatorship.
>
> David Goldberger, "Skokie: Rights or Wrong"

We have thus far laid out the basic arguments that constitute the foundation for our model of tolerance judgments. First, as Chapter 2 revealed, previous research has clearly established the strong influence of antecedent considerations, such as personality, education, and commitment to democratic principles, on people's current tolerance judgments. Such predispositions and standing decisions presumably set boundaries on people's willingness to be tolerant or intolerant at any given time. But this past research also identifies another potential influence on tolerance: perceptions of threat. While people may have a predisposition to see threat as pervasive, or a standing decision to perceive a disliked group as threatening, threatening stimuli in the environment can also be especially relevant pieces of contemporary information.

As we discussed in Chapter 3, Gray argues that the BIS monitors the environment for threatening stimuli that violate norms of proper, orderly behavior. Therefore, the type and degree of threat a group poses provide people with information that may affect their current tolerance judgment. State of mind, that is, whether people pay attention to their thoughts or feelings, may also affect their

55

contemporary tolerance judgments. Much of the previous discourse would lead us to believe that responding out of passion probably makes people more intolerant and that responding with reason makes people more tolerant. Gray's work and the literature on mood accessibility also posit the importance of state of mind and its impact on attitudes and behavior. We therefore need to take into account people's affective and cognitive states of mind to understand their tolerance judgments.

THE SURVEY-EXPERIMENT

How do these arguments fit together in a clearly specified model of political tolerance judgments? We explicate such a model in this chapter and test it using a survey-experiment design. The use of survey-experiments allows us to examine in depth the effects of predispositions, standing decisions, and contemporary information on political tolerance.

A survey-experiment combines features of an experiment with those of a survey. Traditional laboratory experiments share several characteristics. First, classical experiments usually consist of a pretest, an experimental stimulus, and a posttest. The researcher administers a pretest to the subjects that determines a baseline measure of the dependent variable. The subjects are then exposed to an experimental stimulus – the independent variable – and the dependent variable is once again measured in a posttest. Second, the laboratory usually provides a tightly controlled environment where subjects' attention is focused on the experimental topic itself. Few outside interruptions are permitted. The laboratory setting also allows researchers to use physiological measures such as the galvanic skin response, or advanced technological equipment such as interactive computer programs. Third, researchers often use a fairly small number of subjects in a laboratory experiment, most often students in an introductory psychology class. Finally, experiments often have both experimental and control groups. The experimental group is exposed to the stimulus, whereas the control group completes the pretest and posttest without the intervening stimulus. Including a control group allows the researcher to determine what effect the experimental situation itself has on the subjects and therefore to assess the direct effect of the experimental treatment on the dependent variable.

Surveys, on the other hand, are easily administered to a large number of randomly selected respondents. The traditional survey relies heavily on invariant questions asked of most respondents. The use of the Computer Aided Telephone Interview (CATI) technique, however, has introduced more flexibility into the survey instrument. For example, Piazza, Sniderman, and Tetlock (1989) describe the survey they used for studying racism. The telephone interviewers gave respondents a short description of a person and then asked whether the person should get government assistance. The computer randomly assigned the characteristics of the person described to the respondent, such as his or her race, gender, and dependability. Thus, each respondent was given a randomly selected stimulus and asked to respond to it. Yet even this flexibility does not eradicate a drawback of telephone surveys; the necessity of employing limited information in the survey instrument. For example, Piazza et al. (1989) provided a very limited range of descriptors to respondents, who could not be expected to listen to a long, detailed description of the person.

We combine these two methods in our survey-experiments by relying on an experimental design and using a survey to obtain the data for our study. First, we gave subjects a survey as a pretest, then later gave them the experimental stimuli and a posttest survey. Subjects were randomly assigned to the experimental treatments, as is necessary in an experiment. Second, we used a larger number of subjects than is usual in an experiment but fewer than is usual for a survey. Third, these subjects were exposed to the experiment in large groups, often in a natural setting (such as a classroom, a place of business, and so on). We therefore had less control over the environment within which the survey-experiment took place than is usual in a laboratory experiment. Finally, while we used students for many of our experiments, we also obtained a nonstudent adult sample in order to examine the external validity of our results.

The survey-experiment method we use is highly appropriate for testing our theoretical concerns. As we discussed in earlier chapters, antecedent considerations are the broad array of previously acquired beliefs, values, prejudices, and sentiments that people bring to any new situation demanding tolerance judgments, including commitment to democratic principles, political knowledge, personality, and so on. All of these variables have a strong impact on people's tolerance judgments when they are confronted with a new situation. In a survey-experiment design, we can identify the effects of predispositions and standing decisions by using covariates in an analysis of covariance model.[1]

Yet while antecedent considerations matter, we contend that contemporary information can also be influential. Contemporary information is any new information to which people are exposed in a situation requiring a tolerance judgment. In our survey-experiment, people are exposed to this information through the experimental treatments. We manipulate the content of this information, as well as the state of mind in which people make their judgments, and the manipulations become the main effects in our analysis of covariance model. Some interactions among these main effects also play a vital role in our theoretical model, and can be easily evaluated with analysis of covariance.

Thus, the survey-experiment method, in combination with analysis of covariance, allows us to examine the crucial theoretical underpinnings of our model. Our model holds that a person's current tolerance judgment, the dependent variable, is the combined result of predispositions, standing decisions, contemporary information concerning the threat posed by a group, and a focus on an affective or cognitive state of mind. Predispositions and standing decisions are covariates; contemporary information and attention to state of mind are the experimental treatments. We discuss these two parts of the model in more detail here.

THE MODEL

Antecedent Considerations

The number of possible antecedent considerations we could include in our model is obviously vast. We have chosen to use an "unfolding" strategy to analyze antecedent considerations in order to present the findings in a manageable fashion. The basic findings presented in this chapter do not turn on this choice. The subsequent analyses in the chapters that follow elaborate and augment these findings, but do not overturn them.

In the basic model we include gender as a predisposition. Some research suggests that females are more likely to report fear in response to external threat (Boehnke, Macpherson, Meador, & Petri, 1989; Rabow, Hernandez, & Newcomb, 1990; Schatz & Fiske, 1992) and to report greater emotional intensity than males (Eagly &

Wood, 1991; Fujita, Diener, & Sandvik, 1991). It is therefore likely that females would be less tolerant than males, and that gender will have a direct and an indirect effect on current tolerance judgments.

We also include two standing decisions in our basic model. We argue that people have a tolerance standing decision, based on various predispositions and experiences, that provides a default decision rule whenever they are confronted with a new situation. People who tend to be generally tolerant are more likely to be tolerant in any specific situation, while those who tend to be generally intolerant are more likely to be intolerant in the same situation (McClosky & Brill, 1983; McClosky & Zaller, 1984; Sullivan et al., 1982). This default decision rule reflects a summary decision based on various predispositions including education, gender, long-standing threat perceptions, personality, and so on. It is this standing decision to be tolerant or intolerant that has been most widely studied by political scientists, as we discussed in Chapter 2. We therefore include in our model a measure of tolerance as a standing decision.

We argue that a second standing decision will also have a direct effect on current tolerance judgments: commitment to democratic principles. According to Gray, threatening stimuli increase people's attention to contemporary information. A natural reaction to this threat is intolerance, as McClosky and Brill (1983) argue. In a threatening situation, a strong commitment to democratic principles has the potential to overcome the natural response of intolerance. A commitment to democratic principles therefore will have a direct effect on current tolerance judgments because of the role it plays in overriding a natural inclination to be intolerant in specific threatening situations.

Perceptions of Threat as Contemporary Information

Our model also includes experimental treatments containing contemporary and threatening information. Prior literature suggests the possibility that two aspects of threat may be relevant (Sullivan et al., 1982 and discussion in Chapter 5): the treachery and belligerence of the group and the probability of a noxious group becoming more powerful. We therefore manipulate these two aspects of threat in our experimental treatments.

The first experimental treatment, normative violations, concerns the appraisal of a noxious group's treachery and belligerence (see Chapters 2 and 3). Survey research shows that the extent of a noxious group's violation of the norms of proper, orderly behavior is highly related to tolerance (Sullivan et al., 1982). What explains the strong relationship between normative violations and tolerance? Gray provides an intriguing framework for understanding this relationship. As discussed in Chapter 3, Gray's (1981; 1984; 1985; 1987a, b, c; 1988) theory implies that specific emotional reactions to political groups are based on sensory information provided by the current environment. Changes in mood reflect constant monitoring of the state of contemporary affairs with regard to uncertainty and threat. Gray's model specifies which changes in mood will influence current political tolerance judgments. Specifically, normative violations should increase the sense of threat, which should decrease tolerance.

In our model, the normative violations of the group are the stimuli that evoke threat, which in turn leads to changes in current tolerance levels. Therefore, to the extent that disliked groups violate normative expectations, individuals will be more intolerant. To the extent that individuals feel reassured that disliked groups are predictable and orderly, people will be more tolerant. Thus, the manipulated factor includes a high or *threatening* level of normative violations versus a low or *reassuring* level of normative violations.

The second experimental factor is appraisal of the probability that a noxious group will become more powerful, which should be related to how threatening a person perceives the group to be. Survey research has suggested that assessments of a group's power and strength are not related to tolerance (Sullivan et al., 1982), yet two theoretical traditions highlight the potential importance of such information in influencing people's attitudes. First, rational-actor models emphasize the importance of calculating the probability of an event occurring in people's decision-making processes (Downs, 1957; Enelow & Hinich, 1984; Rabinowitz & MacDonald, 1989). When decisions are made under conditions of uncertainty, risk becomes a major part of the decision-making process, and therefore the probability of an expected outcome becomes a major part of the calculus (Arrow, 1982; Borch, 1968; Ordeshook, 1986). Probability assessments are widespread since most decisions occur under conditions of uncertainty. We might therefore expect probability information to weigh heavily in people's decisions concerning tolerance.

Second, protection motivation theory, a psychological theory, also posits the importance of probability information in changing people's behavior (Rogers, 1983). This theory has specifically been applied to research on fear appeals, but it is also relevant to understanding threat situations. When confronted with a threatening stimulus, people naturally respond by trying to avoid the danger (Leventhal, 1970). This coping response is in part affected by people's assessments of the probability of a noxious event occurring if they do nothing. Applied to tolerance, we can interpret people's intolerance as a coping response. If people are confronted with a threatening stimulus and the probability of a noxious event occurring is high, they will seek a coping response. Society provides cues that restricting the activities of extremist political groups can provide such a coping response. Indeed, collective, regime-level prohibitions will reduce significantly the probability that the noxious effects of the disliked group's platform and ideas will be realized.

Therefore, according to both rational choice theory and protection motivation theory, probability assessments play a major role in attitudinal and behavioral change and should therefore be related to tolerance levels. To the extent the probability of a disliked group obtaining power is perceived to be high, individuals are likely to be more intolerant. To the extent this probability is perceived to be low, individuals are likely to be more tolerant.

Order in which Contemporary Information Is Received

People's reactions to contemporary information may be affected by the order in which they receive that information. We turn to two theoretical arguments concerning order effects, one that predicts order to be a main effect, the other an interaction effect. First, research on schema use and impression formation suggests that we might expect a primacy effect (Jones & Goethals, 1972; but see Fiske & Taylor, 1991). Information received first will lead a person to access a relevant schema, which will then affect the encoding of later information. Based on this research, whatever information is attended to first will likely affect tolerance judgments the most and, therefore, order will have a main effect.

However, this research is primarily cognitive, and we are manipulating some information that is heavily affective. We are more persuaded by a second theoretical argument based on Gray's work. Gray's argument that the BIS cycles continually suggests that unless a normative violation stimulus is corroborated by further information, threat will be dampened. The BIS continuously monitors the

[margin annotation: Complexity of the info. environment]

environment and therefore can quickly take into account the with-drawal of the threat-evoking stimuli. Thus, if people are confronted with such threat-evoking stimuli but see that these stimuli quickly recede, they will be reassured.

This argument can easily be applied to order effects. The two types of information we manipulate are the probability of a noxious group gaining power and the normative violations of the group. If people are confronted with threatening information about the nor-mative violations of a group, but that threatening information is quickly followed by probability information that previous research has shown to be nonthreatening, then the normative violations in-formation should not affect tolerance. On the other hand, if people are confronted with the threatening normative violations informa-tion last, they will be affected by it when making their tolerance judgments. We therefore argue that the order effect will be signifi-cant only as it interacts with the normative violations manipulation.

This discussion of order effects, however, raises the problematic specter of threat being so transitory that its impact on tolerance is severely limited. If the threat induced by normative violations quickly dissipates, why should we be concerned with its effect on tolerance? We believe it is important for two reasons. First, even short-lived, threat-induced anxiety can have an effect on tolerance, which may lead to the serious abridgment of basic civil liberties for disliked groups. In other words, even short-lived threat can have serious consequences. Second, we are rarely confronted with only one piece of threatening information followed by calm. Rather, we are more often confronted with a threatening stimulus in a contin-uous and sustained manner. An obvious example of this phenome-non is the McCarthy era. People were continuously confronted with threatening information about communists and the "red scare." As Stouffer (1955) demonstrated, the threat people felt in reaction to the red scare was strongly related to intolerance, which he concep-tualized as a standing decision. Thus, when people are continuously confronted with threatening stimuli, their current tolerance judg-ment can be significantly affected.

State of Mind

The final experimental factor concerns people's state of mind – whether they attend to their thoughts or feelings. Does attending to thoughts or attending to feelings lead to different tolerance judg-

Reason v. passion

ments? A long-standing debate centers on the differential effects of reason and passion on political judgments (for example, Kant and J. S. Mill emphasize the crowning achievements of reason, whereas Burke and Le Bon find virtue in the role sentiment plays). Since the Enlightenment, a widely shared view holds reason superior to passion: if people give a "sober second thought" to a situation at hand, they will arrive at a wiser tolerance judgment than if they simply react based on their passion (Stouffer, 1955). According to Gibson (1987), "The natural reaction toward something that one opposes is to suppress it. Tolerance requires . . . a 'sober second thought'; that is, reflection about the political benefits of tolerance" (p. 439). These arguments lead us to expect that attending to thoughts will lead to greater tolerance, whereas attending to feelings will lead to greater intolerance.

Research suggests that directing subjects' attention to affective cues – instructing them to attend to their feelings – does yield different judgments from attention to cognitive cues (Kuklinski, Riggle, Ottati, Schwarz, & Wyer, 1991; Millar & Tesser, 1986; Ottati, Riggle, Wyer Jr., Schwarz, & Kuklinski, 1989; Wilson, Dunn, Kraft, & Lisle, 1989). Millar and Tesser (1986) divide attitudes into two components, affective and cognitive, and argue that "when the cognitive component is emphasized by thought, the general evaluation will reflect the cognitive component, and when the affective component is emphasized, the general evaluation will reflect the affective component" (p. 271). The instruction set they used (as did most other researchers working in this area), asked subjects to focus their attention on either their feelings or the *reasons* for their feelings, thereby emphasizing the affective or cognitive component of an attitude respectively. In their experiment, they had subjects play with five different puzzles. Half of the subjects were instructed to analyze *how* they felt while they played with the puzzles, whereas the other half were instructed to analyze *why* they felt the way they did about the puzzles. They found that instruction set was significantly related to attitude–behavior consistency (that is, subsequent playing with the puzzles): subjects who focused on their feelings had a much higher attitude–behavior correlation than did those who thought about reasons. This suggests that our feelings about a subject may give a truer indication of our inclinations than the reasons we proffer. Numerous experiments replicate this finding (Millar & Tesser, 1989; Tesser & Clary, 1978; Wilson, Dunn, Bybee, Hyman, & Rotondo, 1984; Wilson et al., 1989).

While judgments may differ depending on the focus of people's attention, research on mood accessibility gives some clues as to what is actually taking place when people attend to their feelings. Bower (1981) developed the associative network theory of mood-congruence effects, which basically holds that when people are in a distinct emotional state (e.g., anger) they more easily retrieve mood-congruent memories (e.g., memories related to anger). Ehrlichman and Halpern (1988) used odor to induce mood and found that people in the pleasant-odor condition were more likely to retrieve happy memories than those in the unpleasant-odor condition. Numerous other methods have been used to induce moods, including hypnosis, the experience of success or failure, and reading mood-relevant sentences (Blaney, 1986). These studies demonstrate a strong relationship between mood and memory, where positive mood enhances the retrieval of positive memories and, to a lesser extent, negative mood the retrieval of negative memories (see, e.g., Fiske & Taylor, 1991). In our study, we can therefore expect that asking people to focus on their feelings will lead them to retrieve memories congruent with their current mood state (feeling threatened or reassured).

What is the implication? [handwritten annotation]

Much of the research in psychology has been specifically concerned with the effect of instruction set on attitude–behavior consistency, but work in this area has also been done on tolerance. Kuklinski et al. (1991) instructed subjects either to "attend to your feelings" or to "think about the consequences of an action or event." They discovered that respondents who were told to think about the consequences were *less* tolerant than those who were told to attend to their feelings. What were people's concerns when asked to think about consequences? A small number of respondents in the "consequences" condition were asked to record the reasoning behind their tolerance judgments. Kuklinski et al. (1991: pp. 21–22) found that these respondents concentrated on the negative repercussions of allowing people to exercise their basic civil liberties, such as a group brainwashing children. A much smaller percentage of respondents focused on the need to protect civil liberties for all groups, the consequences of their own tolerance judgment or, as Gibson (1987) argues, the consequences of the benefits of tolerance.

Our cognitive instruction set differs from that of Kuklinski and his colleagues. Rather than asking people to "think about the consequences," we asked people to "attend to your thoughts." Asking people to attend to their thoughts may prompt them to give the situation a "sober second thought." It is also likely to make people less attentive to their feelings. We hypothesize that including an instruction set, "attend to your thoughts" or "attend to your feelings," will produce a main effect of greater intolerance when subjects are given the affect instruction, and higher tolerance when subjects are given the cognition instruction.

We therefore devised a model of tolerance judgments that takes into account antecedent considerations and contemporary information. The first three factors are the antecedent considerations people bring into any new situation that requires a tolerance judgment, and these are the covariates in our model: (1) gender, as a predisposition; (2) a standing decision toward tolerance or intolerance; and (3) a standing commitment to democratic principles.[2] Four other factors are manipulated in the experiment and therefore are the main effects in our model: (4) degree of normative violations; (5) probability of power; (6) the order of presentation of the probability of power and normative violations information; and (7) instruction set (attend to thoughts or feelings). Finally, we also included two other variables that control unique experimental effects: (8) the study in which the subjects participated; and (9) the hypothetical group about which subjects read.

THE EXPERIMENTAL DESIGN

The survey-experiment we designed occurred in two stages. First, the subjects in the experiment filled out a pretest survey asking about their feelings toward various groups in the United States, their willingness to accord basic civil liberties to their most disliked group, their commitment to abstract democratic values such as free speech, and about various demographic questions. Two weeks later, the subjects read a scenario about a hypothetical group in the United States that included the experimental manipulations. They then answered a posttest survey that measured their tolerance of the hypothetical group. In order to disguise the true purpose of the study, subjects were told at the beginning of the posttest that we were interested in social networks and therefore wanted to know where people get information and who influences their opinions. After completing the posttest, subjects were debriefed and told the true purpose of the study.

Experimental procedures and conditions

For the concept of tolerance to make sense, we must object to something before we can be said to tolerate it. We must therefore ascertain which group each individual finds most objectionable so that people are asked to tolerate groups toward which they have malice. This procedure ensures a content-controlled measure of tolerance (Sullivan et al., 1982). In the pretest, subjects were presented with a list of eleven extremist political groups and were asked, among other things, to indicate how much they liked or disliked each group, and to select the group they most disliked.

Subjects were then asked to respond to six statements concerning the rights that should be extended to each respondent's most-disliked group. The following statements make up the tolerance scale, with the group included in the bracket corresponding to each subject's most-disliked group (as an example, we use the American Communists):

1. Members of the [American Communists] should be banned from running for public office in the United States.
2. Members of the [American Communists] should be allowed to teach in public schools.
3. The [American Communists] should be outlawed.
4. Members of the [American Communists] should be allowed to make a public speech.
5. The [American Communists] should have their phones tapped by our government.
6. The [American Communists] should be allowed to hold public rallies.

Each tolerance statement had five possible response options: strongly agree, agree, neutral, disagree, and strongly disagree. The most tolerant response was assigned a value of 5 and the least tolerant response a 1. The pretest tolerance scale ranged from 6 to 30.[3]

Subjects also responded to statements about abstract democratic principles (see Appendix B). These questions ascertained people's general commitment to basic civil liberties, such as freedom of speech and assembly, regardless of the specific situation at hand.[4] It is important to note that scholars have distinguished between support for the abstract principles of democracy, such as freedom of speech and minority rights, and political tolerance, which refers to the application of these principles to actual groups and situations. The abstract democratic principles statements measure the former (see Chapter 6).

We have therefore gained four critical pieces of information in the pretest: each subject's most disliked group, his or her pretest score on the tolerance scale, gender, and his or her level of commitment to democratic principles.

The basic experiments are six-way between-subjects analysis of variance designs with three covariates: pretest political tolerance of the initially selected least-liked group, support for democratic principles, and gender. These are the antecedent-consideration surrogates in our model. All covariates and the dependent variable – posttest tolerance – were standardized to a range of scores from 0 to 1. This standardization procedure does not affect variances but does facilitate comparisons of regression coefficients without incurring the problems of using standardized regression coefficients (see King, 1986; Luskin, 1991; Marcus & MacKuen, 1993). The drawback of standardizing variables in this way is that the mean differences appear much smaller when the scale ranges from 0 to 1 than when it has a much larger range, thereby making our experimental manipulations look weaker. In spite of these drawbacks, we think the benefits of standardizing the range outweigh the cost of appearing to have small mean differences.

Two weeks later, as part of the posttest survey, subjects read a scenario about a hypothetical group coming to power in the United States. The least-liked group each subject chose in the pretest determined which scenario he or she read (see Table 4.1). For example, subjects who chose the American Communists as their most disliked group in the pretest read a scenario about a hypothetical group called the New Movement for America. Similarly, those who chose feminists read a scenario about a group called Women for Justice, and so on. Thus, each subject read a scenario about a group toward which he or she felt malice, thereby minimizing differences in the level of malice toward the target group. This procedure also ensured that subjects did not read a scenario depicting a group they might like and support.

We chose to use a hypothetical group rather than an existing group for several reasons. First, our model argues that antecedent considerations and contemporary information influence current tolerance judgments. The scenarios include contemporaneous infor-

Table 4.1. *Target groups, frequencies, and corresponding hypothetical groups*

Least-liked groups selected	N	Scenario assigned
Religious fundamentalists	42	Christians in Politics
Prolife on abortion issue	24	(CP)
American Communists	46	New Movement for
Socialists	1	America (NMA)
Ku Klux Klan	406	White Supremacist Faction
American racists	159	(WSF)
American Nazis	113	Nationalist Party of
		America (NPA)
Prochoice on abortion issue	20	Women for Justice (WJ)
Feminists	11	
Oppose prayer in public schools	7	
Oppose nuclear weapons/	12	Americans Against the
foreign policy		Military (AAM)

mation about the hypothetical group as well as information that should bring to mind antecedent considerations about a real group. If a real group were used, it would be more difficult to isolate the impact of contemporary information to that contained in the scenario because some subjects might be aware of the current activities of the real group and therefore react to the information they already have rather than to the information in the scenario. In other words, people would be more likely to engage in counterarguing, knowing that the real group had not taken the actions depicted in a hypothetical scenario.

Second, if we used a real group, its actions in the interim between the pretest and posttest might unduly affect the experiment. By using a hypothetical group, it is likely that even if a real group took actions that were covered in the media, these actions would only indirectly and tangentially affect the experiment.

Third, it is essential for our experimental design that information provided in the scenario be standardized across hypothetical groups. If real groups were used, we could not ensure this standardization.

Fourth, and most important, we wanted to enhance the verisimilitude of the scenario and could do this only by using a hypothetical group. The probability manipulation varies the probability of a group gaining power in the United States, but fringe groups in the United States tend to be quite small and powerless. Subjects would know, for example, that American Communists do not have a high probability of gaining a great deal of power in the near future, but they may be less likely to question the credibility of a scenario about a hypothetical communist group. These considerations also led us to place the scenario in the future, since again subjects would be aware that a certain type of group was not immediately gaining significant power.

Each scenario began with a brief introductory paragraph:

> Now we would like you to read the following scenario about a hypothetical group that has organized in the United States. While you read the scenario, please think about how you and the people in your social network would react to such a group.

This paragraph informed subjects that this was a scenario about a hypothetical group. We also mentioned subjects' social network to reinforce the cover story we used in our experiment – that we wanted to discover where people obtain their political values and beliefs.

This introductory paragraph was followed by the scenario itself. Every subject who chose a particular group in the pretest as their most disliked read the same scenario. The first paragraph provided a description of the beliefs held by the hypothetical group. The second and third paragraphs outlined actions the group proposed to take to implement their beliefs. We use as an example the White Supremacist Faction for people who chose the KKK or racists as their most disliked group in the pretest.

> Suppose it is the late 1990s and a new political group has been formed in the United States. It is an extremist group that evolved from the Ku Klux Klan of the 1980s. This group – the White Supremacist Faction (WSF) – has pledged to rid the United States of Black influence which they believe has grown too great. They believe that Blacks have been favored by liberal government policies and have taken advantage of the system. Recent evidence of this, they believe, is the massive affirmative-action efforts of recent decades and the various special job training programs in Black neighborhoods and communities, as well as the attempts to integrate schools. They believe that American society has lowered its standards, and blame Blacks for this. They are also beginning to worry more and more about the power and influence of Catholics as well, but have decided to concentrate for now on Blacks.

> The WSF has not been very specific about the actions they propose to take, but there are hints that they would like to restrict the economic and polit-

ical rights of Blacks and perhaps even Catholics. They would like to keep Blacks out of public office, and have stated that they would like to screen other candidates to make sure they do not support programs designed to help disadvantaged minorities. They would like to restrict welfare programs, and have mentioned eliminating many job and welfare programs. They have stated that they will not use violence to achieve their aim of limiting Black influence in America.

Another part of the WSF program seems to be restricting entry into colleges and universities, largely because they perceive them to be the major training ground for the Black middle classes and liberal intellectuals. These Blacks and intellectuals have masterminded the decay of white middle-class values and have assisted in creating and maintaining the Black and liberal stranglehold on the political system in the United States. The WSF would like to restrict the college experience to small, denominational, Christian institutions and to do away with the large research universities across the country. They want to ensure that only the physically and intellectually "fit" are allowed to attend college and to become part of the governing classes in the U.S. Although they have not explicitly said so, it appears likely they would institute a screening program to weed out dangerous college professors.

The first paragraph set the scenario in the future, making it more credible, and explicitly tied the WSF to the Ku Klux Klan. Since the WSF evolved from the Klan, subjects could draw on standing decisions related to the Klan to influence their current tolerance judgment about the WSF. The platform of the WSF also calls to mind the Klan, making the hypothetical group seem more real. We formulated this platform in such a way as to make it hard-hitting and disruptive, but did not include foul or provocative language. The paragraph set up the idea that the WSF blames blacks for many problems in the United States and attacks policy initiatives specifically designed to help blacks. For example, we mentioned affirmative action and school integration, which have strong symbolic connotations and about which people tend to feel intensely. We also mentioned Catholics in this paragraph in order to widen the net of people potentially affected by the WSF and its platform.

The second paragraph laid out the policy proposals of the WSF but left them vague. Leaving the proposals vague allowed subjects to read into them abhorrent policy options that they might associate with a racist group. The WSF was also portrayed as wanting to influence elections, specifically by keeping certain people out of office.

We also mentioned that the WSF would not use violence, which sets up the normative violations manipulation. Any mention of the use of violence in the normative manipulations increases how untrustworthy the group appears to be.

The third paragraph specifically mentioned the WSF's views on colleges and universities to make the scenario more personally relevant to most of the subjects. In essence, we wanted these subjects to believe that WSF policies could have a direct effect on their own lives, and to feel the personal impact of the potential threat posed by the WSF.

The format and general content of the other five scenarios were very similar, differing only in the name of the group and the group's specific beliefs and goals. For example, the scenario for the Christians in Politics (CP) focused on liberal groups and liberal social policies, whereas the Nationalist Party of America (NPA) focused on Jews and the economy. Unlike the WSF's casual mention of Catholics as a potential target group, the CP potentially targeted Jews and the NPA blacks. Appendix A provides the scenarios and manipulations for the other hypothetical groups.

The overriding purpose of these three paragraphs was to provide sufficient threatening information to our subjects that they would attend carefully to the information that followed. According to Gray, if people perceive potential threat in the environment, they will become more alert and responsive to subsequent contemporary information. Since everyone read a scenario about a group they strongly disliked, and the scenario indicated a rather extreme political agenda, our subjects should have been threatened enough to respond alertly to the manipulations that followed.

These three paragraphs provided information that was common across all experimental conditions, and therefore cannot explain the different effects of the manipulations. That is, everyone who chose the KKK or racists in the pretest read these three paragraphs of the WSF scenario. The scenario, however, set up the manipulations (described below) by making them appear as simply more information about the hypothetical group.

Following the scenario were two additional paragraphs that each contained one of the two principal experimental manipulations. One paragraph provided contemporary information about the treachery and belligerence of the group (i.e., violations of the norms of trustworthiness and proper, orderly behavior) and the other about the probability of the group coming to power. The information contained in the manipulation paragraphs is relatively mild because of potential problems with incredulity.

The first manipulation was achieved by creating two versions of a paragraph that varied the degree to which the description of the group and its actions violated established behavioral norms. We adopted the language used in the normative violations paragraph with Gray's arguments in mind – the threatening version emphasized violations of behavioral norms, and the reassuring version emphasized compliant and orderly behavior.

The threatening paragraph:

The WSF has begun to hold public rallies to generate support for their cause. Before their rallies, they refused to cooperate with the police and local authorities but did promise to have peaceful demonstrations according to the conditions of their parade permits. However, they have not always marched along the designated routes and have gotten enmeshed with counter demonstrators and the police. As a result violence has broken out at some of the rallies. Fist fights and rock throwing have resulted in spectators, demonstrators and some police getting hurt. Members of the WSF have shouted "Whites only, down with the Blacks" and "First get the dirty blacks, then Catholics." At the rallies and demonstrations, leaders of the WSF have asked their supporters to take bold actions to pursue their cause.

The reassuring paragraph:

The WSF has begun to hold public rallies to generate support for their cause. Before their rallies, they cooperated with the police and local authorities and promised to have peaceful demonstrations according to the conditions of their parade permits. They have marched along the designated routes and did not cause any trouble with counter demonstrators, spectators or the police. At the rallies and demonstrations, leaders of the WSF have asked their supporters to act vigorously but as lawfully as possible to pursue their cause.

The threatening paragraph portrayed the group as uncooperative with the police and devious with regard to their demonstration plans. It was also portrayed as involved in violence and using inflammatory language.[5] This paragraph was constructed to invoke images of treachery and belligerence, thereby activating subjects' feelings of fear and threat, and does not contain any information about the probability of the group gaining power. According to Gray, stimuli that appear suddenly, particularly in the form of normative violations, will make people feel more threatened. The threatening paragraph introduces this type of stimulus and should therefore encourage intolerance. The reassuring paragraph portrayed the group as cooperative, trustworthy, and peaceful, thereby reassuring subjects that threat was minimal. Subjects should therefore have expressed more tolerant attitudes because they were reassured.[6]

The second manipulation, the probability of power paragraph, varied the extent to which the group was popular and likely to come to power, and had a higher and lower version:

The higher-probability paragraph:

The WSF has already amassed large sums of money for a sophisticated and subtle advertising campaign. Public opinion polls show that although they are not likely to win any major national elections soon, more and more people – particularly young people – are beginning to listen to their message and to find some value in it. Most people do not agree with everything they say, but do find some points appealing. This is evidenced by some electoral gains that the WSF has begun to register in local elections in some parts of the country, particularly Chicago, Southern California, and parts of the South. Some public opinion polls indicate that as much as 10% of the public feels sympathy for the WSF and its point of view, and the percentage appears to be on the rise. Several Black organizations, including the NAACP, are taking the threat very seriously indeed and have begun an urgent campaign to combat the WSF.

The lower-probability paragraph:

The WSF has tried raising money for an advertising campaign, but public opinion polls show that few people are paying much attention to them. In fact, many people find their views objectionable, and most people are apathetic about the group and its agenda. The group has grown some in recent years, but most political analysts have classified it as another in a long line of extremist groups in the U.S. that simply do not appeal to the bulk of the moderate American public. Analysts agree that they might indeed do harm to some Black groups and individuals but they have little chance of gaining any significant political power.

These paragraphs differed systematically in information about the effectiveness of fund-raising and the degree of public responsiveness to the group's appeals, not the group's belligerence or treachery.[7] They also differed in the group's electoral success and the significance accorded to it by appropriate monitoring organizations. We emphasized in these paragraphs information about the realistic degree of danger presented by the hypothetical group.[8] Rogers (1983) contended that <u>probability information is a key determinant of</u> <u>whether people change their attitudes or behavior in the face of</u>

threatening stimuli. If people were confronted with the threatening stimulus (the hypothetical group) and assessed the group's potential for gaining and wielding real power, then those who read the higher-probability paragraph ought to be less tolerant than those who read the lower-probability paragraph.

As we mentioned earlier, the order of presentation of these two paragraphs may significantly influence tolerance, either as a main effect or as a second-order effect. We therefore varied the order of the probability and normative violations paragraphs. Half of the time the probability paragraph preceded the normative violations paragraph and half of the time it followed.

After reading their scenario and the manipulated paragraphs, subjects read an instruction set preceding the tolerance questions that told them to pay attention to their feelings or to their thoughts. The instructions – adapted from Kuklinski et al. (1987) – read as follows.

Focus on feelings:

Instructions. We have found that people's attitudes and opinions are reported most accurately when they do not think carefully about the statements. It is more accurate for people to simply base their judgments on the feelings, or emotional reactions, they experience when they read the statement. Therefore, in evaluating each of the propositions you will read, try to base your responses on your *feelings*, or emotions, not your thoughts.

Focus on thoughts:

Instructions. We have found that people's attitudes and opinions are reported most accurately when they ignore the feelings, or emotional reactions, they experience when they read the statement. It is more accurate for people to simply think carefully and base their judgments on the thoughts they have when they read the statements. Therefore, in evaluating each of the propositions you will read, try to base your responses on your *thoughts*, not your feelings.

The instruction set occurred *after* reading the scenarios and therefore could not influence how the subjects perceived and encoded that information, only how and what they retrieved and used in making judgments. The mood-congruence literature leads us to expect that when subjects are asked to attend to their feelings, they will retrieve memories congruent with their mood. When asked to focus on their thoughts, subjects are likely, given the same literature, to think about the reasons for or benefits of their judgments.[9]

The subjects then responded to the six tolerance statements included in the pretest; but in the posttest these statements specifically referred to the hypothetical group in the scenario. For example, if the subjects read a scenario about the Christians in Politics, one of the tolerance statements was "Members of the Christians in Politics should be allowed to make a public speech."

Contemporary information is manipulated by our four main experimental variables, each of which has two levels. This design enables us to evaluate whether exposure to particular kinds of contemporary information influences individuals to express more tolerant or less tolerant views. These manipulations reveal the impact on tolerance of (1) normative violations; (2) the probability of power; (3) the order of the information presented; and (4) attending to feelings or thoughts.

By incorporating both antecedent considerations and contemporary information in our experimental design, we can examine the extent to which subjects' predispositions, standing decisions, and contemporary information influence current tolerance judgments. If these judgments are solely the result of antecedent considerations, then the experimental manipulations should be insignificant in our analysis. If, on the other hand, contemporary information determines tolerance, then the antecedent considerations should be insignificant. We actually expect the results to fall somewhere between these two extremes. We know from the literature that predispositions and standing decisions should have a strong impact on current tolerance level, but Gray's work (and that of others) suggests that contemporary information should also affect tolerance.

Subjects

We conducted the basic experiment three times – an original experiment and two replications. In the first experiment, conducted in the spring of 1989, the subjects were 219 students in five introductory American Government classes at the University of Nebraska. A year later, a second experiment was conducted that used 339 students in introductory American Government classes at the same university. It is important to note that these students at Nebraska represent a fairly wide range of interests and backgrounds since every incoming student must take a humanities or social science elective, of which the introductory American Government course is one option.

Yet students share special characteristics, such as scholarliness or inexperience, that could make them react to the experimental manipulations differently from the population at large. Because we wanted to ensure that our results were not applicable only to students, we conducted an experiment during the summer of 1991 with 362 nonstudent adults living in Lincoln, Nebraska. We chose subjects from three groups. The largest number of subjects came from office staff, custodians, and groundskeepers at the University of Nebraska. We randomly selected 400 names from the university staff directory (excluding professors and students) and sent them a letter briefly describing the study; 176 of the 400 people contacted completed both the pretest and the posttest. The second group was drawn from staff or customer volunteers at six small- to medium-sized businesses in Lincoln; 140 of the subjects came from this group. The last group consisted of people involved in leisure or recreational activities (members of a community play, members of a sports team, and the like); 46 subjects came from this group. We asked the nonstudent adults either to come to the Political Science Department, in which case we paid them ten dollars at the completion of the posttest, or we went to the work or recreation site. While these subjects do not constitute a random sample of adults in the Lincoln area, we were able to escape the more extreme homogeneity of the student samples.

THE RESULTS

In all three experiments, we found identical results. We therefore combined the data from the three experiments into one data set and weighted the samples (to an N of 219 for each study).[10] The reason for weighting the samples is that we did not want any one study – in particular the adult study which had the largest number of subjects – to disproportionately affect the results. The following data analysis is based on the weighted sample.

The results confirm our expectation that both antecedent considerations and contemporary information help explain people's levels of political tolerance. The predisposition and standing decision covariates are all significantly related to tolerance (see Table 4.2). People tend to be more tolerant or less tolerant over time, and approach any new situation with a baseline level of tolerance or intolerance ($p < .01$). Therefore, the standing decision to be tolerant or intolerant, derived from the many variables discussed in

Table 4.2. *Antecedent considerations, contemporary information and political tolerance: analysis of covariance with posttest political tolerance*

Variables	Unstandardized regression coefficient	F	p
Antecedent considerations (covariates)			
Pretest tolerance	.50	222.8	<.01
Democratic norms	.18	11.3	<.01
Gender	−.03	4.5	.04
Contemporary influences (main effects)			
Normative violations		10.1	<.01
Probability of power		1.0	.33
Order		0.2	.89
Instruction set		27.4	<.01
Study		6.2	<.01
Scenario group		2.6	.02
Significant interaction[a]			
Normative violations by order		4.8	.03
Total weighted N (excluding cases with missing data) = 614			

[a]All other interactions in the analysis of covariance, except one five-way interaction, were insignificant and are therefore excluded from the table.

Chapter 2, has a strong and lasting effect on any current tolerance judgment.

People also bring to any new situation their specific standing commitment to the abstract principles of democracy. People who believe in basic civil liberties, such as freedom of speech, bring this commitment into new and threatening situations, and it affects their judgments ($p < .01$). As we argued earlier, this direct effect on current tolerance level means that commitment to democratic norms has a unique effect on tolerance in a specific threatening situation above and beyond the indirect effect it has through tolerance standing decisions. In a highly threatening situation, this commitment may help people overcome their natural inclination to be intolerant. Indeed, the correlation between commitment to democratic norms and pretest tolerance is .51 ($p < .01$).

Finally, females tend overall to be more intolerant than males ($p = .04$) in threatening situations requiring new judgments. Females have a very weak tendency to hold less tolerant standing decisions than males (the correlation between pretest tolerance and gender is $r = -.09$, $p < .05$), but they also apparently react more intolerantly to the hypothetical groups in the current environment than males.

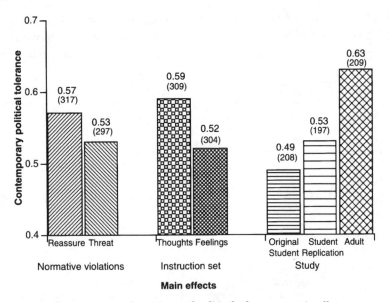

Figure 4.1. *Contemporary information and political tolerance – main effect mean scores on posttest political tolerance (weighted N's in parentheses – combined data set)*

These results emphasize the importance of antecedent considerations in people's current tolerance levels; people confront novel situations with certain predispositions and standing decisions. Given their significance, however, what impact can information about threat, available in the immediate environment, have on people's current tolerance judgments? The four experimental manipulations indicate which types of new information have an impact and which do not. In short, Table 4.2 shows significant effects for normative violations, instruction set, and the normative violations by order interaction. Probability of power has no effect. In addition, the study and the scenario have significant effects.

First, as Figure 4.1 shows, when people read information about a hypothetical group that depicts the group violating norms of peaceful, orderly behavior, they respond with greater intolerance. When people are reassured about the group's normative behavior, on the other hand, they react with greater tolerance ($p < .01$). Subjects who read the threatening paragraph were basically at the midpoint of the tolerance scale, whereas those who read the reassuring paragraph were on the tolerant side of the scale. People seemed to respond to the emotional content and context of contemporary information; evocative language depressed tolerance, whereas reassuring language increased it. Therefore, our hypothesis about normative violations, based on Gray's work and prior survey analysis, is supported by the data. When people are confronted with a group that violates the norms of proper, orderly behavior, the increased perception of threat leads them to respond with intolerance, a natural reaction according to McClosky and Brill (1983).

Second, probability of power information does not appear to be related to tolerance judgments ($p = .33$), although those who read the higher-probability paragraph were less tolerant than those who read the lower-probability paragraph. This result leads us to question the application of Rogers' protection motivation theory to the study of political tolerance. Probability information simply is not very important in people's tolerance decisions, both in this study and in prior survey research. We can therefore question whether people are driven primarily by pragmatic considerations when it comes to tolerance. If people were merely pragmatically tolerant – being tolerant only when the group in question was weak and ineffectual – they would rely heavily on probability information to determine their tolerance judgments.

Third, Table 4.2 shows no significant main effect for the order of presentation of the two manipulated paragraphs. The paragraph people read first did not significantly affect their tolerance judgments. The primacy effect therefore does not hold in this study: information read earlier does not appear to access relevant schemas that affect further interpretations of information. And, of course, the recency effect also does not hold, as the paragraph they read second did not significantly affect tolerance judgments.

However, the two-way interaction between normative violations and the order of presentation of the manipulated paragraphs is significant. When the normative violations paragraph is presented before the probability of power paragraph, there is no significant difference between the reassuring and threatening (means of .56) conditions. When the normative violations paragraph is presented last, however, the difference between the two conditions is large and significant: people who read the reassuring paragraph last are much more tolerant toward the hypothetical group (mean of .59) than those who read the threatening paragraph last (mean of .51). Thus, while order is not significant as a main effect, its interaction with the normative violations information has a significant impact on tolerance (see Figure 4.2).[11]

Gray's work can help us interpret these results. As we discussed

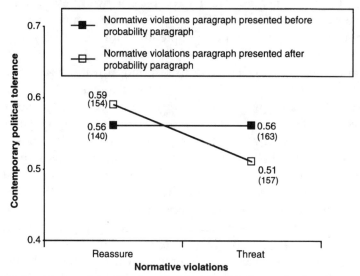

Figure 4.2. *Two-way interaction between normative violations and order of presentation of treatment paragraphs*

earlier, since the BIS cycles continually, the impact of the threatening stimulus (normative violations) might be potent but short-lived. The probability information is obviously not threatening to people, which may be why it is not significantly related to tolerance in our survey-experiments. When the probability paragraph follows the normative violations paragraph, it dampens feelings of threat evoked by the normative violations paragraph that subjects read first. When the normative violations paragraph is read last, however, it directly affects responses to the tolerance statements.

Fourth, the instruction set has the strongest impact on tolerance of the manipulated variables (see Table 4.2 and Figure 4.1). Subjects who are told to pay attention to their feelings are significantly less tolerant than those who are told to pay attention to their thoughts. This finding is consistent with the notion that a "sober second thought" leads people to reconsider their automatic response, which is a natural intolerance toward groups and ideas they find objectionable. When paying attention to how they *feel*, which is invariably negative toward their least-liked group, respondents access moods and memories that make it difficult to be tolerant. When actively *thinking* about the issues involved, specifically the benefits of tolerance, as Gibson (1987) contends, they more often think it wise to be tolerant. Indeed, they may be less alert to threat and, because of their thoughts, more inclined to tolerance.

Finally, the mean tolerance levels of subjects differ depending on which experimental study the subjects were involved in and which scenario they read. The student subjects tend to be less tolerant than the adult subjects: a mean of .49 for the students in the original study, .53 for students in the replication, and .63 for the adults. Why might tolerance levels differ by study? Part of the explanation may lie in the ideological leanings of the subjects. We found that the students were significantly more conservative than the nonstudent adults ($p < .02$), which may explain some of the difference in tolerance scores. More important, the students were significantly less committed to abstract democratic principles than were the adults (mean democratic principles scores were .64, .67, and .73 respectively for the original student, student replication and adult studies; $p < .01$). Although the overall tolerance levels differ by study, the results already discussed hold in each of the studies (moreover, using the study that subjects participated in as a main effect, that is as a treatment variable, showed that study does not interact with the other main effects). The differential effect of scenario may also be a matter of relevance. Even though we made the scenarios as similar as possible across hypothetical groups, some of the groups were simply more easy to tolerate than other groups.[12]

DISCUSSION AND CONCLUSIONS

Although it is clear that people respond to contemporaneous information about a group's treachery and belligerence and react differently if attending to thoughts or feelings, it is unlikely that people create their tolerance judgments anew each time they are confronted with a noxious group. The shifts in tolerance that occur due to the manipulations are shifts away from a meaningful *baseline* level of tolerance.[13] Therefore, it makes sense that pretest tolerance, abstract democratic norms, and gender are significantly related to people's tolerance level measured in the posttest about the hypothetical group. Some people *tend* to be tolerant while others *tend* to be intolerant, but contemporary information and moods (normative violations and instruction set) can elicit judgments that differ from people's standing decisions.

Our findings, while modest in magnitude, are highly robust: not only are the two manipulations significant in the combined data set, they are also significant in each of the three experiments. Even the modest threat introduced by the threatening normative violations paragraph led to significant, although small, differences in mean tolerance levels. Similarly, asking people to attend to their thoughts or feelings had a highly significant effect on tolerance judgments. When asked to attend to their feelings, they may focus on their dislike of the group and therefore react naturally with intolerance. When asked to attend to their thoughts, they may focus on the benefits of tolerance, thereby superseding their natural instinct to be intolerant.

The results of the tolerance experiments can be interpreted as consistent with Gray's explanation: people feel more threatened when they read the information contained in the threatening normative violations paragraph than they do with the probability paragraphs. The reassuring normative violations paragraph may actually reduce perceptions of threat. People may be aware of the probability information, but such information may not affect their threat perceptions or their tolerance.

Naturally, this paper-and-pencil test does not directly confirm the application of Gray's theory to the study of political tolerance judgments. As noted in Chapter 3, Gray's work provides a useful metaphor about the role of contemporary threat information in such judgments. The direct application of his theory would take us far afield from the central concerns of political scientists and political psychologists, and into the realm of physiological psychologists. As a result, we have concentrated on the importance of threat perceptions for understanding citizens' decision making. It is important, we believe, to understand the role of affect in political judgments, and how such feelings influence the political process. But that does not mean that we must take direct measurements of limbic-system activity.

Having said this, it is nevertheless important to establish that our experimental manipulations really "work." By work, we mean not that they can be directly linked to limbic activity, but that contemporary information led to differing perceptions of the group. However, the probability of power manipulation was not significant. It may be that people who read the high-probability paragraph believed that the group had a relatively high probability of gaining power, whereas those in the low-probability condition believed the group was relatively weak; nevertheless, that information did not affect their judgments. An alternative explanation of our results is that people who read the high- or low-probability paragraphs did not believe or retain this information on probabilities. In this instance, the finding that probability is unrelated to tolerance could be explained easily: the probability manipulation did not work. We assume the former, and we make similar assumptions about the normative violations paragraphs. This manipulation significantly affects tolerance; but do people really view the group as more threatening when they read the threatening paragraph? Are they more reassured when they read the reassuring paragraph? In Appendix 4A, we test whether these assumptions are valid. We examine the results of various survey-experiments in which we test whether our probability of power and normative violations manipulations had the effect we intended.

Readers comfortable with our results and interpretations to this point might choose to skip Appendix 4A and turn to Chapter 5. In Chapter 5 we explore more fully the role of threat in shaping contemporary tolerance judgments.

APPENDIX 4A: THE BASIC EXPERIMENTS–
MANIPULATION CHECKS

In this appendix, we present results from survey-experiments designed to assess the impact of normative violations, probability of power, and affective or cognitive cues on tolerance judgments. As we discussed in Chapter 4, we conducted the same basic experiment three times, and the results were the same each time. Normative violations and instruction set had consistent and significant effects on tolerance judgments, whereas probability of power manipulations had no effect.

Skeptics might suggest that we may not have successfully manipulated people's perceptions of the likely future power of the hypothetical groups in our scenarios. Perhaps people's perceptions of their actual least-liked group determined their perceptions of the probability that these hypothetical groups would achieve power. For example, if they disliked the KKK and believed it had no chance to obtain power, then they may have discounted the possibility that the WSF could gain some power, even if they read the high-probability paragraph. Thus, it is possible that the paragraphs we asked the subjects to read may not have affected their perceptions of the hypothetical group's power. If so, then the probability of power manipulations failed to affect tolerance judgments because they did not influence people's perceptions of the group's likely power. Respondents' perceptions of power actually might relate to tolerance judgments, but our scenarios might have been unable to shape these perceptions.

The normative violations and instruction-set manipulations appeared to work quite well because they led to statistically significant and plausible differences in tolerance judgments. After conducting a manipulation check on the probability of power paragraphs, however, these considerations led us to conduct survey-experiments to verify that these manipulations "worked" in another sense.[1] For example, did people who read the threatening normative violations paragraph really feel more threatened, and did they perceive the hypothetical groups to be more threatening and unpredictable, than people who read the reassuring paragraph? Did people who were instructed to pay attention to their thoughts really do so more often than those who were instructed to pay attention to their feelings?

In this appendix, we describe several small survey-experiments designed to show that the treatments discussed in Chapter 4 actually

84

manipulated subjects' perceptions. We present an initial check of the probability of power manipulation that was designed to determine whether subjects in the high-probability condition had greater estimates of the likelihood that the hypothetical group would obtain power, of how much power it would be likely to obtain, and of the perceived threat posed by the group.

Next, we present an initial check of the normative violations manipulation. This initial check was designed to determine which of the two paragraphs made people feel more nervous. Then we present a third manipulation-check study designed to verify and expand the initial manipulation checks of the probability and normative violations paragraphs.

We also examine our instruction-set manipulation in two different ways. First, we assess whether respondents actually pay attention to thoughts or feelings. Second, we determine whether the instruction set is as effective when given as an encoding instruction before people read the scenarios as it is when it is given at the time tolerance judgments are made, as in the studies presented in Chapter 4. Finally, we conduct an experiment to determine whether using a hypothetical group in the scenarios affects people's posttest tolerance judgments. It is important to ascertain the effects of using a hypothetical group if we are to claim that our results apply to the real world.

MANIPULATION CHECK OF THE PROBABILITY OF POWER PARAGRAPHS

The finding – repeated in several different studies – that the probability of power paragraph has little if any effect on political tolerance could mean one of two things. First, it could mean that the paragraphs did not affect subjects' estimates of the likelihood that their least-liked group would gain power or pose a realistic threat in our political system. Perhaps this part of the message in the scenario was unconvincing. Second, it could mean that estimates of the probability of power do not constitute central elements of the perceptions of threat, and therefore do not affect levels of tolerance. This is the conclusion we drew in Chapter 4.

To test these alternate explanations, in the spring of 1992 we conducted a manipulation check (Study 1) of the probability of power paragraphs.[2] The subjects in this study were 122 Introductory American Politics students at the University of Minnesota. They answered a questionnaire designed to check whether the two paragraphs successfully manipulated students' perceptions of the probability of power.

Minnesota undergraduates had an overwhelming tendency to select the Klan, Nazis, racists, or white separatists as their least-liked group.[3] As a result, in the posttest, all students read a scenario about the White Supremacist Faction (WSF). This simplified the administration of the survey-experiment. Students were assigned randomly to read either the high- or the low-probability of power paragraph. Later in the analysis, we will compare the responses of students who selected, in the pretest phase, a racist least-liked group with those who selected a nonracist least-liked group.

After people read the WSF scenario, they rated the amount of power they thought the WSF would obtain in various parts of the country and in the country as a whole. We combined these items into a "power potential" scale with a coefficient alpha of .60. We also asked subjects to rate how much the WSF would be able to hurt people of color. As a final measure of perceived power, we asked subjects to rate the chance (between 0 and 100%) that a group like the WSF would ever achieve significant power in the United States. As a final manipulation check, we had subjects rate the WSF on the measures of perceived threat that we used in our survey research. These are semantic differential adjectives: honest/dishonest; trustworthy/untrustworthy; dangerous/safe; nonviolent/violent; and good/bad. These items formed a scale with a coefficient alpha reliability of .70.

Our findings are unequivocal. These two paragraphs clearly manipulated perceptions of probability. Students who read the paragraph suggesting that the WSF might have some success rated the likelihood that the WSF would obtain power significantly higher than those who read the paragraph minimizing its influence (mean differences are reported in Figure 4A.1). The high-probability paragraph led subjects to increase their estimates on the power potential scale ($p < .01$); to reach a higher estimate that the WSF might hurt people of color ($p = .05$); and to estimate a higher probability (21% v. 13%) that the WSF might achieve significant power in the United States at some future date ($p < .01$). These results show that the probability of power manipulation is effective – it influences people's estimates of how powerful the hypothetical target group is likely to become.

However, reading the probability paragraphs did not affect the traditional measure of perceived threat ($p = .90$). This supports the

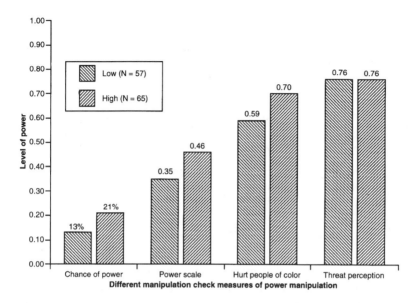

Figure 4A.1. *Manipulation check – probability of power treatment study 1 (spring 1992: N = 122)*

argument that the survey research measures of perceived threat, which correlate highly with tolerance, do not incorporate perceptions of power about the political system. The perceived-threat measures relate more closely to the treachery and belligerence of the group, information we manipulated in the normative violations paragraphs.

Finally, we compared the responses of people whose least-liked group was one of the racist groups with those of people who selected a nonracist group. People who had target groups other than racists did not differ significantly from those who selected racist least-liked groups.[4] Reading the high-probability paragraph affected both types of respondents the same way – it increased their perceptions of the WSF's likely power. Thus, people's inferences about power were based on the information we presented to them, not on their judgments or feelings about the group.

THE NORMATIVE VIOLATIONS PARAGRAPHS
AND ANXIETY

In the summer of 1992, we investigated whether the normative violations paragraphs worked so well because they manipulated state anxiety (Study 2). As in the probability of power manipulation check, we asked all of the participants about the WSF. Using fifty University of Nebraska students from an Introduction to American Government class, we first did a simple check. We randomly assigned half the students to read both normative violations paragraphs. They then assessed which of the two paragraphs made them feel more nervous. There were two conditions, randomly assigned. In the first condition students read the reassuring paragraph first, and the threatening paragraph second; in the second condition, the order was reversed. Under the first condition, four students said the reassuring paragraph made them feel more nervous, but fully twenty-one said the threatening paragraph did; under the second condition, the numbers were six and nineteen, respectively. Under both situations, the differences are statistically significant ($p < .01$).

When we conducted this simple manipulation check, we also randomly assigned the second half of the class – another fifty students – to another manipulation check. In this second experiment, half the students read the reassuring paragraph only and half read the threatening paragraph only. They rated how nervous they felt about the WSF. For the full sample, the differences were not significant.

As in the probability of power manipulation check, however, we divided the sample into two groups, those who selected a racist least-liked group and those who selected a nonracist group. We did this because all participants read the scenario about the WSF. Overall, participants selecting a racist least-liked group had higher nervousness scores after reading their scenario than did those who selected a nonracist group. In addition, for the students who selected a racist group as their least-liked, the manipulation check worked: as Figure 4A.2 shows, those who read the reassuring paragraph reported a nervousness mean score of .71, while those who read the threatening paragraph reported a mean of .93 ($p < .01$).

This latter finding led us to examine additional data collected during the probability of power manipulation check (Study 1) described in the previous section. In that study, after reading the scenarios, students rated their state of anxiety using four adjectives (nervous, upset, afraid, and distressed). The resulting scale had a coefficient alpha of .84. Examining the results (Figure 4A.2), we found that there were significant mean differences in anxiety between those selecting racist and nonracist least-liked groups (means of .64 and .55, respectively).

This confirms the results of the normative violations manipulation check. It shows that when respondents focus on their least-liked

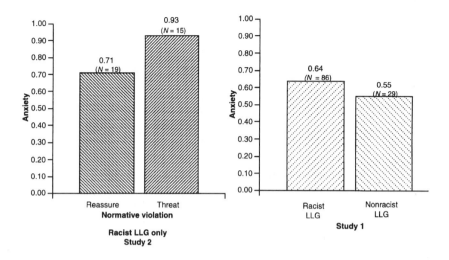

Figure 4A.2. *Normative violations manipulation check studies (summer, 1992 – N's are in parentheses)*

groups, they are more emotionally engaged and responsive than when they focus on a non–least-liked group. People become more nervous and anxious under the former condition than the latter (see the results in Chapter 7 for further confirmation of this point).

Regardless of contemporary information, then, people feel a more general sense of anxiety concerning their least-liked group than they do for a non–least-liked group. When we provide additional information about the normative violations in the environment, then an even more significant difference exists between respondents who read about their least-liked group and those who do not. The former become even more anxious if their least-liked group is presented as belligerent and treacherous, whereas the latter are unaffected by such information. Of course, in the studies described in Chapter 4, all respondents read about hypothetical target groups that were based on their least-liked group. For all of them, then, the threatening normative violations paragraph should have increased their anxiety.

A JOINT MANIPULATION CHECK

After conducting the two separate studies described, we designed another study to replicate and expand these two manipulation checks. This study again used only the WSF scenario. In the spring

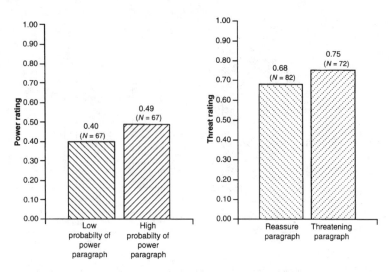

Figure 4A.3. *Joint manipulation check (1993 – N's are in parentheses)*

and summer of 1993, 288 Introductory American Politics students at the University of Minnesota were assigned to one of two groups. We randomly assigned one group to read either the low- or high-probability of power paragraph. Then they rated the WSF's potential power in the country as a whole and in various regions. We combined these two items to create a scale with a coefficient alpha of .63.

We randomly assigned the second group of students to read either the reassuring or the threatening paragraph. Then they rated the WSF on five adjectives: treachery, belligerence, dishonesty, untrustworthiness, and dangerousness. We combined these ratings in an overall scale with a coefficient alpha of .73. In surveys, these adjectives were strongly related to tolerance judgments (Sullivan, Piereson, & Marcus, 1982). Having earlier established that the threatening paragraph increases anxiety, we also wanted to establish that the normative violations paragraphs affect respondents' specific threat perceptions of the group.

Again, as Figure 4A.3 shows, the results consistently support the validity of our manipulations. Students who read the low-probability paragraph estimated the WSF's potential power lower (mean of .40) than those who read the high probability paragraph (mean of .49). The difference is significant ($p < .01$). Again, these differences are about the same for students who selected racists and those who selected nonracists.

Students who read the threatening normative violations paragraph estimated that the WSF was more threatening on the five adjectives (mean of .75) than those who read the reassuring paragraph (mean of .68). This was also a significant difference ($p = .02$). Again, when we separated students who selected racists from those who selected nonracists, the results were significant only among the former students. The pattern is quite clear – probability judgments are information-based and do not vary between those who are particularly disturbed by the target group and those who are less disturbed by it. On the other hand, reactions to normative violations are more affective, and information that is reassuring or threatening will significantly affect those with more malice toward the target group by altering their threat perceptions.

A MANIPULATION CHECK FOR INSTRUCTION-SET CUE

Our final set of manipulation checks focuses on the instruction-set cue. Whether people pay attention to their thoughts or their feelings significantly affects their contemporary tolerance judgments (see Chapter 4). That particular manipulation showed that those who paid attention to their thoughts had significantly higher tolerance levels on the posttest than those who attended to their feelings.[5]

To validate this manipulation, we need to know if those told to pay attention to their thoughts really did so, and whether those who were told to pay attention to their feelings were instead more centered on their emotions. This would give us some confidence that people receiving cognitive or affective instruction sets were performing as we asked them.

During the winter of 1993, we conducted another validation study with ninety-three American Government students at the University of Minnesota. The study was similar to those described in Chapter 4. Students filled out a pretest questionnaire and two weeks later read a hypothetical scenario about an extremist group. This study differed from the experiments in Chapter 4 in several ways. First, we used scenarios about only two hypothetical disliked groups. Those who selected racists, Nazis, or the Ku Klux Klan as their disliked group read about the White Supremacist Faction on the posttest. We used the Feminist and Gay Faction as a target for those who selected homosexuals, feminists, and prochoice groups on the abortion issue.[6] Those who selected other target groups as their most disliked group read the scenario about the White Supremacist Faction.[7] Second, we updated the information in the scenario about the WSF to reflect recent events, particularly the Rodney King verdict and the candidacy of David Duke for governor of Louisiana. The normative violations paragraph always followed the probability paragraph.

As our validation check, we concluded the questionnaire by asking students the following two open-ended questions:

Recall the scenario about the White Supremacist Faction [the Feminist and Gay Faction]. What emotional reactions do you have toward the group? That is, describe your *feelings* about the WSF [FGF].

And,

Recall the scenario about the WSF [FGF]. What thoughts do you have toward the group? Describe your *thoughts* about the WSF [FGF].

We coded student responses as purely cognitive, purely affective, or mixed.[8]

Students had difficulty articulating their emotional reactions to the open-ended questions – there were no significant differences by instruction set. However, instruction set did make a significant difference when answering the question about their thoughts. Students who read the cognitive instructions were significantly more likely to give a completely cognitive response with no affective content at all ($t = -2.46$, $p = .02$). Students who read the affective instruction set were more likely to give a mixed response including both thoughts and feelings. Many students were unable to express their emotional responses toward the group. Only 34 percent of the students responded purely affectively when asked about their emotional reactions to the scenario. Another 39 percent had a mixed response, but a quarter of them responded with answers that seemed purely cognitive.

Purely emotional responses included those who simply noted how they felt, without any particular explanation of why. One student noted about the WSF that "I am disgusted and disheartened. I also feel anger. I empathize with the blacks and wonder how furious it must make them feel." Another student said, "It makes me sick to my stomach when I think of groups like that [WSF]. They absolutely make me angry." The most common emotions mentioned (among those with either emotional or mixed responses) were anger (31%), disgust (21%), dislike (21%), sadness (18%), and hate (13%). A small minority responded by noting that despite their feelings, the group had the right to demonstrate. For example, one student said, "Although I disagree with the WSF's beliefs, I feel no hatred or bitter feelings towards them. I just feel they are demonstrating their right of free speech."

However, many students had difficulty describing their emotional responses, and reported largely cognitive responses. Students seemed to believe that they were discussing their feelings if they simply wrote "I feel" followed by their thoughts. For example, one student responded to the question about feelings, "I personally feel that their convictions are wrong. Given the power, they would take the freedom of many individuals away. However, since that will probably never happen, I choose to just ignore them." Another student responded to the emotions question similarly, saying "I think that there [sic] aims and goals are not to [sic] enlightening yet I feel that they're free to express their opinion peacefully." These students were typical of the large percentage of students who responded cognitively to the affective question.

In fact, nineteen students (20%) directly commented on the difficulty of separating their thoughts from their feelings. As one person said, "My thoughts are the same as my feelings." Her response to the question showed her mixed emotions: "I believe that the people in this group are mostly uneducated. I feel frustration towards their attitudes." One student pointed to the very emotional nature of the issue: "How does one separate thought from emotion when the very issue is about one of the strongest emotions humans know? (hate) See above answer." That answer was, "I can't tolerate intolerance. I am angered and saddened by the group. I would like to hate them, for things they say and do, but how can you hate someone with an illness?"

The responses of six students illustrated this difficulty in separating thoughts and emotions. As they read the second question asking about their thoughts, they realized that in response to the first question they had already expressed their thoughts, but not their feelings. Those students drew arrows between the questions to indicate their misunderstanding of the first question. One person, for example, wrote in response to the feeling question that "they are very ethnocentric and prejudiced and I personally feel sorry for them." Then, realizing her mistake, she wrote her emotions in the second space "anger, frustration, exasperation."

In contrast, students followed the cognitive instruction more easily. Two-thirds answered with only thoughts, and another fifth answered with both emotion and cognition. Only 2 percent answered purely emotionally when asked to provide their thoughts.

Purely cognitive responses generally focused on the rights of the group. As one student said, "I don't think that their Constitutional rights should be taken away. They should have the same rights as everyone else." Another said, "I strongly disagree with their beliefs. But in order to have the freedom we all want, they need to be able to express their views, no matter how insane those ideas may be." Another student provided a mixed response: "Even though I hate them, they have the right to speak." Some students did suggest banning the group or limiting their rights if violence erupted, but most admitted the groups had a right to exist and to demonstrate their views. "I do not believe that some of their goals are within the laws of this country," wrote one student, "but I do respect and would grant them the rights that are preserved and due to all free citizens of this country. They should be able to express themselves in an appropriate manner."

Students also seemed to need explanations for extremist behavior. One wrote: "When I think of people like this, I wonder what made them this way. Who put so much hatred and stupidity into the minds of these people and whether there is a way to change them." One theme that emerged was that those in such groups were "ignorant" and "uneducated." "I feel they are an ignorant group of pigs that are scared of their own shadow," wrote one student, while another said, "They're small-minded, ignorant people, full of hatred who are trying to find a scapegoat for the plight of their miserable lives." Others attributed the group members' views to their lack of self-esteem. One student said, "They are insecure whites who blame 'America's problems' on the entire black race," while another said that "people in WSF probably have insecurities about other races. They feel weak without a group to be in. The WSF probably supplies the group, which allows its members to feel stronger."

Students also suggested how members of such groups might be "cured" of their extremism. Several students suggested that education is the answer: "I think that the only way to combat and prevent such a thing from happening would be an increase in education." Another student suggested further exposure to the people they hate: "I think they need help – something like letting them talk to and get to know one of the people they think they really hate." But a few students suggested harsher means of solving the problem: "I really think they should [be] banned from society because [these] kind of behaviors are not normal," and "I would like to remove ALL of their constitutional rights and exile them to an island or something. I hate them."

While responding to their thoughts and feelings about the scenario, the students often made general comments about the hypothetical group and situation. Their comments indicate that the scenario was believable and compelling. Many students referred to the disliked group by its initials, and none of them said that the scenario was impossible to imagine. Students seemed convinced by the scenarios, and perhaps a bit frightened by them. The students particularly seemed to fear that the group might take over the educational system: "The WSF is a potentially dangerous faction considering the state of the economic and social structure of the country at the present time. If they were allowed to hold public office or teach in our schools then it is possible that the group could have serious harmful effects on innocent members of our society." Another student expressed fear of such a group because "the way they are organized and their plan for 'takeover' seems much more 'acceptable' than the ideas of the KKK. This could lead to a more receptive response from people who are [deceived] about the group's intentions."

Most students, regardless of instruction set, had difficulty describing their feelings and often misinterpreted the question to refer to thoughts. This suggests that, in everyday discourse, Americans tend not to be aware of, or explicitly introspective about, their emotional state. Of course, as we argued in Chapter 3, we are always in an emotional state whether or not we are consciously aware of it or can describe it to ourselves and others.

Although this validation check provides mixed support for the validity of our instruction-set cue, it generally bolsters our findings. Students who received the feelings-or-thoughts instructions did give different types of answers to the open-ended question asking them to describe their thoughts about the hypothetical target group. Those given the feelings instructions were significantly more likely than those given the thoughts instructions to answer this question with reference to both thoughts and feelings. Those given the thoughts instructions gave answers that were more exclusively cognitive. This suggests that, regardless of the level of introspection or awareness of feelings, students who read the feelings instructions did in fact access and use their feelings to a greater extent in making their tolerance judgments. The major impact of the "pay attention to your thoughts" instruction set may have been to inhibit *any* reliance on affect. These students gave almost exclusively cognitive answers to both of our questions about the target group – the thoughts-and-feelings questions both elicited purely cognitive responses. This focus presumably led them to offer more tolerant views.

Much of the impact of instruction-set cue appears to be nonconscious. This is consistent with Zajonc's (1980) conclusion that affective reactions are difficult to verbalize. He argues that affect is often not transformed into semantic content. This makes it extremely difficult for most students to communicate their affective reactions to the scenarios even when asked to do so. Nevertheless, the experiments show that subjects' reactions to instruction cues have very powerful effects on their tolerance judgments.

Students' comments suggest that the scenarios we used were believable and compelling. These remarks indicate that students really "got into" the scenarios and reacted with intensity and concern to the WSF/FGF. The ease with which students are able to envelop themselves in role playing situations – even extreme ones (Haney, Banks, & Zimbardo, 1983) – also suggests that our hypothetical scenarios were effective.

INSTRUCTION SET: ENCODING OR RETRIEVAL EFFECTS?

When we collected the open-ended data on instruction sets, we also told another 101 students to pay attention to their thoughts or their feelings *before* reading the scenario. Recall that in our basic experiments, the instruction set occurred after reading the scenario. The instruction set produced the strongest and most consistent findings in the experiments.

Analysis of these data showed that, when read before the scenario, instruction set had no impact on tolerance judgments. The impact of thoughts and feelings appears to be in the retrieval stage, not in encoding. People who focus on their thoughts as they are learning about the situation do not make more tolerant decisions when someone later asks them to make a judgment. When they focus on their thoughts as they are making that judgment, however, they do make more tolerant decisions than those who are focusing on their feelings.

People's state of mind when they are learning about a group or situation does not in and of itself affect their judgment. However, after the encoding process, if they later attend to their feelings, they will make a less tolerant decision than if they attempt to be thoughtful about the situation.

THE REAL WORLD VS. THE HYPOTHETICAL WORLD

We argued in Chapter 4 that we needed to use a hypothetical group in the scenarios for several reasons: to have greater control over the information to which subjects react; to lessen the impact of real-world events on subjects' judgments during the experiment; to standardize information across groups; and to increase the verisimilitude of the experimental manipulations. But what if subjects' tolerance judgments are unduly affected by the fact that the group discussed in the scenario is hypothetical? Perhaps subjects would react differently to a scenario about a real group.

To test this possibility, we conducted an experiment at the University of Nebraska in the summer of 1993 with students in Introduction to American Government classes. As with the basic experiments, students were given a pretest and two weeks later a posttest. The relevant manipulation concerned the scenario subjects read. Half of the students were randomly assigned to read the scenario about the hypothetical White Supremacist Faction. The other half read a scenario about a real group, the Ku Klux Klan. The subjects then answered the posttest tolerance questions about either the WSF or the KKK, depending on which scenario they read.

If the hypothetical nature of the basic experiment scenarios had an impact on subjects' tolerance judgments, we would expect that those who read about a fabricated group would answer the posttest tolerance questions differently from those who read about a real group. Specifically, a hypothetical group is likely to be less threatening than a real group and therefore more likely to be tolerated by subjects. Does the type of scenario group make a significant difference on tolerance judgments?

Our findings indicate that the answer is no. Confining our analysis to subjects who chose a racist group as their least-liked, we ran a difference-of-means test on posttest tolerance scores for those who read about the WSF (twenty-five cases) or the KKK (twenty-two cases). Their tolerance scores did not differ, with a mean tolerance score of .50 for both experimental groups ($p = .99$). We can therefore conclude that using a hypothetical rather than a real group in our scenarios did not have an effect on people's tolerance judgments. This corroborates what we garnered from the open-ended responses in the instruction-set manipulation check: the subjects in our experiments seem to believe in the veracity of the scenarios and therefore respond as if they are reacting to a possibly real situation.

DISCUSSION AND CONCLUSION

Our main manipulation checks show that the primary experimental effects – probability and normative violations – do indeed affect subjects' perceptions of threat information. These manipulation checks allow us to feel confident that our interpretation in Chapter 4 is correct: probability information is simply not critical in making contemporary tolerance judgments. Information on normative violations, however, proves central to people's contemporary tolerance judgments. In addition, the instruction-set cue, when given after the scenario but prior to the tolerance statements, appears to focus subjects on their emotions or their thoughts. Finally, our scenarios appear believable and engaging to the subjects, validating our general approach.

Having established that our manipulations appeared to work as we intended, in the next several chapters of the book we will examine individual differences in how people responded to our experiments. In Chapter 5, we examine threat perceptions as antecedent considerations as well as contemporary information. In Chapter 6, we probe the role of democratic norms in vitiating the impact of contemporary threat perceptions on tolerance judgments. We also explore how different levels of support for democratic norms affect individuals' responses to the information we provide in the survey-experiments. In Chapter 7, we reevaluate some of our findings and explore the role of political knowledge in shaping civil liberties judgments. In Chapter 8, we investigate the role of personality differences in political tolerance judgments and identify personality differences that influence people's responsiveness to contemporary information.

PART III

Refining the Model – The Role of Antecedent Considerations as Individual Differences

OUR PREVIOUS SECTION ESTABLISHED that predispositions, standing decisions, and contemporary information all contribute to tolerance judgments. What we have described to this point is people's aggregate response, yet we know that differences exist among individuals. For example, when confronting contemporary information, a person who is very thoughtful and politically aware will respond differently than someone who is less thoughtful and politically ignorant. Such differences may affect how people make tolerance judgments in a number of dimensions, which we explore in this section.

Chapter 5 focuses on the key issue of threat. While threatening contemporary information is part of our basic model, it also seems likely that certain individuals may have a propensity to feel threatened. We highlight two types of threat. First, we examine threat as a predisposition, that is, as a generalized tendency to perceive the world as dangerous. Second, we examine threat as a belief that a particular disliked group is highly threatening. Both are significantly related to tolerance judgments.

Chapter 6 turns to a discussion of the paradoxical nature of democratic norms. Most people support abstract democratic principles, but fail to support the civil liberties claims of noxious groups. In this chapter, we focus on democratic principles in two ways. First, we report the results of another experiment to explore whether information about the meaning of democratic principles matters in the contemporary environment. Second, we compare individuals who are strong and weak in their support for democratic principles, because it seems likely that those who strongly support democratic norms would not change their views in response to contemporary information.

Chapter 7 builds on both our basic model presented in Chapter 4 and the findings discussed in Chapter 6. First, we validate our model using a new experiment. Second, we explore the issue of source credibility by varying the status of the source of the democratic norms information. Third, we investigate expertise as an important predisposition related to tolerance. Finally, we test our conceptualization of tolerance that requires objection to a group by differentiating those who disliked the hypothetical group from those who did not feel strong malice.

Chapter 8 turns to the individual difference of personality. Gray's model of personality includes three dimensions: neuroticism, extraversion/introversion, and openness to experience. We expect that personality will be strongly related to tolerance judgments. However, for the most part personality is encapsulated by other attitudes, such as standing decisions about tolerance and support for democratic principles.

CHAPTER 5

Threat and Political Tolerance

Or in the night, imagining some fear, How easy is a bush
suppos'd a bear!

William Shakespeare, *A Midsummer Night's Dream*

A puzzle prompted our research. As we noted in Chapter 2, earlier
survey research indicated that the single variable most strongly related to tolerance, perceptions of threat, is exogenous (Sullivan et
al., 1982). This suggested that threat perceptions may be a contemporary judgment formed by relying on contemporary information,
not an earlier acquired antecedent consideration. The findings in
Chapter 4 are consistent with this hypothesis. Exposure to threat in
the form of normative violations caused subjects to modulate their
current tolerance judgments.

The 1978 NORC national study (shown in Figure 2.2) measured
threat perceptions by asking respondents to describe on a seven-
point scale their least-liked group using a list of polar adjectives.
The adjective pairs were selected to represent a variety of familiar
terms that respondents might find relevant in describing their appraisal of the objectionable group they confronted. Table 5.1 presents the bivariate correlations between political tolerance and these
measures of threat, including a further measure, "How likely do you
think it is that (group named) will be more popular in the future:
very likely, somewhat likely, or very unlikely?"

There are two clusters of threat measures. The top group contains
measures that reflect negative or positive normative evaluations.
People judged the group to be trustworthy or untrustworthy, violent
or nonviolent, and so forth. The bottom group of measures includes

Table 5.1. *Correlations between political tolerance and threat measures (1978 NORC)*

Political tolerance scale	Correlation coefficient
Normative measures of threat	
Violent/nonviolent*	−.24
Dangerous/safe	−.26
Untrustworthy/trustworthy	−.30
Unpredictable/predictable	−.34
Dishonest/honest	−.31
Bad/good	−.27
Average correlation of normative measures	**−.29**
Strength measures of threat	
Strong/weak	−.14
Important/unimportant	.17
Likely to become popular	−.05
Average correlation of strength measures	**−.01**

Note: The first item in each adjective pair is assigned the higher value. In the survey, some of the items were reversed to inhibit response bias. Source: Sullivan, Piereson, & Marcus (1982).

evaluations of the strength of the objectionable group. Some people judged their least-liked group to be relatively powerful, while others judged theirs to be relatively weak.

As Table 5.1 shows, the normative measures consistently relate to political tolerance judgments. The correlations are moderately strong and statistically significant. People are unwilling to tolerate groups perceived to be more belligerent or untrustworthy, while they would tolerate groups they judged to be more benign and trustworthy. This pattern of findings seems, on its face, consistent with Gray's depiction of what people identify as threatening – intrusive and disruptive normative violations.[1]

The second group of threat measures seems to have no influence whatsoever on political tolerance judgments. The latter correlations do not differ significantly from zero. These survey data suggest that variations in perceptions of the least-liked group – as strong rather than weak, important rather than unimportant, and more likely to become popular – are unrelated to levels of tolerance. And, as these items make no reference to norms, the failure of these items to correlate with political tolerance judgments is also, on its face, consistent with Gray's account of how the behavioral inhibition system monitors threat.

Thus, these survey findings mirror what we found in our survey experiments (Chapter 4): normative violations are significant factors that influence political tolerance judgments, whereas assessments of strength and probability, absent any mention of norms, are not influential. However, the survey-based data cannot identify whether all or part of this influence is rooted in standing decisions, predispositions, or contemporary information. Our results in Chapter 4 suggest the importance of contemporary information. In this chapter, we assess whether threat perceptions are – in part – prejudicial sentiments that shape political tolerance judgments beyond their source in contemporary observations.

The results in Chapter 4 do not necessarily mean that the apprehension of threat is *solely* a function of contemporary assessments. Indeed, others have consistently treated perceptions of threat as a personality-like predisposition or a long-standing belief (Kinder & Sears, 1981; Nunn et al., 1978; Stouffer, 1955). Much like being risk-averse, people who feel generally threatened might respond intolerantly to civil liberties dilemmas. Such individuals may project their general predisposition to experience the world as uncertain and dangerous onto tolerance judgments about specific groups. For example, Altemeyer (1988) found that a "dangerous-world orientation" is strongly related to right-wing authoritarianism. Thus, those who generally expect a high level of threat in their environment may react more fearfully to pernicious groups. If that is the case, then our manipulation of threat information does not incorporate the full impact of threat on tolerance. Sensitivity to threat might also be a personality trait that we would classify as a predisposition. And, indeed, Gray's full account of the emotional systems provides for threat sensitivity as an important part of personality.[2]

In addition, sensitivity to threat might be a standing decision, a previously learned set of beliefs about specific groups. To the extent we have learned that some groups are generally placid and unobtrusive, we may form the belief that they are relatively safe. On the other hand, to the extent that we conclude that some groups – or types of groups – are generally inclined toward violence and disruption, we may come to believe they are threatening.

In this chapter we consider the theoretical and evidentiary basis for the view that perceptions of threat are preexisting as well as contemporary. We will evaluate two measures of threat to determine how threat influences political tolerance judgments. Our model includes threat as a predisposition, as a standing decision, and as contemporary information. We also explore whether the inclination to perceive a group as threatening and, more generally, to perceive the overall environment as threatening, modifies how people react to contemporary information.

SYMBOLIC RACISM AND THREAT PERCEPTIONS

Kinder and Sears (1981) offered an extensive and thoughtful theoretical and empirical examination of threat. During the 1969 and 1973 campaigns for the mayor's office in Los Angeles, which matched a white conservative incumbent (Samuel Yorty) against a liberal black city councilman (Thomas Bradley), they conducted surveys in two Los Angeles districts. The surveys included a variety of measures of threat, which they correlated with candidate preference. The general presumption was that the more that whites felt threatened, the more likely they would vote for the white candidate, or against the black candidate.

Kinder and Sears reported an extensive series of sophisticated analyses showing that candidate preferences were essentially unaffected by perceptions of the actual likelihood of threatening events occurring. Instead, candidate preferences were powerfully influenced by deeply held, emotionally dense beliefs they called "symbolic racism." Further, they reported that racial threat measures based on personal vulnerability influenced neither candidate preferences nor the cluster of beliefs called "symbolic racism." They concluded: "We could uncover little evidence that [measures of personal vulnerability] threat affected voting behavior or generated more symbolic racism," and "Our findings imply that the white public's political response to racial issues is based on moral and symbolic challenges to the racial status quo in society generally rather than on any direct, tangible challenge to their own personal lives" (1981: 427 and 429).

Although Kinder and Sears used very different measures than we do in this study, and relied on survey research data rather than experimental methods, their findings are in one respect similar to ours. Assessments of probability, the likelihood that a specific threat is imminent, did not seem to influence political tolerance judgments, racial beliefs, or candidate preferences. On the other hand, specific normative beliefs did influence these sorts of judgments and seem to have a rich affective content (in the words of Kinder and Sears, these beliefs are "moral feelings").

A crucial theoretical issue in the "symbolic politics" approach is the treatment of affect. Kinder and Sears concluded that because "symbolic attitudes" are affectively dense, they must have been formed at some earlier period. But survey research is not the best methodology either to establish or to challenge that claim. If affective reactions ebb and flow with changing circumstances, or if such reactions are a complex mixture of established beliefs that may be modified through attention to contemporary information, then survey research methodology is ill-suited to disentangle these components. Gathering data on one survey cannot determine whether responses to survey questions depend on matters of the moment or have their genesis in an earlier time period.[3]

To understand threat fully we need to consider whether perceptions of threat derive solely from a contemporary assessment (i.e., perceptions of threat that have no predispositional component) or are formed both by antecedent considerations and by contemporary observations.

EVALUATING THE ROLE OF THREAT AS AN ANTECEDENT CONSIDERATION

In this chapter we again analyze the combined data set from the three basic studies described in Chapter 4.[4] We included two sets of questions to evaluate whether some aspects of threat perceptions represent antecedent considerations. In the pretest questionnaire we included a series of questions about a wide variety of possible target groups. (See Appendix B for the listing of these questions.) We asked the respondents, "How threatening do you believe each group is to our country as a whole?" Ratings of ten of the eleven groups listed, socialists excluded, formed an acceptable scale with a reliability of .70 (coefficient alpha). This scale measures perceived threat from a series of diverse groups, revealing how strongly people believe the world around them is populated with dangerous political groups. Because these groups form a diverse set, not specifically related to the hypothetical group the respondent read about in the scenario, this measure fits within our category of a predisposition.[5] People with high scores have a diffuse sense of being threatened by a wide variety of unconventional groups.

Figure 5.1 shows the distribution of the threat predisposition scale. The distribution of scores on threat as a predisposition is roughly normal, with a mean of .48 and a median of .49 (very near

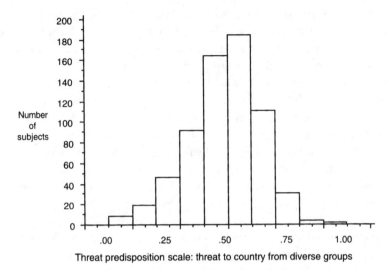

Figure 5.1. *Distribution of threat as a predisposition scale (weighted combined data)*

the midpoint of .50). Some people see threat to the country ema-
nating from many nonconformist groups across the ideological spec-
trum, while others see such threat from only a very few such groups.
Most people are in the middle, perceiving threat from some extremist groups (not just one or two), but not others.

To measure standing decisions on threat, each respondent assessed his or her least-liked group on several polar adjectives,
including honest/dishonest, trustworthy/untrustworthy, safe/dan-
gerous, nonviolent/violent, and good/bad (Sullivan et al., 1982). A
scale with a reliability of .70 was created from these five assessments.
This scale measured threat as a standing decision.[6] As with the first
measure of threat, this measure cannot be influenced by the contemporary information contained in the scenarios, because that
information was not presented until two weeks later, in the posttest.

As Figure 5.2 shows, this distribution is highly skewed. The mean
value, .82, is well above the midpoint of the scale and the mode is
1.00, the highest possible score. This is not surprising, as the focus
of evaluation is the least-liked group specifically identified by each
subject. Clearly, most people believe that their least-liked group is
very threatening.

Conceptually, we are distinguishing among three different types

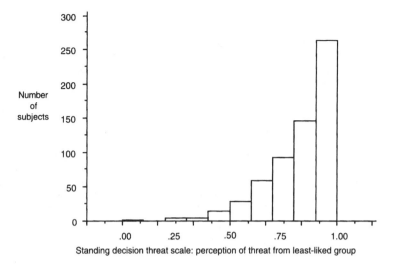

Figure 5.2. *Threat as a standing decision (weighted combined data)*

of threat. The first, threat as a predisposition, is a general assessment that is independent of any specific group or context but generates a tendency to perceive the world as dangerous. The second, threat as a standing decision, is meant to summarize respondents' attitudes about the belligerence and untrustworthiness of their least-liked group and other similarly situated groups. In this respect threat as standing decision is a far more specific measure of threat than the predispositional measure. Finally, threat as contemporary information refers specifically to a sense of threat with reference to an interaction between a specific group and a context that is available only from the immediate environment. Our scenarios provide the *current* specific information that can form the basis for a concurrent threat assessment. These three measures allow us to compare and distinguish among the three sources of threat – the predispositions that respondents bring to the survey-experiment as enduring attitudes and beliefs, standing decisions respondents have made concerning their least-liked group, as well as contemporary assessments based on information provided in the scenarios (see Table 5.2).

Figures 5.1 and 5.2 show that the two distributions of the two threat antecedent considerations are very different. The predispo-

Table 5.2. *The conceptions of threat as antecedent considerations and as contemporary threat perceptions*

	Antecedent considerations (gathered in pretest survey)		Contemporary information (presented in the experiment)
Conception	Predispositions	Standing decisions	Contemporary threat perceptions
Construct	*Threat predisposition*	*Threat standing decision*	*Normative violations*
Operational Definition (measures)	Index of the amount of "threat to the country: summed across a variety of groups – a *global* measure of threat as an antecedent consideration	Scale of semantic differential items measuring the belligerence and untrustworthiness of self-selected least-liked group – a *specific*, or focused, measure of threat as an antecedent consideration	Responses to the threatening and reassuring paragraphs embedded in scenarios

sition measure of threat is more typical of personality characteristics in its normal distribution. The measure of threat targeted on the least-liked group, the standing decision to attribute belligerent and treacherous qualities to their least-liked group, has a highly skewed distribution. These differences suggest that each may have a unique impact on how people make tolerance judgments.[7]

FINDINGS

The bivariate correlations suggest that both antecedent considerations – threat as a predisposition and as a standing decision – influence contemporary tolerance judgments. The global predisposition measure of threat correlates with posttest tolerance judgments ($r = -.23$; $p < .01$), as does the standing decision that the least-liked group is a threat ($r = -.26$; $p < .01$). In each case, the greater the perceived threat, the less tolerant subjects are of the group depicted in their scenario.

Table 5.3A presents the results for a model that includes our two threat antecedent considerations. It shows that both threat measures have substantial effects on posttest tolerance judgments. Both regression coefficients are substantial: $b = -.28$, for threat predisposition and $b = -.34$ for threat standing decision ($p < .01$). These coefficients suggests that those who anticipate threat, that is, who bring threatening antecedent considerations to their judgments, are more likely to make less tolerant civil liberties decisions. The effect of contemporary information remains consistent with our findings in Chapter 4 (i.e., normative violations and instruction set are significant).[8]

Table 5.3B presents a fully specified model with the three antecedent consideration measures – the standing decisions of tolerance, democratic norms, and gender – with the contemporary information (treatment) variables. The effects of threat, defined either as a predisposition or standing decision, have modestly independent influences on contemporary tolerance judgments.[9] The generalized sense of threat, threat predisposition, is influential ($p = .02$), whereas the influence of standing decision threat is more marginal ($p = .09$). The magnitude of threat antecedent considerations is far less substantial than when only threat covariates are considered. The regression coefficient for threat as a predisposition loses more than half its magnitude as a predictor of contemporary tolerance judgments when other covariates are included, and the coefficient for threat as a standing decision shrinks to about one-fourth of its original size (the reduction in explained variance is even greater). This suggests that the influence of threat antecedent considerations is encapsulated, to some extent, in a standing decision to be intolerant. Perhaps a standing decision to be intolerant of the least-liked group acts as a summary of a range of predispositions and other deeply held beliefs.

We can conclude that previously learned threat convictions do shape contemporary civil liberties judgments. The general inclination to see the world populated by threatening groups decreases support for the rights of specific noxious groups in specific contemporary circumstances. Similarly, though marginally significant, the specific prior beliefs about a particular group affect contemporary tolerance judgments as well. The regression coefficients suggest that the influence of threat predisposition and threat standing decisions are weaker ($b = -.12$ and $-.09$) than those of the tolerance standing decision ($b = .46$) and the standing commitment to democratic beliefs ($b = .18$). Nonetheless, these two effects, taken together, suggest that malice embedded either in a general threat expectation or in fears about a specific group, do make the support of civil liberties more difficult.[10]

Table 5.3. *Analysis of covariance of current tolerance judgments adding threat antecedent covariates (weighted combined data)*

A. *Without Controls for Standing Decisions (N = 611)*

Variables	Unstandardized regression coefficient	F	p
Antecedent considerations (covariates)			
Predisposition threat	−.28	22.3	<.01
Standing decision threat	−.34	37.2	<.01
Contemporary Influences (main effects)			
Normative violations		4.7	.03
Probability of power		1.5	.22
Instruction set		14.9	<.01
Order		.2	.69

B. *With Controls for Standing Decisions (N = 589)*

Variables	Unstandardized regression coefficient	F	p
Antecedent considerations (covariates)			
Pretest tolerance	.46	159.0	<.01
Pretest democratic norms	.18	11.1	<.01
Gender	−.02	2.8	.09
Predisposition threat	−.12	5.3	.02
Standing decision threat	−.09	3.0	.09
Contemporary influences (main effects)			
Normative violations		8.9	<.01
Probability of power		.5	.47
Instruction set		25.1	<.01
Order		.0	.99

HOW ANTECEDENT THREAT CONSIDERATIONS CONDITION ATTENTION TO CONTEMPORARY INFORMATION

Another means of assessing the effects of threat would be to explore differences between individuals. If some people are particularly attuned to threat, they might be much more influenced by contemporary signs of it because they are predisposed to be attentive to threatening information. On the other hand, other people might be oblivious to threatening information and disregard evidence of threat in the contemporary environment. The underlying logic of these speculations is that antecedent considerations of threat, in addition to the general influence they have on current tolerance judgments, might interact with how people process contemporary threat information.

Again, we turn to Gray's conception of a threat-monitoring system, the behavioral inhibition system, to inform our discussion of how threat as a predisposition might influence people's response to contemporary information. If, as we have argued, attention to threat provides an ongoing assessment, then highly threatened people ought to be most alert and responsive to contemporary signs of novelty and threat. After all, predispositions are habitual response patterns. By this logic, then, those who are sensitive to threatening environments should be most influenced by contemporary circumstances.

This implies an interaction between an antecedent consideration and contemporary information, which we will also encounter in subsequent chapters. To determine the significance of such interactions, we divide the sample into two groups, high and low, on the antecedent consideration in question.[11] This creates a dichotomous variable that can be entered as a main effect into our basic model, and also as interaction terms with our treatment manipulations. This approach enables us to preserve all of the cases in our combined data set and to test the significance of all the predicted interactions.

First we will examine the results for threat as a predisposition. Gray's theory suggests that people who expect the world to be a very dangerous place will be more responsive than other people to contemporary information about threat. In this study, that leads to the expectation that a significant interaction will occur between the threat variables and the normative violations manipulation. Specifically, those most threatened will show a greater difference than others in tolerance levels depending on whether they read the reassuring or the threatening paragraph.

The interaction illustrated in Figure 5.3 is in the expected direction ($p = .08$ level). People high in threat as a predisposition are less tolerant than those less threatened, and this difference is greater if they have read the more threatening paragraph. This confirms two sets of implications from Gray's theory – people high in threat will be less tolerant, shown as the distance between the two lines in Figure 5.3, and those high in threat will be more responsive to threatening information from the contemporary environment, shown as the steeper negative slope among respondents higher in threat predispositions.[12]

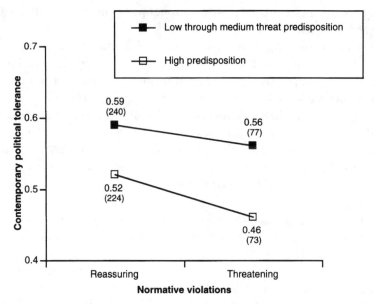

Figure 5.3. *Normative violations by levels of threat predisposition (combined data set –*
N*s are in parentheses)*

Gray's theory might lead us to derive the same expectations of
threat as a standing decision and as a predisposition. However, as
Figure 5.2 shows, almost everyone in the sample perceived their
least-liked group as extremely threatening. This lack of variance vi-
tiates the potential conditioning effect of standing decision threat
on contemporary information processing. Since almost everyone is
high on this measure of threat, everyone should be relatively responsive to information about normative violations of their least-
liked group. In fact, this is the case. There were no significant
interactions between threat as a standing decision and any of the
experimental manipulations we conducted. The overall pattern of
findings described in Chapter 4 holds up across the different levels
of threat as a standing decision.

DISCUSSION

Most social scientists argue against reliance on prejudices (Allport,
1954; Devine, 1989; Devine et al., 1991; Kinder & Sears, 1981) because prejudices tend to be both unfair and negative. Moreover,
many social scientists, especially those who study how people from

one group, or nation, perceive people in other groups or nations, are concerned with the propensity to project prejudices onto outgroups (LeVine & Campbell, 1972; Staub, 1989; Volkan, 1988). It is often held that those who are most nervous and suspicious are most likely to project those fears onto the world around them (and see a bush as a bear).

Both threat as a predisposition to see many groups as dangerous to the country and as a standing decision to assess the least-liked group as particularly threatening can operate as prejudices. They have direct influences on contemporary tolerance judgments (see Table 5.3). In both instances, the higher the level of threat, the less likely people are to make a tolerant decision about civil liberties. Yet, those who are most threatened are most attentive to contemporary information and thus are able to be either reassured or threatened by new information.[13] Those who are *less* threat sensitive are *less* responsive to the relevant contemporary information before them. This suggests that certain antecedent considerations actually *enhance* the attention people pay to current circumstances (see also Marcus & MacKuen, 1993).

Gray's theoretical model has been very helpful in directing our work in a number of ways. First, Gray has helped call our attention to the types of stimuli that are apprehended as threatening (i.e., behavior that is belligerent, treacherous, or disruptive to the normal evolution of expected events). Second, Gray has identified emotional response as a principal mechanism by which people apprehend threatening stimuli.

In the next chapter, we turn our attention to another major consideration that influences how civil liberties decisions are made: support for democratic principles. Throughout the literature on tolerance, a paradox exists between generally high levels of support for abstract democratic principles and much more modest support for concrete manifestations of those principles. Attention to the various interpretations people can give to democratic norms may be crucial to understanding how contemporary tolerance judgments are made. We explore that possibility in Chapter 6.

CHAPTER 6

Democratic Values as Standing Decisions and Contemporary Information

> Clearly the American civil liberties record has deep flaws
> in it, especially in social and racial justice and toleration
> of radical political expression, and clearly the record is
> not as pristine as American ideals are. Yet it must also be
> remembered that the record would probably not be as
> good as it is if American ideals were not so high, for they
> act as a constant standard and constant challenge.
>
> Robert Justin Goldstein (1987)

The study of political tolerance remains intriguing, to a great extent, because of a paradox found repeatedly in empirical studies. Americans express strong support for abstract ideals such as free speech and minority rights. The standing decision on democratic principles, absent any context, seems to be one of tolerance. Yet, when faced with unpopular groups exercising particular rights in a particular situation, many people want to limit the freedom of such groups. Everyone should have a right to march to express their political ideas, but not the Nazis in Skokie – or a group I dislike in my town! This disparity could occur because decisions about particular groups conflict with standing decisions about democratic values. It could also occur because contemporaneous information about a particular group and its behavior lead people to arrive at judgments that differ somewhat from their standing decision.

In this chapter, we begin to take seriously that most people actually believe their expressions of democratic ideals. The strength of their democratic convictions can influence their levels of tolerance, but contemporary information may also be important. Commitment to democratic norms constitutes one facet of people's standing decision, but appeals to these same norms can be interjected by participants in any particular situation and thereby become contemporary information. Introducing this nuance into our experimental model allows us to assess how contemporary information can bring into play democratic norms, and how these norms influence political tolerance for disliked groups. In effect, we broaden our model to include another type of contemporary information, reconsideration of the meaning of democratic principles. We consider how and when individuals react to the broader discussions that often accompany controversial contemporary events, especially those that focus on civil liberties.

THE NORMS OF DEMOCRACY AS STANDING DECISIONS

Prothro and Grigg (1960) argued that people must believe in general procedural norms of democracy and then apply these norms to concrete situations in order for a democracy to function. In fact, they said that democratic principles are not strongly supported in a population unless people support both abstract norms and the concrete application of them. Prothro and Grigg presented subjects from Ann Arbor, Michigan, and Tallahassee, Florida, with statements about the "fundamental" nature of democracy, majority rule, and minority rights, such as "Democracy is the best form of government," and "The minority should be free to criticize majority decisions." Then, subjects responded to statements concerning more specific situations, including "If a communist were legally elected mayor of this city, the people should not allow him to take office," and "A communist should not be allowed to run for mayor in this city." Prothro and Grigg claimed that these abstract and specific statements were so clearly linked that respondents must see the logical necessity of agreeing with the concrete statements if they agreed with the abstract idea. However, while people overwhelmingly supported the abstract norms of democracy – about 90 percent of the subjects agreed with those statements – the specific applications had less support. Only 44 percent of the subjects would have allowed a communist to speak in their community and only 42 percent of them would have allowed a communist to run for mayor.

McClosky's (1964) work found essentially the same results: a general consensus exists about abstract democratic principles, but disagreement emerges when those general principles are expressed in more concrete form.[1] The conclusion that McClosky drew from this disjuncture in beliefs, which supports Prothro and Grigg, was that our democracy may be in some danger because it does not rest on a firm foundation of public understanding, acceptance, and application of abstract *and* concrete democratic principles.

The work of these researchers can be criticized on two levels. First, their theoretical assumption that the stability of democracy rests on the consistent acceptance of the abstract and applied principles is certainly troubling. Theorists have long debated the nature of democracy, and it remains a hotly contested subject to this day (Dunn, 1979; Hanson, 1989). In fact, one reason the nature of democracy remains controversial is that our understandings of democratic principles can and do change. For example, for many years voting was limited to white male property owners, and was only gradually expanded to include minorities and women. We would not agree to such a limitation on the franchise today. But does that mean that the United States was then not a democracy?

Second, McClosky, as well as Prothro and Grigg, failed to recognize fully the conflicting values inherent in a democracy. As democrats, we believe in the general notion of minority rights, but we also believe that the majority has rights. When examining a statement that allows a communist to speak in the town, democratic values collide, leaving citizens with difficult choices to make between order in the community and the freedom of the individual, or between threat to the democratic regime and the civil liberties of the Communist Party members. Individual citizens will weigh these principles differently, and therefore make different choices about whether to support freedom of speech or the sanctity of a democracy threatened by communism. McClosky as well as Prothro and Grigg failed to grapple with this important paradox.

Later Studies of Tolerance and Democracy

These studies in the 1950s and early 1960s laid the groundwork for more methodologically sophisticated studies of political tolerance and democratic values in the 1970s (McClosky & Brill, 1983; McClosky & Zaller, 1984). McClosky and Brill (1983) changed the terms of the debate in order to eliminate the paradox. Support for abstract ideals means little, they argue. Americans can easily support a statement endorsing free speech for everyone because it costs nothing. The true attitudes that Americans hold toward democracy show up in their failure to enact those high ideals when faced with concrete situations involving specific groups.

McClosky and his associates derived their empirical data from two national polls conducted during the late 1970s. The Opinion and Values Survey, conducted in 1976–77, involved a nationwide survey with 938 respondents and an elite sample drawn randomly from mailing lists of twenty-three national organizations and *Who's Who*. The Civil Liberties Study, conducted in 1978–79, included a national sample of 1,993 adults and an additional 1,891 community leaders. The format of the questions asked required respondents to select one of two choices – one supporting and one denying civil liberties. Several hundred questions were asked on the surveys; more than fifty questions were used to assess the level of support for democratic principles. Examples include the following:

1. A person who publicly burns or spits on the flag:
   a. Should be fined or punished in some way.
   b. May be behaving badly but should not be punished for it by law.
2. Should demonstrators be allowed to hold a mass protest march for some unpopular cause?
   a. No, not if the majority is against it.
   b. Yes, even if most of the people in the community don't want it.
3. A humor magazine which ridicules or makes fun of blacks, women, or other minority groups:
   a. Should lose its mailing privileges.
   b. Should have the same right as any other magazine to print what it wants.
4. Free speech should be granted:
   a. To everyone regardless of how intolerant they are of other people's opinions.
   b. Only to those who are willing to grant the same rights of free speech to everyone else.

Responses to the fifty civil liberties questions were used to divide respondents into groups with generally high, medium, or low support for freedom of speech, which was then related to levels of political sophistication. McClosky and Brill found that those with higher levels of political sophistication or knowledge tended to support freedom of speech more strongly. In fact, 44 percent of those with high political sophistication strongly supported free speech, compared with only 15 percent of those with low political sophistication (p. 84).

In addition, McClosky and Brill (1983) showed that the gap between elites and the mass public persists; community leaders supported civil liberties 15 percent more than those in the general public. Among the legal elite of judges and lawyers, McClosky and Brill provided even stronger evidence that elites have different attitudes from the public concerning support for civil liberties. In general, the legal elite were 15 percent more tolerant than the community leaders and more than 35 percent more tolerant than the mass public. This difference persisted even when level of knowledge was controlled. Of those with high knowledge of civil liberties, the legal elite supported freedom of speech 80 percent of the time, while community leaders expressed support 73 percent of the time and the general public only 48 percent of the time.

The importance of the legal context and structure in the United States is also clear. If the courts have set a clear precedent, then the legal elite in society are more likely to agree that this is an acceptable exercise of civil liberties. The views of the legal elite are important because they provide cues to the less-informed public about the acceptability of various activities that push the limits of legally protected civil liberties. McClosky and Zaller (1984) found a difference between the issues on which the courts have set a clear precedent supporting civil liberties and issues not addressed clearly by the courts. For example, the courts have supported the rights of groups like the Nazis to march, and for the community to provide political protection for such groups. Support for that right among the legal elite in their survey was at 66 percent, compared to 34 percent among those of high sophistication in the community, 20 percent among those with moderate sophistication, and a mere 7 percent among those with low sophistication (pp. 52–53). However, in areas in which the courts have not set a clear precedent, such as whether undercover agents may secretly join far-right or far-left political groups, or whether a radio or television station must provide a balanced view on the issues, the legal elite and community leaders do not differ significantly in their support of rights.

At this point three primary findings stand out. First, consistency does not always exist between belief in abstract notions about democracy and specific situations requiring their application. Second, leaders and elites exhibit more consistency between the abstract principles they endorse and the concrete actions they claim they would allow. Third, cues from political elites may prove influential in shaping the opinions of attentive audiences.

McClosky and his colleagues, however, failed to address whether the *strength* of support for civil liberties would have any impact on political tolerance. They relied, instead, on dichotomous choices to accept or reject democratic principles, which provided no indication of the intensity of people's acceptance of those principles.

Sullivan, Piereson, and Marcus (1982) directly addressed the idea that the strength of people's support for general norms of democracy may play an important role in their political tolerance. To create a scale that measured intensity of support for abstract principles of democracy, they asked subjects to indicate their support for a variety of items on a five-point scale ranging from "strongly agree" to "strongly disagree." When this democratic-norms scale was introduced into a multivariate model explaining political tolerance, support for democratic values was a strong and significant predictor of political tolerance (see Figure 2.1). The path coefficient was .33, indicating a strong positive relationship between the two variables. Contrary to McClosky and Brill's (1983) claim, endorsing abstract democratic norms means something: those who weakly support the norms tend to be intolerant, while those who express strong support tend to be tolerant. These differences indicate that expressing strong support for such principles does indeed constrain a person's reaction to a specific situation requiring a tolerance judgment. Standing decisions about democratic principles *do* matter.

Transmission of Norms

Why is it that U.S. citizens overwhelmingly accept the general norms of democracy, even though many individuals do not apply them in specific situations? McClosky and Zaller (1984) explained this phenomenon using social learning theory. Social learning theory operates on the premise that through repeated exposure to ideas, people comprehend and internalize them. Elites – particularly legal elites – are exposed more often to concrete examples of groups pushing the boundaries of their legal rights. Through such exposure, and through their legal training, they become aware of the connection between those general principles and specific applications of rights. They develop a standing decision that favors democratic principles.

Other researchers suggest that among the non-elite, some people have stronger beliefs in democratic norms than others. Those with stronger beliefs have attitudes that will be more cognitively available and accessible (Fazio & Williams, 1986; Higgins & King, 1981).

Once an attitude or belief is stored in long-term memory – once it is internalized – it remains available. But the extent to which it is accessible and easily retrieved depends on a number of factors. For example, if the idea is important to a person or is used frequently, then the belief will be more readily accessible. If a value has been recently accessed, it may come to mind more readily in other circumstances (Fazio & Williams, 1986; Higgins & King, 1981).

Alternatively, contextual factors may be important in triggering democratic principles. If a dispute is framed as concerning support for freedom of speech, then even individuals with weak democratic attitudes may access those attitudes and give a tolerant response. On the other hand, if a dispute is framed as dangerous or threatening to the rights of others, then different democratic attitudes, perhaps those favoring majority rule and law and order, might be accessed and people will give an intolerant response. As we noted in Chapter 2, Lawrence (1976) found that decisions based on general norms were more important than contextual information such as the nature of the issue or the group, but that such contextual information did have an effect beyond the initial standing decision. The context in which the dispute arises, in other words, may be an important determinant of whether most people will support civil liberties.

We might expect such contextual details to be important for a number of reasons. First, many people have conflicting attitudes about democratic values that they never fully explore (Sullivan et al., 1982). For example, they may endorse majority rule without fully realizing the implications of such views for the rights of minorities. Second, most people compartmentalize their views and thus fail to link all of their beliefs about democracy into a coherent whole (Fiske & Taylor, 1991). As noted in Chapter 2, Gibson (1987) found that contextual factors mattered to many gay activists in Houston when the KKK planned to march in the gay quarter. Many of those who would restrict the march gave specific reasons connected with the Houston march to account for their decisions, such as the potential for violence along the proposed route and the cost of police prevention. This means that contextual details may be important for determining which particular beliefs about democracy will be used when making tolerance judgments in concrete situations.

Thus, if people are reminded of the importance of free speech, then those attitudes may play a more consequential role in their judgments. Once attitudes about freedom of speech are accessed and considered, individuals may make different choices about allowing rights than they would if different attitudes had been accessed.

MANIPULATING DEMOCRATIC VALUES

Most people support democratic rights and principles, but the variation in intensity that exists among individuals is highly significant. The intensity of the standing decision to support democratic norms enhances their level of tolerance.

Just as perceptions of threat may change depending on the particular context, so too can the nature of democratic debate. For example, when the Nazis wanted to march in Skokie, both those favoring the rights of the Nazis (e.g., the American Civil Liberties Union) and those wishing to place restrictions on the Nazis (e.g., the Jewish survivors of the Holocaust who lived in Skokie) used the media as a public forum for debate. Similarly, the issue of whether city and state governments should be allowed to regulate "hate speech" (such as cross burnings) drew attention during 1992 when the Supreme Court decided *R.A.V.* v. *the City of St. Paul.* Public debate on the issue included the views of those who advocated laws restricting hate speech because such speech hurts others and makes no meaningful contribution to public debate, as well as the opinions of those who believed that any restriction on free speech based on content is unconstitutional. These examples highlight that contradictory discussions occur concerning democratic ideals when civil liberties issues are debated. Many citizens have "democratic principles" attitude structures that are not chronically accessible because of rare usage, but that remain available and can be accessed when people are reminded through the course of public debate about such issues (Higgins & King, 1981).

Our first three experiments suggest that contemporary perceptions of threat toward least-liked groups can be manipulated, that these manipulations affect levels of tolerance, and that the emotional elements of perceived threat are relatively potent. Survey work on the topic (McClosky & Brill, 1983; Stouffer, 1955; Sullivan et al., 1985) also has shown that perceptions of high threat reduce levels of tolerance. However, this same research also indicates that a strong commitment to democratic principles can override the negative impact of threat perceptions for some people. Since perceptions of threat are uncorrelated with support for democratic principles, commitment to the principles increases tolerance both among those who are highly threatened by unpopular groups and those who are not (Gibson, 1987; Green & Waxman, 1987; McClosky & Brill, 1983; Sullivan et al., 1982, 1985). Conversely, even political elites will become intolerant if they believe a group poses a serious threat to democracy itself (Sullivan et al., 1993).

This chapter focuses on understanding how contemporary information about democratic norms might influence tolerance judgments. As noted earlier, in the everyday world of political discourse, democratic principles can be evoked either to promote or to inhibit tolerant responses. When confronted with the difficult question of whether Nazis should be allowed to march in Skokie, people could apply democratic principles in ways that would justify quite different conclusions about tolerance. Some people argued that the Nazis should not be allowed to march because they do not themselves accept the principles of free speech and minority rights. Freedom of speech should only exist for those who endorse democratic values. Others argued that the rights of free speech mean nothing if they are not applied equally to all groups. Clearly, then, appeals to democratic norms can either exhort people to be more tolerant or warn them of the dangers some extremist groups can pose to a democracy.

Another nuance is that appeals to democratic norms can be made on both cognitive and affective grounds. Perhaps appeals based on an affective attachment to democratic rights are more effective than those that simply lay out cool, cognitive arguments.

Finally, prompting consideration of democratic values without any positive or negative content and without a clear cognitive or affective tone could show the impact of a reminder without a substantive message. Simply invoking the idea of democracy and suggesting that people consider democratic norms when thinking about the rights of those involved in this situation may allow them to access democratic attitudes.

Our procedures in this experiment were identical to those of the basic experiments described in Chapter 4, with the following exceptions. We dropped the order and the probability paragraph manipulations and replaced them with paragraphs that reminded people about the ideals of freedom of speech, minority rights, majority rights, and pure tolerance. We chose to modify our design and drop those two manipulations for two reasons. First, neither the order nor the probability paragraphs had significant main effects in the basic studies we reported in Chapter 4. Second, modification of the scenarios to include democratic norms made the order manipulation nonsensical, because the democratic-norms manipulation focuses on a reaction to the rally described in the normative violations paragraph. Thus, the democratic-norms manipulation must always follow the normative violations manipulation, making it impossible to explore the second-order interaction we discussed in Chapter 4 between order and normative violations.

The democratic-norms manipulation has five variations, each designed to remind people of the importance of democratic principles. After people had read the scenario and a normative violations paragraph, but before they read the instruction-set manipulation and responded to the tolerance statements about the hypothetical group, we inserted a scene designed to set up a "democratic norms" manipulation. Using the White Supremacist Faction as an example, respondents read the following paragraph:

During rallies of the, (WSF), television reporters often interview bystanders for their reactions. Some people think the rallies should not be allowed, while others think they should be allowed. At one rally, a student who was interviewed said:

Respondents were then randomly assigned to read one of the following paragraphs:

Affectively focused negative norms:

I love America and the freedoms we have and in my way of seeing things, that means groups like the (WSF) shouldn't be allowed to say the things they're saying. The (WSF) is a real threat to people's rights and freedoms. If people like that get into power, it's just too scary to think about what they would do. They'd destroy this great democracy and would take away our Constitution and Bill of Rights. After all, the majority of people in America hate the (WSF) and the majority has rights too. I feel very strongly that we need to protect our civil liberties, and that means keeping these idiots from saying whatever they want.

Affectively focused positive norms:

I love the American way of life and the freedoms we have, and in my way of seeing things that means groups like the (WSF) can speak their minds freely. I care about free speech, it makes me feel good that I live in a country that has free speech. If you lived in South Africa or China you wouldn't see this kind of thing, but that's why I'm glad I live in the USA. Millions of Americans have lived, and many have died, so that we'd have the opportunity to live in this great democracy. The wise Founders of our nation saw to it that our Constitution and Bill of Rights guarantee my right to say what I want to. And, no matter how much I dislike these jerks, I feel strongly that they should have the freedom to say what they want to as well.

Cognitively focused negative norms:

The (WSF) does not seem to respect the rights of others. In fact, it presents an outright danger to some law abiding citizens in our country. I think that groups like (WSF) which present a real threat to other people's civil rights and civil liberties, should not be given such rights themselves. If the (WSF) came into power, they would do away with freedom of speech and persecute those who disagree with them. People like that should not be given a chance to destroy the very rights that protect them. Our system is based on majority rule, and the majority objects so strongly to the (WSF's) notions that they ought to be silenced. Furthermore, ideas like theirs can cause political disorder and affect the stability of society. So if we truly believe in free speech, we should not allow (WSF) to have free speech in this case.

Cognitively focused positive norms:

The right to political expression is established in our legal framework through the First Ten Amendments to the Constitution and through court cases. Minority groups like the (WSF) should, in a healthy society, have the right to persuade people that their views should be the majority view. Free speech in our system is supposed to invite dispute. In fact, free speech might be at its finest when it creates dissatisfaction or discomfort. People should have access to a variety of ideas, so that they can make up their minds based on full information. After all, if people don't agree with an idea, they can always reject it. A lack of dissent in a society may indicate weakness, while dissent itself may point to a stronger society. All of these ideas lead me to conclude firmly that the (WSF) should be allowed to have their say.

Neutral:

I don't want to tell people what they should think or feel about this issue. I believe people should consider it carefully, and they should also examine their feelings on the issue. At a minimum, when deciding what to do about the (WSF) the good citizen should think about democratic values. What does democracy mean? How important are democratic values like freedom of speech to our country? How important are democratic values in comparison to other competing values? And, finally, we should ask ourselves, "what do my thoughts and feelings about democracy have to say about my view of the (WSF's) activities?"

Although it is not possible to separate completely cognitive and affective appeals to democratic norms, we have attempted to provide more emotionally rousing content in the affective paragraphs and more reason-oriented content in the cognitive paragraphs. For example, in both of the affectively focused paragraphs, we included emotionally charged language such as "love America," "too scary," "feel strongly," and so on. In the cognitive paragraphs, we attempted to present language that relied more exclusively on intellectual reasoning. In the neutral paragraph, we tried not to present a position, but simply to raise the issue of the meaning of democracy and its connection with the group's activities.

The differences between the positive and negative norms are more obvious. The positive-norms paragraphs contend that the group should be allowed to speak, while the negative paragraphs suggest that the demonstrations should not be allowed. The positive paragraphs speak of individual rights and the importance of dissent, while the negative paragraphs focus on the rights of the majority.

While we might expect to be able to manipulate people's attitudes about democratic values, based on our previous research, standing decisions would clearly still matter. As before, we measured support for abstract democratic norms and political tolerance on the pretest in order to obtain measures of standing decisions.[2] The tolerance and democratic-norms statements are reported in Appendix B.

RESULTS

This experiment was conducted with 400 freshman-through-senior undergraduates at the University of Minnesota during winter quarter 1990. The mean tolerance level for the students at Minnesota was .67, which is higher than the overall mean at Nebraska in the experiments described in Chapter 4. The most likely reason for this is political culture: Minnesota's political culture is more liberal and supportive of civil liberties than is Nebraska's.

In examining the results of our new democratic-norms manipulation, it was clear that the mean tolerance scores of those reading negative statements about democratic norms were substantially lower than the means of those who read positive statements. The mean scores for the cognitive and affective versions of both positive and negative statement paragraphs were virtually identical. When people who read the positive and negative norms were compared, however, real differences occurred in tolerance levels ($p = .02$), suggesting that contemporary tolerance judgments are influenced by appeals to democratic principles. It was the substance of the message – either positive or negative – that mattered, rather than the tone – affective or cognitive – used to deliver it. Further analysis will therefore drop the distinctions between cognition and affect, and focus on the difference between positive and negative norms.

Those who read the neutral-norms paragraph had a mean tolerance score that was not significantly different from those who read the negative norms. That the neutral-norms statement is closer to the negative norms suggests at least two possible interpretations of the neutral- and negative-norms manipulations. First, the neutral paragraph did not serve as a prime. The mere mention of a principle such as freedom of speech, with no substantive content, apparently does not provide enough impetus for a "sober second thought" that results in greater tolerance for civil liberties. When no substantive message is provided about how to actually apply democratic values, the default option is less tolerance. Perhaps, in fact, the neutral paragraph caused reflection about the actions of the group, explaining the less tolerant decision (Kuklinski et al., 1991). Second, the negative manipulation may have failed to persuade people, leading them to fall back on their standing tolerance decision. However, it is impossible to determine whether those who read the neutral-norms paragraphs are responding in the same manner as those who read the negative-norms paragraphs. Thus, we will drop the neutral subjects from our subsequent analysis (rather than adding them to the negative-norms group) so that our analysis will not be confounded by what could be two very different processes that lead to similar tolerance judgments.

Table 6.1 shows the results of an analysis of covariance that incorporates the three antecedent considerations (tolerance, democratic values, and gender) and contemporary information (democratic norms, normative violation, and instruction set), so we can analyze the democratic norms both as standing decisions and as part of the contemporary context. First, as in the experiments discussed in Chapter 4, standing decisions about tolerance and abstract democratic principles remained important covariates ($p <$ .01). The basic standing decisions that these students made concerning civil liberties remained important even as they responded to the experimental conditions. Students entered the experiment with views about many political issues including civil liberties, and these views remained relevant even when students were confronted

Table 6.1. *Democratic norms – the effects of antecedent considerations and contemporary information (democratic norms data set, 1990, N = 400)*

Variables	Unstandardized regression coefficient	F	p
Antecedent considerations (covariates)			
Pretest tolerance	.46	153.7	<.01
Pretest democratic norms	.27	24.9	<.01
Gender	−.03	2.7	.10
Contemporary influences (main effects)			
Democratic norms		11.4	<.01
Instruction set		4.4	.04
Normative violations		1.2	.27

with information about a new situation and group. Their standing decisions about tolerance and democratic values were the standard by which they processed the contemporary information contained in the scenarios.

As Table 6.1 shows, contemporary information, as represented by the manipulation of democratic norms, had a significant effect ($p < .01$). Those reading positive arguments about democratic norms are more tolerant, .69, than those who read negative arguments about how to apply democratic norms, .65 (see Figure 6.1).

Political debates that raise concerns about democratic principles can obviously affect tolerance, even when people feel threatened and some ambiguity remains about the possibility of disorder being involved in an unpopular group's exercise of its rights. Political elites' discussions of democratic principles may therefore affect how citizens respond to these situations. Framing the issues in terms of a marketplace of ideas, stressing the positive role of dissent, and noting historic freedoms in the United States can increase support for tolerance, even when the group involved is extremely unpopular. It should also be clear that democratic values can be invoked to argue against political tolerance. If the issue is framed in terms of the group's desire to abrogate the rights of others, then people express less tolerant views. This replicates our finding in Chapter 4 that threat perceptions can be influenced by contemporary considerations. Much as emotional appeals can reassure or threaten, democratic values can limit or expand support for civil liberties.

The effect of the normative violations paragraph was – as expected – not as great as it was in the first three experiments, and

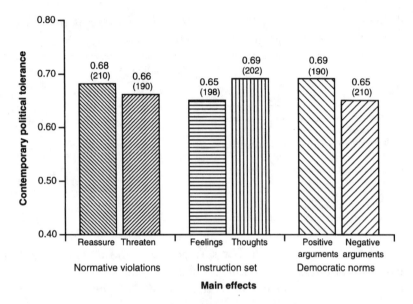

Figure 6.1. *Democratic norms experiment – main treatment effects (N's are in parentheses)*

although the mean differences are in the expected direction, they are not statistically significant ($p = .27$). Although the impact of the normative violations paragraphs was greatly diminished it would be premature to assert that placing the "hard cases" into a context of democratic norms will eradicate the influence of contemporary threat on individual judgments. The effect of threat or reassurance may be mitigated by a discussion of democratic norms, especially since the democratic-norms manipulation always followed the normative violations paragraph.[3] Framing issues of tolerance within the broader domain of democratic values can diminish the role of threat and the particular features of the target group (Sullivan et al., 1993).

The instruction-set manipulation, however, works much as it did in the earlier experiments: those receiving instructions to attend to their feelings were significantly less tolerant (.65) than those instructed to attend to their thoughts (.69).

This experiment shows the importance of considering both standing decisions and contemporary information in order to fully understand contemporary tolerance judgments. Standing decisions about tolerance and democratic norms had an important impact on people's tolerance decisions concerning a new hypothetical group. But contemporary information about democratic norms in the context of a particular event was also important. Thus, standing decisions about democratic values are only part of the story: reminding people about the values they hold as part of the context of an event can modify how those standing decisions are applied in a particular situation.

DEMOCRATIC PRINCIPLES AS STANDING DECISIONS: EFFECTS ON RESPONSE TO CONTEMPORARY ARGUMENTS ABOUT THE APPLICATION OF DEMOCRATIC VALUES

As we saw in Chapter 5, not all people will be equally responsive to contemporary information. McGuire (1985) suggested that the extent to which people are open to influence may be nonmonotonic across a number of dimensions of personality and attitudes. He found that "maximum persuadeability [*sic*] occurs at intermediate levels on many dispositional variables such as age, self-esteem, anxiety and intelligence" (1985: p. 286).

The nonmonotonic nature of openness to political appeals was addressed more recently by Zaller (1992), who applied this argument to such political concepts as political involvement, political sophistication, and partisan stability. Two processes underlie McGuire's theory of persuasion as applied to politics by Zaller. First, people vary in their exposure to persuasive messages, and those with little or no exposure will neither receive the message nor change their beliefs. Second, responsiveness to the persuasive message is related to the strength of salient prior attitudes and knowledge, so that those who have very strong convictions are least likely to respond to a message that challenges firmly held antecedent considerations. For example, Zaller (1987) and Geddes and Zaller (1989) found those with moderate levels of involvement most open to persuasive appeals during a campaign. While those who are more involved with politics may be exposed to partisan arguments, they also have enough knowledge and sophistication to counterargue the new information and thus maintain their original preferences. Those with low involvement do not pay enough attention to politics to hear the campaign appeals. The moderates, on the other hand, pay at-

tention to the appeals but do not have enough information to counterargue successfully the information they receive. Thus, the
moderates remain most open to political persuasion.

In the context of our survey-experiments, exposure does not vary
because all of the subjects received the message. Therefore, we expect to find, in our experiment, variation only in the responsiveness
to the persuasive message contained in the scenarios. Only those
with a strong commitment to democratic principles will be unaffected by the message contained in the scenario due to their ability
to counterargue. Regardless of whether they received positive or
negative messages, we expect that they would remain unchanged
due to their strong commitment to democratic values.

Those with moderate to low support for democratic principles (as
measured on the pretest) should be most responsive to the influence of the positive and negative democratic-norms manipulations.
This theoretical analysis leads us to expect a significant interaction
between antecedent support for democratic principles and the democratic-norms manipulation.

To test this hypothesis, we created a dichotomous variable that
placed those with high support for democratic principles into one
group and those with moderate to low support for democratic principles into another group. Figure 6.2 shows the significant interaction between the democratic norms-manipulation and the antecedent level of support for democratic principles ($p = .06$).

Reading a democratic-norms paragraph was inconsequential
among those who were already firmly supportive of democratic principles. Those who read the negative argument had exactly the same
response as those who read the positive argument. These individuals
all had strong commitments to democratic values and may have
been able to counterargue effectively the negative-norms message.
However, those with less strongly established beliefs in democratic
principles were significantly affected by the manipulation. The arguments proved to be persuasive and altered their standing tolerance decision.[4]

While our measures differ from those of McGuire or Zaller, our
general findings support their work. Change is least likely to occur
among those who are strongly committed to democratic principles.
They are closed to persuasive messages. And, as we shall see in Chapter 9, intensity plays an important role, in a more general way, when
we consider the relationship between attitudes and behavior.

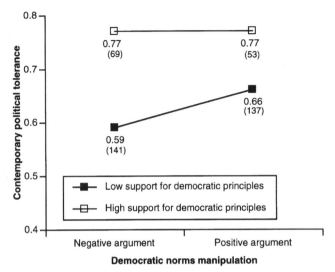

Figure 6.2. *Interaction between antecedent support for democratic principles and contemporary arguments for and against support for tolerance of the target group (N's are in parentheses)*

DISCUSSION AND CONCLUSION

We began this chapter by focusing on the disjuncture between people's abstract support for democratic norms and their seemingly contradictory refusal to support concrete manifestations of such norms. Our results show that reminding people about democratic values and their interpretations serves to modify their contemporary tolerance judgment in relation to the rights of disliked groups. Reminding people, particularly those less supportive of democratic norms, about their general abstract beliefs tended to persuade subjects to support or limit civil liberties in a particular context, depending on the type of message they received.

An important finding of this study is that both standing decisions concerning democratic principles and the new information about how to implement them made a difference for people's tolerance judgments. The democratic-norms paragraphs could have had no impact on tolerance beyond that of the democratic-norms standing decision (i.e., on established beliefs). The most striking result of the manipulations is that the positive manipulation increased tolerance significantly over both the negative and neutral paragraphs. Active guidance may be necessary to engender a positive application of free speech norms. Given that most people believe in abstract principles regarding freedom of speech and individual rights, persuasion directed at those general beliefs is most likely to be successful in effecting change in tolerance decisions.[5] In fact, norms of freedom of speech are simply stronger than those toward egalitarianism or group rights, reflecting the individualism of American society (McClosky & Zaller, 1984).

The finding that those who are less strongly committed to democratic principles are open to persuasive messages that often surround contemporary events, such as those that provoke public attention to the activities of noxious groups, has normative implications. Opinion leaders and political elites bear a special responsibility when they articulate how democratic principles ought to be applied. They are most persuasive among those least committed to those principles. Should they formulate arguments in favor of weakening support for the universal application of these principles, they are likely to find a receptive audience among those already least committed to democratic principles. On a more positive note, if they articulate a strong defense of democratic principles, they can raise the level of support precisely in that stratum of the population that most needs such encouragement.

Next we turn to the issue of political knowledge. How do individuals with greater knowledge about the world of politics respond to the challenge of noxious groups compared with those with less political knowledge? Democratic theorists have hoped that as people become more knowledgeable about the world of democratic politics they would also be more mindful of the responsibilities of democratic citizenship. Chapter 7 explores this question, among others.

CHAPTER 7

Source Credibility, Political Knowledge and Malice in Making Tolerance Judgments – The Texas Experiment

Since we conducted our original experiment in 1989, a number of events have occurred to alter the political environment related to the study of political tolerance. The Los Angeles riots following the Rodney King verdict, the murder of doctors by prolife advocates, and the rise and fall of David Duke provide prominent examples of dramatic events involving political tolerance issues that have occurred since our initial experiments. Highly visible and salient incidents can activate citizens' attitude structures – stimulating cogitation and arousing emotional reactions – that under more mundane circumstance would remain dormant. These sensational events raised the salience of political, social, and racial tolerance issues. It is therefore vital to establish that the subsequent change in political context did not alter in fundamental ways the processes by which citizens arrive at their tolerance judgments. In short, a substantial replication of our basic findings from the late 1980s and early 1990s would provide greater confidence that our results are not entirely time bound, but can be generally applied to the process of making political tolerance judgments.

In addition to attempting to verify the basic findings obtained in the studies described in Chapters 4 and 6, the research described in this chapter was designed to test a more completely specified model of political tolerance judgments. This research incorporated an examination of the role of source credibility and political expertise.

First, the research on tolerance judgments reported in Chapters 4 and 6 demonstrates an important role for contemporary information; the ostensible source of that information should also have a significant effect. Although there are often confounding factors, in general a high-credibility source has a greater impact than a low-credibility source (Larson, 1985: p. 27). In the Texas study, we examine source credibility in terms of the status and expertise of the messenger.

Second, in a fully functioning democracy, citizens ideally would be interested in politics and well-informed about the major issues of the day. The realities in the United States are quite different. While some citizens are politically knowledgeable, many are not. When it comes to fundamental issues such as political tolerance, a central question thus becomes whether political experts and novices arrive at different judgments and/or rely on different decision-making processes. As we will note, there are reasons to expect that they do, which raises wide-ranging implications for democratic theory. For example, if novices rely less on standing decisions and more on media cues and other contemporary information, then the general prevalence of political expertise would play an important role in determining tolerance judgments' malleability and susceptibility to political context.

In this chapter, then, we present four different analyses. First, although we introduce some modifications in our basic design, we check the robustness of our principal findings. Second, we examine the role of source credibility by varying whether the democratic-norms messages introduced in Chapter 6 affect subjects differently depending on whether the message comes from a high-status expert or a lower-status non-expert. Third, we explore how political expertise affects tolerance judgments. Finally, we examine whether our conceptual standard for tolerance, forbearance of noxious groups, identifies a distinct psychological decision-making process.

THE TEXAS STUDY

In fall 1993, we conducted another survey-experiment at the University of North Texas, with 783 undergraduate respondents from the American and Texas Government classes. Since every Texas undergraduate is required to take these classes, the students represent a diverse group. We followed the same basic procedures as in our earlier experiments, as described in Chapter 4, with six modifications. The six changes included: (1) having all students read about the White Supremacist Faction; (2) making slight modifications of the normative violations manipulation; (3) using only positive and negative democratic norms manipulations; (4) eliminating the probability manipulation; (5) adding an order manipulation; and (6) adding a source credibility manipulation. We now explain those modifications.

First, the experimental treatment differed from previous experiments in that all students read an updated scenario about the White Supremacist Faction, rather than a scenario about a hypothetical group based on their least-liked group.[1] We chose this procedure partly because it greatly simplified the administration of the surveys and partly to examine more directly our least-liked group procedure, which we will discuss in a later section.[2] How strongly would standing decisions affect tolerance judgments if those judgments were made about a group that was not a least-liked group to some respondents? What types of contemporary information would affect those who read about a group that they may not dislike as intensely as others? This survey-experiment design allows us to explore these questions.

Second, we slightly modified the normative violations paragraphs. The full texts are available in Appendix 7A. The reassuring version of the normative violations paragraph added one sentence explicitly suggesting that the group can be trusted and is not dangerous, whereas the threatening paragraph noted the opposite. In the threatening version, we made two additional modifications. The first clause now refers specifically to the Rodney King verdict and Los Angeles riots; we modified the specific reference to violence that occurred in the first version by simply describing what happened at the rallies. These changes were introduced to make the normative violations manipulation more potent.[3]

Third, we reduced the previous affective and cognitive democratic-norms treatments to create one positive and one negative version. As noted in Chapter 6, the affective and cognitive aspects of the democratic-norms messages were overwhelmed by the positive and negative nature of the manipulation. Since cognition and affect made no difference, we simplified our design to include only positive and negative paragraphs. As in the earlier study, the manipulation begins by suggesting that these comments are made at a public rally.

Positive democratic-norms statement:

The First Amendment of the Constitution says that we have freedom of speech, so that members of groups like the WSF can speak their minds freely. Freedom means allowing minority groups like the WSF to persuade people that their views should be the majority view. After all, free speech in our system is supposed to invite dispute. Really, free speech might be at its finest when it creates dissatisfaction or discomfort. A lack of dissent in a society actually indicates weakness, while dissent itself allows a stronger society to develop. One great quality of the United States is that our freedom is far greater than in other countries, like South Africa or China. The Bill of Rights guarantees everyone's right to express their views, so no matter how much I dislike the message of this group, the members should have the freedom to speak out on public issues.

Negative democratic-norms statement:

While the First Amendment protects freedom of speech, those rights are not absolute. Groups like the WSF shouldn't be allowed to say the things they're saying because the group does not seem to respect the rights of others. In fact, it presents an outright danger to the rights and freedoms of law-abiding citizens in our country. If people like that get into power, they would do away with freedom of speech and persecute those who disagree with them. They would destroy this great democracy and would take away our Constitution and Bill of Rights. People like that should not be given a chance to destroy the very rights that protect them. After all, this is a democracy, and in a democracy the majority sets the rules that everyone has to follow. Those rules mean protecting all of us from extremists in the minority. Furthermore, their ideas can cause political disorder and instability. In order to protect civil liberties for most of us, we need to stop these extremists from misusing freedom of speech.

The positive paragraph focuses on the importance of dissent and the rights of all groups to be involved in public discourse. The negative paragraph emphasizes the values of majority rule and order, suggesting that the First Amendment does not apply to groups that may take away the rights of others.

Fourth, we dropped the probability manipulation. Through all of our basic experiments this manipulation of contemporary information failed to significantly influence contemporary political tolerance judgments. It seemed best, therefore, to keep this already complex design as simple as possible.

Fifth, we varied the order of presentation of the normative violations and democratic-norms paragraphs. The democratic-norms manipulation always appeared last in the 1990 study reported in Chapter 6. However, the basic study, discussed in Chapter 4, showed an interaction between order and normative violations, suggesting that the normative violations information is more potent when it is read after the probability paragraph. Varying the order in this study allows us to determine whether it makes a difference to have the democratic-norms or normative violations manipulation last.

Sixth, we introduced source credibility as an additional piece of information. In the democratic-norms experiment discussed in Chapter 6, we told subjects that a student made the remarks conveyed in the democratic-norms paragraph, which means source credibility did not vary. In this experiment, we told subjects either that a bystander made the comments (low source credibility) or that an expert, a state judge, made the comments (high source credibility).

The literature disagrees about the extent to which source credibility matters. McGuire (1969) suggested that information given by high-credibility sources is thought to be more factual, grammatical, and fair than the same message ascribed to a low-credibility source. Some research, however, has raised the possibility that the salience of the subject matter may condition the impact of source credibility. Researchers have suggested that source credibility is relatively unimportant if the issue engages the subjects' interest. College students, for example, did not pay attention to the credibility of the source when the message concerned raising college tuition (Rhine & Severance, 1970). Petty and Cacioppo (1986) found similar results in an experiment concerning whether comprehensive senior examinations should be adopted.

Zaller (1992) questioned the application of the Petty and Cacioppo experiment to the real world of politics, arguing that the students are vitally concerned with issues dealing with student life. But Zaller agreed with Petty and Cacioppo's finding that low salience led to greater reliance on source credibility. Most people pay limited attention to politics and are therefore likely to rely on peripheral cues relating to the status and position of the advocate (Zaller, 1992; p. 47). In our experiment, most students are presumably not vitally interested in civil liberties, and the democratic-norms messages (positive and negative) are meant to be equally strong, so we expect source credibility to play an important role in the students' judgments.

Our results in this experiment verify those reported earlier for the basic and democratic-norms experiments.[4] Antecedent considerations and contemporary information both matter when people make contemporary tolerance judgments. Table 7.1 shows the main findings, limiting the sample only to those who selected a racist least-liked group. As before, pretest measures of standing decisions on

Table 7.1. *Analysis of covariance of basic model with racist least-liked group subjects only (Texas data set)*

Variables	Unstandardized regression coefficient	F	p
Antecedent considerations (covariates)			
Pretest tolerance	.45	166.3	<.01
Pretest democratic norms	.20	13.6	<.01
Gender	−.07	4.6	.03
Contemporary influences (main effects)			
Normative violations		20.9	<.01
Democratic norms		44.4	<.01
Source expertise		<.1	.81
Instruction set		11.1	<.01
Order		.8	.37
$N = 550$ (excluding cases with missing values)			

political tolerance and democratic norms along with gender are significantly related to contemporary tolerance judgments. People's decisions to tolerate a group are heavily influenced by the attitudes, values, and beliefs they bring to the decision-making process.

In addition, as we found in earlier studies, contemporary information makes a meaningful and significant contribution to the final tolerance decision. As Table 7.1 shows, normative violations, the democratic-norms manipulation, and instruction-set cues strongly affect levels of tolerance ($p < .01$). Figure 7.1 shows that those who read the positive democratic-norms paragraph are more tolerant than those who read the negative paragraph. The instruction-set cue also works as before: those who are told to attend to their thoughts are significantly more tolerant than those who are told to attend to their feelings. In the normative violations condition, those who are reassured are more tolerant than those who are threatened. Indeed, the magnitude of that difference is greater than that presented in Figure 4.1. This result may seem surprising because in Chapter 6 the impact of normative violations was overshadowed by the democratic-norms manipulation. As noted earlier, however, in the Texas study the normative violations treatments were successfully modified to enhance their potency. This shows that normative violations, if sufficiently strong, can continue to play a role in contemporary tolerance judgments even when placed in the context of a debate on democratic principles.

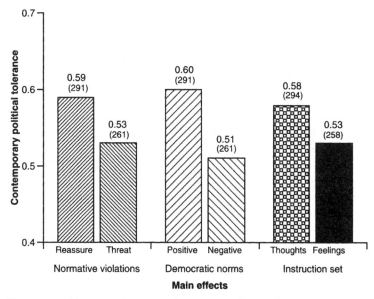

Figure 7.1. *Texas experiment – main treatment effects (N's are in parentheses)*

Order is not significant as a main effect or as an anticipated interaction effect. In this experiment, the democratic-norms information is a highly salient consideration, providing persuasive cues regarding how best to respond to the normative violations information. As a result, order is unimportant and the democratic-norms information has the same effect whether read before or after the normative violations paragraph.

Our new manipulation, source credibility, has no effect on level of tolerance. Even in the low-involvement setting, where Petty and Cacioppo as well as Zaller expect source credibility to be most likely to have an effect, the substance of the message overwhelms the impact of the status of the messenger. The content of the democratic principles themselves, rather than the source that enunciates those principles, is the significant variable for the subjects.

Thus, our basic findings are validated with an updated scenario and a different pool of subjects. Our goal with this study was to replicate and extend the findings reported in Chapters 4 and 6, which we have done. Normative violations, democratic norms, and instruction-set cues are all significant contemporary influences that matter to the tolerance judgments of individuals.

From this analysis, we argue that our results reflect some rather basic psychological processes that are not altered in fundamental ways by changes in the political context. The dramatic events involving racial and political intolerance that we identified at the opening of this chapter do not appear to have changed the role of contemporary information in citizens' decision-making processes.

We also found that the status and expertise of the source of contemporary information about the application of democratic values did not seem to make any difference to most respondents. The second aspect of expertise – the respondents' status as politically knowledgeable or ignorant – may, however, play an important role in making tolerance judgments. In the next section, we test its effects, later turning our attention to the importance of respondents' choice of least-liked group.

POLITICAL SOPHISTICATION, KNOWLEDGE, AND EXPERTISE

Political scientists have long argued that political sophistication is a central determinant of how and whether citizens structure their political beliefs. Converse (1964) argued that political elites and the more sophisticated members of the general public structure their political attitudes along a liberal–conservative dimension, whereas less sophisticated citizens might be better characterized as holding nonattitudes and as providing random responses to public opinion questions. The literature on the concept of political sophistication burgeoned after Converse's classic was published, much of it updating and some of it questioning Converse's theory or methodology (Kinder & Sears, 1985). Many different measures of political sophistication were used, including the classic "levels of conceptualization" measure introduced in *The American Voter* and used subsequently by many political scientists (Lyons & Scheb, 1992; Pierce, 1993). Others have focused on political interest, political knowledge, education, and various related measures of political sophistication (Luskin, 1990).

Political psychologists have focused their efforts on the concept of political expertise rather than that concept of political sophistication. They make a distinction between political experts and novices based on how much individuals know about politics and their level of interest and involvement in political issues (e.g., Fiske, Kinder, & Larter, 1983; Judd & Krosnick, 1989). Whereas political scientists' major concerns revolved around whether nonsophisticates had coherent belief systems, political psychologists' major concerns have been with how experts and novices process political information and arrive at political judgments. Our interest here is more directly related to the latter concern.

Political psychologists have argued, and in many cases have demonstrated, that political experts process information differently than novices do (i.e., experts have greater on-line processing capacity than novices; e.g., McGraw & Pinney, 1990; Fiske et al., 1983).[5] More specifically, researchers have shown that political experts are less responsive than novices to persuasive political messages because they have stronger information-based opinions on most political issues and hence are better able to counterargue information they receive through the media and by word of mouth (Zaller, 1992). Zaller, in an adaptation of McGuire's argument, tested the proposition that novices are less attuned to political information and hence will be relatively unresponsive to such messages; experts will receive more political information but will be better able to resist any implications for opinion change, and hence will be relatively unresponsive; and those in the middle – who are not experts but who have some interest in and knowledge about politics – will exhibit the most change as the result of political information received from their environment. They will receive more messages than novices because they are somewhat interested, but they will resist the implications of these messages less than experts because they have less knowledge and their attitudes are less well-developed. Zaller's (1992) evidence strongly supported McGuire's argument.

In the survey-experiment, this formulation needs to be modified, as we noted in Chapter 6. Zaller's argument was based on differences in both information reception and information responsiveness by level of expertise, relying almost exclusively on poll data. In our research, everyone reads a scenario that contains contemporary information, even if they are novices who are uninterested in politics. As a consequence, information exposure is unrelated to expertise, unlike in the "real world" of politics. The major effect we expect expertise to have, then, is in responsiveness to the information provided. Experts should be less responsive than novices to the contemporary information to which they are exposed. For example, Judd and Krosnick (1989) and Lavine, Thomsen, and Gonzales (1994) found that experts hold more tightly organized attitudes and that these attitudes are more strongly related to abstract values. As a result, in our experiments, experts' predispositions and standing decisions should be more firmly grounded in political values, and hence their current judgments should be less easily swayed by contemporary information or transitory feelings.

Political expertise has been measured in several different ways. Recent research, however, has begun to suggest that some measures are better than others. Fiske, Lau, and Smith (1990) factor analyzed measures of political knowledge, education, political activity, media usage, and self-schemas as measures of expertise. They found that political knowledge per se was the core variable affecting general political expertise and political information processing, including variables such as recall. As a result, we focus on objective measures of political knowledge.

Delli Carpini and Keeter (1993) analyzed the reliability and validity of a large number of measures of political knowledge. They found that five objective questions about general political knowledge create a reliable summary scale. Those questions focus on national governmental institutions, such as by asking subjects to identify the party with the most members in the House of Representatives, the number of votes required to override a presidential veto, and the office held by Al Gore. However, since the students in our study may have already taken one-half of the two-semester American and Texas Government sequence, we asked additional questions requiring greater depth of knowledge (for example, identify William H. Rehnquist) as well as questions requiring students to categorize a number of well-known political figures as liberal or conservative (for example, Ronald Reagan and Michael Dukakis). A complete list of expertise items together with the scale reliability is reported in Appendix B.

Here we explore two hypotheses. First, we will determine whether political experts and novices make different contemporary tolerance judgments. Previous research suggests that they do (McClosky & Brill, 1983; McClosky & Zaller, 1984; Sullivan, Piereson, & Marcus, 1982). McClosky and his colleagues argue that experts have more strongly internalized democratic principles because their political activity and awareness increase their exposure to and understanding of political norms in general. As a result, they are more likely to support civil liberties.

Second, we will examine whether political experts and novices process and use contemporary information differently when making political tolerance judgments. We expect to find that experts respond less than novices to contemporary information because of their increased ability to counterargue and the deeper connection between their values and opinions. Adding an interaction term to our model allows us to specify the type of contemporary information used, or not used, by novices and experts.

Table 7.2 presents the results. When only political knowledge is included as a covariate, the regression coefficient is .38 (Table 7.2A). As expected, knowledge about politics is significantly and strongly related to citizens' contemporary political tolerance judgments. When the other standing decisions are added to the model as covariates (Table 7.2B), the regression coefficient for knowledge drops to .17, remaining an important covariate of tolerance judgments ($p < .05$). This indicates that much but not all of the effects of expertise are encapsulated in other standing decisions. Experts are generally more tolerant than novices going into the experimental situation, and they remain so even controlling for other standing decisions.

To examine whether experts respond differently from novices to contemporary information, subjects who were low and medium in expertise ($N = 560$) were compared with those who were high in expertise ($N = 197$). Figure 7.2 shows the only significant two-way interaction between expertise and contemporary information, specifically normative violations ($p < .05$). Those who were high in expertise had the same contemporary tolerance judgment regardless of whether they received a reassuring or threatening normative violations paragraph (.68). By contrast, novices showed a significant difference depending on whether they read the reassuring (.59) or threatening (.53) normative violations paragraph.[6]

These results confirm our expectations. Novices were most responsive to normative violations information while those higher in expertise found the normative violations information irrelevant. The reason for this is probably that experts have firmer commitments to both democratic norms and tolerance as standing decisions and are better able to counterargue contemporary information. Figure 7.3 shows this conclusively. Two weeks before reading the scenarios, experts demonstrated significantly greater support than novices for democratic values (.77 versus .71), despite the generally consensual status of these values in American society. They also had a stronger level of tolerance as a standing decision. In fact, while novices' standing decisions were intolerant (.43, well below the midpoint of .50), those of experts were tolerant (.57). As a consequence of these preexisting commitments to democratic values, experts were not af-

Table 7.2. *Analysis of covariance of basic model with political knowledge as an antecedent consideration (Texas data set)*

A. *Without Controls for Standing Decisions* (N = 767)

Variables	Unstandardized regression coefficient	F	p
Antecedent considerations (covariates)			
Political knowledge	.38	107.6	<.01
Contemporary influences (main effects)			
Normative violations		11.2	<.01
Democratic norms		25.2	<.01
Source expertise		<.1	.86
Instruction set		9.0	<.01
Order		<.1	.99
Racist group dummy variable		53.4	<.01

B. *With Controls for Standing Decisions* (N = 757)

Variables	Unstandardized regression coefficient	F	p
Antecedent considerations (covariates)			
Pretest tolerance	.41	137.7	<.01
Pretest democratic norms	.18	14.8	<.01
Gender	−.05	15.0	<.01
Political knowledge	.17	23.8	<.01
Contemporary influences (main effects)			
Normative violations		12.3	<.01
Democratic norms		42.9	<.01
Source expertise		<.1	.98
Instruction set		8.5	<.01
Order		<.1	.81
Racist group dummy variable		42.3	<.01

fected by reading threatening information in the scenario. Novices, on the other hand, became less tolerant when they read information suggesting that the group was untrustworthy and dangerous. Novices were less firmly committed in the first place.

Researchers have hypothesized that the greater ability to offer counterarguments sets experts apart from novices (Zaller, 1992). After answering our tolerance questions, subjects were asked to explain why they would or would not allow the WSF to hold a public rally. Counterarguments would be most likely to occur among those who received a negative-norms message: they have been given the arguments against civil liberties, so that any statement made about extending rights to the group could be considered rebuttal. In the negative-norms condition only, we identified the thirteen people

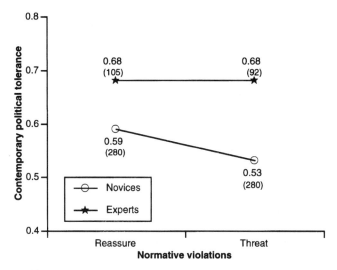

Figure 7.2. *Two-way interaction between normative violations and expertise (Texas data set − N's are in parentheses)*

with the lowest expertise and the fourteen with the highest. By examining the open-ended responses of those with very low and very high expertise, we can determine whether experts are less responsive to contemporary information because they offer counterarguments.

The differences are striking. Those with high expertise exhibit a much stronger knowledge and discussion of democratic norms than those with low expertise: thirteen of fourteen make statements endorsing freedom of speech. As one person stated, "Even though I in no way agree with groups such as the WSF, I firmly believe that they have the same rights as I in expressing their views." Another individual agreed: "By allowing the WSF to hold public rallies, it keeps the organization from going underground where it would be far more dangerous." In contrast, only six of the thirteen novices mentioned freedom of speech as their rationale for allowing the group to hold a rally (or not). They were far more likely to mention violence or the potential for harm in the audience as a reason for restricting the rights of the group. One respondent said, "It would set off more and more anger against the people who are against them, and also it would influence riots and hatred and hurt." Another student agreed: "No [they should not hold a rally], because it causes hatred among people and brings out too much negativity."

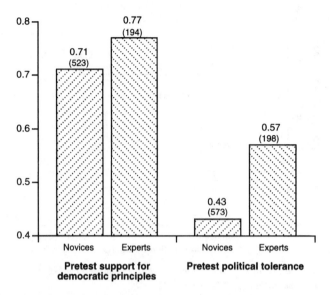

Figure 7.3. *Pretest support for democratic principles and pretest political tolerance – novices versus experts (Texas data set – N's are in parentheses)*

Thus, the experts are far better able to counter the negative-norms arguments than those who are less informed.

Therefore, our expectations concerning expertise have been confirmed. Experts respond with greater tolerance than novices, adding a significant new standing decision to our arsenal. Additionally, experts process information differently than do novices, making them less responsive to contemporary information.

The next section turns to the final variation in the Texas experiment: the extent that mustering objection to the target group matters when making a contemporary tolerance judgment. As we did concerning political expertise, we will consider whether the degree of animus felt made the substance of the tolerance decision different, and whether the tolerance judgments were derived by different psychological processes.

LEAST-LIKED GROUP EFFECTS

Central to our conceptualization of political tolerance is the notion of forbearance. Liking a group and granting it rights is not tolerance but outright support; disliking a group and granting it basic civil liberties is the true test of tolerance. In this section, we explore whether a different dynamic operates when citizens make judgments about their least-liked group versus one that may not be as strongly disliked.

Gray's theory suggests that different processes occur for those who strongly dislike a group and for those who feel less dislike, indifference, or even approbation. The operation of the behavioral inhibition system (BIS) implies that only those confronted with a disliked group would feel the requisite threat that would draw their attention to the contemporary information presented in the scenario. Only those who strongly disliked the group would be sufficiently anxious to be responsive to the new information about normative violations and democratic norms. Therefore, we expect that those who did not select a racist least-liked group would not be affected by the contemporary information that they read and would likely support the rights of the hypothetical racist group, given that these individuals are not necessarily opposed to its goals. Thus, their civil liberties judgments will differ substantively, as will the process used to make the judgment.

Recall that in our previous experiments, we accounted for variation across disliked groups by providing scenarios about groups we knew each respondent disliked. As reported in Chapter 4, we had six such groups. However, in this experiment everyone read about the White Supremacist Faction, greatly simplifying the administration of the second phase of the survey-experiment.

Table 7.3 shows the results for those who selected a nonracist group as their least-liked. These subjects are the first we have encountered whose tolerance standing decision is not significantly related to their contemporary tolerance judgment. The tolerance standing decision is expressly linked to each subject's least-liked group, whereas the contemporary tolerance judgment is based on a group that may generate only mild dislike, indifference, or perhaps even sympathy. Tolerance refers to the willingness to give an objectionable group its basic civil liberties. While subjects who did not select a racist least-liked group were strongly influenced by their level of commitment to democratic principles, they were not influenced by their political tolerance standing decisions. Thus, there is no evidence and little reason to expect that a standing decision of tolerance toward a particular group is generalizable except insofar as support for democratic principles applies universally.

Most surprising is the extent to which, for those who dislike a

Table 7.3. *Tolerance judgments of those not selecting a racist group (Texas data set)*

Variables	Unstandardized regression coefficient	F	p
Antecedent considerations (covariates)			
Pretest tolerance	.06	.7	.41
Pretest democratic norms	.34	14.7	<.01
Gender	−.08	8.8	.07
Contemporary influences (main effects)			
Normative violations		<.1	.84
Democratic norms		2.0	.15
Source expertise		.8	.38
Instruction set		<.1	.93
Order		<.1	.95
$N = 221$ (excluding cases with missing values)			

nonracist group, the contemporary information in the scenarios is irrelevant. These subjects simply rely on their own standing decisions about democratic principles to make a civil liberties judgment. As noted in our discussion of Figure 3.1, something (i.e., threat) must intrude to capture people's attention in order for them to respond to threatening information. The racist scenario itself fills that attention grabbing function for those who dislike racists. However, those who do not choose a racist least-liked group are unaffected by the normative violations statement or the arguments about how to apply democratic norms. Rather, their previously formed conclusions about civil liberties and democratic principles provide sufficient basis for them to express a civil liberties judgment.

In order to identify different types of respondents, we used two different sets of information to establish malice against racist groups. First, respondents were asked to identify their least- and second least-liked groups. Second, respondents were asked to rank all of the target groups on an eleven-point like/dislike scale. We used these two pieces of information to categorize four types of individuals based on their level of animus toward racist groups. The first – and largest – type of individual selected a racist group as his or her most least-liked ($N = 562$). The second type selected a racist group as its second least-liked group ($N = 101$). Among those who did not select a racist least-liked group as either a first or second choice, we distinguished between those who strongly disliked racist groups (*N*

= 68) and those who did not strongly dislike them (N = 46).[7] This creates four types of individuals – those who selected a racist least-liked group as their first choice, those who selected a racist group as their second choice, those who strongly disliked racist groups, and those who did not strongly dislike racist groups.

Figure 7.4 presents the level of tolerance, level of threat perceived from racist groups, and level of dislike toward racist groups by the four types of respondents.[8] Two patterns can be seen in the results. First, the two middle types are virtually identical to each other and different from the other types. Their scores are identical in considering contemporary tolerance judgments and the level of dislike for racist groups, and are not significantly different in perceived level of threat. The two different operationalizations identify those who objected to the racist group but not as vehemently as those who selected a racist group as their least-liked. These two different operational paths lead to identical results.

The second pattern is the linear progression from those who strongly dislike racists to those who felt less malice. When comparing tolerance scores, those who selected a racist group as least-liked were the least tolerant (.56), followed by those who selected a racist group as a second choice or displayed malice (.64), while those who had low malice toward the group exhibited high tolerance (.81), one of the highest mean tolerance scores we have identified.[9] These scores are particularly interesting compared to the standing decision on tolerance that is tied to the most disliked group. Those with low malice scored .50 on the tolerance pretest when asked about their least-liked group, compared with .45 for those who selected a racist group as their first choice on the pretest. It is also noteworthy that the level of dislike and perceived threat from the racist group was significantly lower among those with low malice toward racists, dropping below the midpoint.

On the average, respondents who were lowest in malice toward racists actually *liked* or were *neutral* toward racist groups. They were not threatened by these groups, and according to Gray's theory, if people do not feel threatened they are more likely to rely on habit, or standing decisions, and less likely to monitor the environment carefully for current information. His theory predicts, therefore, that respondents lower in malice toward racists would be less responsive to the experimental manipulations presenting contemporary information about racist group activities.

To explore this hypothesis further, we collapsed the two middle

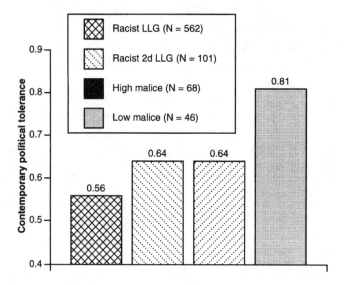

Figure 7.4. *Levels of contemporary political tolerance, dislike of three racist groups, perceptions of threat of three racist groups among those who selected a racist group as least-liked, second least-liked, and those who did not (Texas data set) (See also next page)*

malice groupings into one, creating high-, medium-, and low-malice categories. The hypothesis based on Gray's theory is that an interaction will occur between the malice category and the contemporary information manipulations in our experiment, reflecting different processes of decision making between those who most greatly dislike and are highly threatened by racists, and those who are not.

Figure 7.5 shows a significant interaction among group malice, the democratic-norms manipulation and the normative violations manipulation ($p < .01$). First, consider those respondents who selected a racist least-liked group (represented by squares in Figure 7.5). These people are responsive to both contemporary information about normative violations and democratic norms. The similar slopes of the two groups ($-.05$ for those who read a positive democratic norms paragraph and $-.07$ for those who read a negative democratic norms paragraph) show nearly identical reactions as they move from reassuring to threatening normative violations. The difference between those who received positive and negative democratic-norms paragraphs (represented by the space between the two parallel lines in Figure 7.5) is also essentially the same. These individuals react as expected based on the previous experiments described in Chapters 4–6.

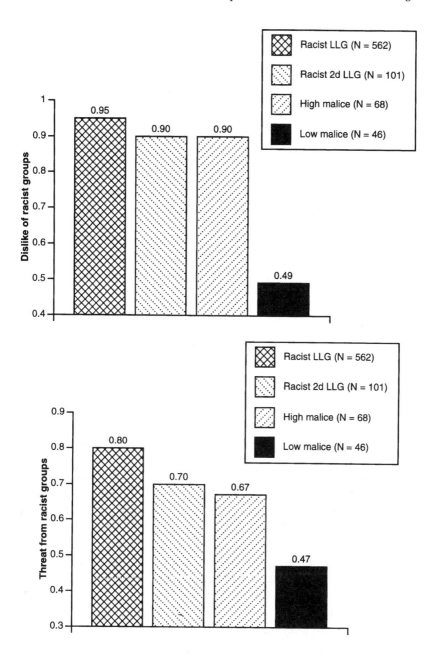

Second, consider those who either picked a racist second least-liked group or who strongly disliked racists (represented by triangles in Figure 7.5). Among this medium-malice category, those who read positive or negative democratic norms have very different re-

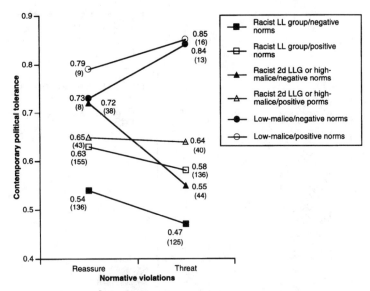

Figure 7.5. *Interaction among group malice, democratic norms, and normative violations treatments (Texas data set – N's are in parentheses)*

sponses. Those who read a negative-norms statement are very responsive to the normative violations paragraphs, with a steep slope between the reassuring and threatening conditions. They dislike racists, and when they read a persuasive argument limiting the group's civil liberties, they are highly receptive unless they are reassured. Among those in the middle-malice category, the negative democratic-norms statements and the threatening normative violations are reinforcing, although if reassured they can overcome the negative-norms message. Those in the positive-democratic norms condition present a sharp contrast. For those individuals, reading the reassuring or threatening condition makes very little difference; the slope is essentially flat. For these respondents, the positive-norms message overwhelms the normative violations message and they do not shift their position due to differences in perceived threat. Therefore, we can see that those with medium malice rely on a more complex process to make their tolerance decision than those who selected a racist group as their first choice. Their tolerance decision depends on the precise contemporary information offered, perhaps partly because their malice toward the racist group is less strong.

Respondents in the low-malice category behave very differently from the other two groups. The high- and medium-malice respondents are less tolerant when threatened and more tolerant when reassured. The low-malice respondents, however, act the opposite way – the more threatening the scenario, the more tolerant they become. This finding is striking We can also see that those who read the positive democratic-norx statement are slightly more tolerant than those who read the negative democratic-norms statement. The starkly different pattern of response among those with low malice indicates that different psychological mechanisms occur among those who respond to a least-liked group, or even a second least-liked group, than occur when the decision is made by those with no strong dislike toward the group in question.

That the underlying dynamics of decision making differ greatly across levels of dislike for racist groups illustrates the importance of our conceptualization of tolerance as requiring serious objection. Among respondents who do object to racists – who dislike them and feel threatened by them – contemporary information plays the usual role in their decision making, as predicted by Gray's theory of emotional response. Threatening contemporary information decreases tolerance, whereas reassuring contemporary information increases it; negative-norms information decreases tolerance, whereas positive-norms information increases it. However, among respondents who do not object to racists – who in fact, according to Figure 7.4, neither dislike them nor feel threatened by them – the role of contemporary information is altered and their decision making differs in significant ways. These findings suggest that the low-malice respondents actually identify with racists rather than seeing them as antagonists.

According to our conceptualization of tolerance, then, the low-malice group does not tolerate racists. Instead, these people actually have some level of identification with and support for racists. As a result, their apparent "tolerance" scores are actually support scores.[10]

With this interpretation in mind we can return to the findings just noted and offer a more compelling interpretation of them. Recall that, among the low-malice respondents, their "tolerance" of racists was actually higher under the high-threat normative violations condition than under the reassuring normative violations condition. If we interpret these as "support" scores, this makes much more sense. Under the high-threat condition, the racists are on the attack, aggressively promoting their views and confronting authorities and their intended victims. Under the reassuring condition, the racists are being cooperative and expressing their views in a more calm and compliant manner. A fairly high proportion of the low-malice respondents actually like the racists, and under this identification, they rally to support the racist group more strongly when the racists are in a more intensively conflictual situation. Under the reassuring condition, the racists are less in need of a supportive response from the low-malice subjects.

Further evidence for this interpretation can be obtained from examining their responses to open-ended questions in the pretest and posttest. We asked them, in both questionnaires, to state their reasons for supporting or not supporting a public rally held by their least-liked group (pretest) or the WSF (posttest). While many of those with low malice supported the WSF and offered explanations involving free speech, a substantial number of those in the low-malice group showed striking differences between their responses when asked about their least-liked group and when asked about the WSF. One man wrote about the WSF: "This is a right that all groups have. I feel that they should be able to hold rallies regardless of their attitude toward blacks and jews." But, when confronted with his least-liked group (homosexuals) on the pretest, the same man wrote, "I feel that homosexuality is immoral and do not feel that these people should be given the right to assemble." Others used the same reasoning. With regard to the White Supremacist Faction, one woman said, "It is my opinion that all groups should be able to hold public rallies as long as they are non-violent and do not infringe on the rights of others"; but with regard to homosexuals, she noted, "Because I disagree with the whole concept of homosexuality, I have no sympathy towards them and their rights to promote their repulsive lifestyle." Another man echoed this response: "We have a right to free speech in this country," he wrote, but also said, "Homosexuals are absolutely disgusting to me and they should all be rounded up and put on a desolate island together."

Many respondents who selected a racist least-liked group, or had high malice toward such groups, distanced themselves from the stated goals of the group even while supporting the group's civil liberties. Those who had low malice toward racists, however, did not. Typical of the former were statements denigrating the goals of the group even when supporting its civil liberties, such as, "Although I disagree completely with their beliefs, it would be wrong to deny them the right to speak," or "Although I don't agree with their group, everyone should have free speech, besides they just show what idiots they are." These types of distancing statements were notably missing from most of the low-malice respondents. As one woman said, "Let them say what they want, its [sic] their Constitutional right, on some issues I agree with them." Another woman stated more bluntly: "It is our constitutional right to hold them. No matter who disagrees with what. It's the same as the Black Panthers holding a rally. They are just as racist as white supremists [sic] and just as dangerous. But because they are black supremists [sic] they are okay. You don't hear very much about them, do you?" Notice the word "our." This woman appears to identify with the views of the WSF, in spite of referring to them by implication as dangerous.

The data in Figure 7.6 corroborate this argument. First, the low-malice respondents' ideology differs significantly from that of the others, with those who selected racists as their least-liked group being on the liberal side (.54), those who selected racists as their second choice or who have high malice being moderately conservative (.40), and those with low malice being very conservative (.32). This ideological pattern is also reflected in their dislike of the leftist groups on the survey, most notably homosexuals and feminists. The levels of dislike and threat shown concerning homosexuals is much stronger among low-malice respondents than among those who strongly dislike racist groups. A similar pattern, not shown in the graph, holds for dislike of feminists, suggesting that these respondents direct their malice toward the left, particularly feminists and gays. It is interesting to note that those low in malice toward racists are predominantly males (67% of this group is male compared to only 40% of those who selected a racist least-liked group).

A question to consider is whether this same pattern – increased support for the group under the threatening normative violations condition – would occur for any segment of individuals asked about a group they like. We believe that the behavior of these right-wing individuals differs from the type of reaction we would have obtained from asking liberals about homosexuals or feminists. Two lines of research support this view. First, Altemeyer (1988) shows that authoritarian aggression is a characteristic of a subset of right-wingers rather than left-wingers. This suggests that right-wingers – more so than liberals – would support the more aggressive type of action described under the more threatening scenario. They would be more likely to become defensive and to "cheer on" the racists when the scenario is threatening than when it is reassuring. The liberals

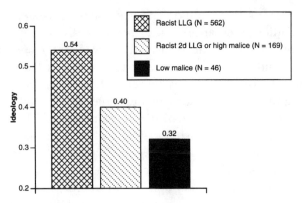

Figure 7.6. *Comparison of ideology and level of malice of and threat from homosexuals by group selected as least-liked (Texas data set) (See also next page)*

would probably be less responsive to the normative violations manipulation if the group in question is homosexuals or feminists, because they have less "authoritarian aggression" according to Altemeyer. A second reason for this expectation is Brady and Sniderman's (1985) finding that extreme conservatives "contrast" their perceptions of the left's ideological position more than liberals do of the right wing's ideology. Thus conservatives see the left as farther to the left than it really is, while liberals distort the position of the right a bit less. As a result, defensiveness may be a quicker reaction for conservatives than for liberals. Both of these findings are consistent with the argument that our finding about the low-malice respondents' levels of support for racists would not be replicated using different respondents and different target groups. Therefore, reversing the target group by giving left-wing scenarios to liberals would likely result in a flat line, rather than an upward slope as we see with the low-malice group in Figure 7.5.

Thus, our conceptualization of tolerance derives support from these results. Those who are low in malice toward racists react very differently from those who dislike racists to our scenarios about the White Supremacist Faction. As Gray would predict, they are not threatened by the group – many of them support such groups – and so they do not respond like others to the contemporary information on normative violations. Rather than deciding whom to tolerate they are deciding whom to support. So their increased support scores reflect enthusiasm for the aggressive efforts of a group they like rather than their forbearance of a group they dislike.

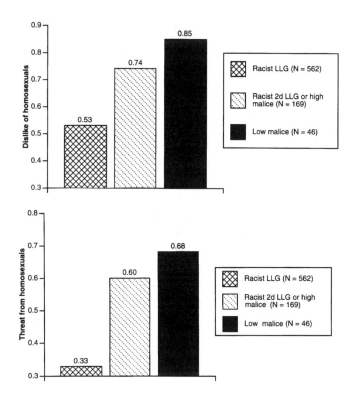

DISCUSSION AND CONCLUSION

This chapter has focused on three contributions of the Texas experiment. First, the experiment replicated and extended our basic findings. The Texas study confirms that antecedent considerations have important influences on contemporary tolerance judgments. Contemporary information, particularly concerning how to apply democratic principles, or the extent of normative violations, remains influential in shaping contemporary tolerance judgments. Although we used updated scenarios, in a changed political environment the main experimental effects remain extremely robust. Source credibility, however, had no impact on contemporary tolerance judgments.

Second, the experiment showed the centrality of expertise in making tolerance judgments. An individual's level of political knowledge is strongly and significantly related to his or her final tolerance judgment. Experts not only make substantively different tolerance decisions, but also use a different process to come to those judgments. Novices remain far more open to the effects of contemporary information while experts discount new information because of their greater ability to counterargue.

Third, these data support our argument that tolerance requires forbearance. Those who do not object to a group's ideas and ideals are not tolerating its activities, but may instead be expressing support for the group. An examination of the low-malice group shows that a different psychological process is used in making a decision to support rather than a decision to tolerate.

In Chapters 4–7 we have demonstrated that tolerance judgments are generally made by relying on four antecedent considerations: political tolerance beliefs, support for democratic principles, threat convictions and, to some extent, gender. To this we can add a fifth: expertise. While some of the effects of threat convictions and expertise are encapsulated by tolerance beliefs and support for democratic principles, both retain a direct impact on tolerance judgments. In the following chapter, we will explore the encapsulation hypothesis more fully as we turn to a sixth antecedent consideration – personality.

APPENDIX 7A: TEXAS STUDY – REVISED SCENARIOS

Reassuring normative violations:

The WSF has begun to hold public rallies to generate support for their cause. Before their rallies, they cooperated with the police and local authorities and promised to have peaceful demonstrations according to the conditions of their parade permits. The police have suggested that they can be trusted and are not dangerous. The WSF have marched along the designated routes and did not cause any trouble with counter demonstrators, spectators, or the police. At the rallies and demonstrations, leaders of the WSF have asked their supporters to act vigorously but as lawfully as possible to pursue their cause.

Threatening normative violations:

After the Rodney King verdict, and in wake of the Los Angeles riots that followed, the WSF began to hold public rallies to generate support for their cause. Before their rallies, they refused to cooperate with the police and local authorities but did promise to have peaceful demonstrations according to the conditions of their parade permits. However, they have not always marched along the designated routes and have gotten enmeshed with counter demonstrators and the police. The police have suggested that they cannot be trusted and might be dangerous. In fact, at some of the rallies, fist fights and rock throwing have resulted in spectators, demonstrators and some police getting hurt. Members of the WSF have shouted "Whites only, down with Blacks," and "First get the dirty N———, then the Jews." At the rallies and demonstrations, leaders of the WSF have asked their supporters to take bold actions to pursue their cause, that the ends justify the means.

CHAPTER 8

Individual Differences – The Influence of Personality

> Certain inner psychological states . . . may help to deter-
> mine whether an individual will be disposed to allow or
> suppress the exercise of freedom by people whose opin-
> ions, conduct, or social characteristics offend him or her.
>
> McClosky and Brill, *Dimensions of Tolerance*

Throughout this book, we have distinguished among the roles of predispositions, standing decisions, and contemporary information in shaping tolerance judgments. We conducted three basic experiments in which we examined the impact of contemporary threat perceptions on tolerance judgments, and we replicated these findings in a subsequent study. We assumed that the cumulative impact of predispositions generally was encapsulated in standing decisions, as measured by respondents' pretest tolerance and their support for democratic norms.

Much of our purpose in Chapter 4 was to analyze threat perceptions as contemporary information that provides meaningful guidance for people when they make concurrent tolerance judgments. In Chapter 5, however, we also analyzed the influence of global threat perceptions that constitute predispositions, and of least-liked group threat perceptions that constitute standing decisions. We found that these antecedent considerations are strongly related to political tolerance. Global threat perceptions and least-liked group threat perceptions lead some people to be less tolerant, independent of contemporary information, and affect how people process contemporary information and arrive at current tolerance judgments.

As noted in Chapter 3, Gray's emotional mood theory suggested how threat perceptions may affect political tolerance. We will also rely on Gray's theory and the circumplex model to examine the role of more stable personality traits. Positive and negative affect represent different tendencies in individuals, not just swings in mood due to limbic-system processing of contemporary information. Thus, although most people become more distressed and fearful in the presence of threatening stimuli, some individuals tend to be higher in negative affect (hostility, fearfulness, distress) than others, all else equal. In other words, individuals begin at different baselines. The same is true for positive affect.

In this chapter we will attempt to accomplish three goals. First, theories of personality, including Gray's, lead us to expect that certain personality types will be more (or less) inclined to be tolerant. We will therefore examine the direct effects of personality as a predisposition to tolerance. Second, although we expect personality to be related to current tolerance judgments, the model we have developed allows us to explicate and test an important caveat to this relationship. We expect that personality as a predisposition has only an indirect effect on current tolerance judgments when standing decisions are included in the analysis. In essence, the effects of personality are encapsulated in people's standing decisions. Finally, personality is important not only in its effects through antecedent considerations, but also in how people process contemporary information. What information people pay attention to and how they use it is affected by personality. First we turn to the theoretical treatment of personality.

GRAY'S MODEL OF PERSONALITY

Modern psychologists have suggested that there are two primary models of personality: discrete and dimensional. Dimensional models recognize many intermediate possibilities between the polar ends that define a dimension, and research based on dimensional models finds that most people cluster more to the center of the various dimensions rather than at the extremes. Discrete models place people into a smaller number of particular types such as extrovert or introvert. Our conception of personality falls into the dimensional model.

Dimensional models also share the presumption that a biological foundation underlies these stable patterned differences (Cloninger,

1986, 1987; Gray, 1987a; Zuckerman, 1991). For example, Gray's state theory, presented in Chapter 3, has a firm biological foundation.

Gray's theory also has a personality, or trait, component. His theory links each of the three biologically based mood systems to a specific basic dimension of personality, thus yielding a three-dimensional model of personality. In his formulation, emotional reactions lie at the center of what he calls moods, and they also undergird his personality theory.

Gray conceives of the behavioral inhibition system (BIS) and behavioral approach system (BAS) as having both a trait and a state component. We have already discussed the "state" component of his theory as that portion of the BIS and BAS that controls the individual's moods. Here, we present the trait, or personality, component of his model.

To develop the trait component, Gray (1987c) builds on the work of Eysenck. He identifies three dimensions of personality. Each of these dimensions is built on an explicit neurological model. The first two dimensions, neuroticism and introversion/extraversion, are the trait components of the BIS and BAS respectively. Neuroticism is part of the BIS, which generates the moods of anxiety and reassurance. The trait component of this system is the general orientation to be nervous, worried, and anxious on the one hand, or to be calm and secure on the other. The introversion/extraversion dimension of personality relates to the BAS, which generates the moods of enthusiasm, elation, and depression. The trait component of this system is the general orientation to be sociable, lively, and venturesome (extraversion), or withdrawn, passive, and shy (introversion).

Figure 8.1 presents the first two dimensions of personality in Gray's model. In this figure we have included two hypothetical individuals. Person A is an extravert, someone who is generally ebullient, sociable, and lively. She is also, to a lesser extent, anxious. Note that this description of Person A is a "trait" description. Person A approaches most situations with eagerness yet with a tad of concern; she approaches most people with energy and social engagement. She has a BAS that has helped her acquire the social and physical skills to master most common social situations. She also has a BIS that creates an alertness to the external environment.

Person B is calm, shy, and retiring. She has a BIS that is quick to disengage from novel people and situations. She seeks to avoid such

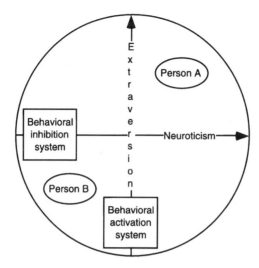

Figure 8.1. *Gray's model and the first two dimensions of personality*

situations. Moreover, she has a BAS that in the past has not helped her to secure a masterful repertoire of social skills. Thus, she finds most social circumstances intimidating and unpleasant.

The collection of personality traits, or dimensions, provides a baseline orientation for each individual. This baseline describes each individual's personality. In these examples, Person A finds most social circumstances to be enlivening and engaging, while Person B finds these same circumstances to be overwhelming and potentially immobilizing.

Recent experimental research confirms that each of these two basic personality dimensions – neuroticism and extraversion – is linked to cognate dimensions of mood – negative affect and positive affect (Larsen & Ketelaar, 1989, 1991; Williams, 1990). In Gray's formulation, however, the state and trait components of the BIS and BAS can function relatively independently of each other. That is, the trait component may describe a general inclination to be calm or to be anxious, but it does not necessarily predetermine responses to changing contemporary circumstances. For example, in Figure 8.1, Person A is more anxious than Person B. However, both people – whether basically calm or anxious – will respond to novel or threatening stimuli by becoming more anxious (MacLeod & Mathews, 1988; Mogg, Mathews, Bird, & Macgregor-Morris, 1990).

Gray's formulation links the third dimension of personality to the fight/flight system. Eysenck calls this dimension "psychoticism" (see Figure 8.2).[1] This system manages unmediated responses to the direct experience of punishing stimuli (i.e., either fight or flight). Those who are low on this dimension are more constrained, conservative, and likely to cling to the familiar. They also choose to be more generally constrained in the way they live their lives. The personality differences identified by this dimension deal with a general disposition to be aggressive or to withdraw in the face of difficult circumstances.[2] We have displayed this dimension as one that shrinks the circumplex space as one moves from low to high psychoticism.

In the next section, we discuss the theory and hypotheses that suggest why and how personality affects political tolerance. We will describe the measures we used to test these hypotheses and the results of our tests.

PERSONALITY AS PREDISPOSITION

In this section, we examine two general hypotheses. First, we argue that personality dimensions have an impact on political tolerance. Previous research and general theory lead to the expectation that different types of individuals will be more or less predisposed toward intolerance as a consequence of the kind of person they have become. Second, we expect that most or perhaps even all of the effects of personality predispositions will be encapsulated in standing decisions such as support for democratic principles and values. These standing decisions are more specific to the topic at hand – political tolerance – than are general predispositions such as personality. In general, standing decisions reflect attitudes and values that are, in part, a product of a broader socialization process and of personality development. As a result, we expect that standing decisions ought to summarize much of the impact of personality on tolerance.

From the dimensions formulated in Gray's model, we derive several specific hypotheses relating personality to making contemporary tolerance judgments. First, people at the high end of the neuroticism dimension – those who are high on trait anxiety – are predisposed to respond to a broader range of stimuli with greater anxiety than are those who are low on neuroticism. Those at the low end of this dimension are less predisposed to find threat and novelty upsetting. More individuals with high scores on this dimension will, therefore, perceive unpopular political groups to be threat-

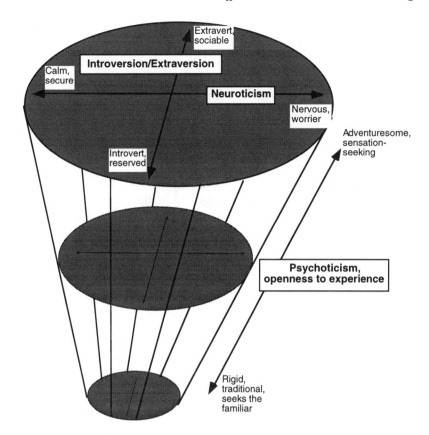

Figure 8.2. *The big three dimensions of personality and Gray's model*

ening and will respond with anxiety and intolerance. Neuroticism ought, therefore, to have a direct (and negative) effect on political tolerance judgments.

Second, countervailing expectations exist concerning individuals who are high on extraversion compared to those low on this dimension. One can be enthusiastically tolerant or intolerant. There are, however, some reasons to expect greater enthusiasm from individuals who are intolerant than from those who are more tolerant. People who are intolerant are more intense in their attitudes (Sullivan et al., 1982, 1985). Therefore, as we show in Chapter 9, they are more predisposed to take action if public policy abrogates their view. These findings suggest that extraversion, like neuroticism, will be negatively correlated with posttest tolerance scores. On the other hand, people who are socially isolated – alienated from society and other people – tend to be more authoritarian, dogmatic, and intolerant (Altemeyer, 1988; McClosky & Brill, 1983). This might lead one to expect a positive correlation between extraversion and contemporary tolerance judgments.

The third personality dimension, openness to experience, is directly linked to tolerance.[3] Individuals who have low scores on this dimension are more restrained, conservative (in the sense of being most comfortable with that which is familiar or traditional), and generally prefer to live more constricted lives. Theoretically, people low in openness to experience are expected to be less tolerant than individuals who are more open and adventurous. Tolerance requires open-mindedness and the willingess to allow, if not accept, the expression of uncomfortable ideas by groups of strangers. Individuals who tolerate such expressions must have a certain boldness and perhaps even audacity. Considerable research on personality characteristics that are negatively related to openness to experience shows them to be strongly related to political intolerance. For example, Altemeyer (1988) shows that authoritarianism relates negatively to diversity of experience and willingness to accept nonconformists. Other studies show that openness, self-esteem, and related concepts have a strong impact on tolerance (Gibson, 1987; McClosky & Brill, 1983; Sniderman, 1975; Sullivan et al., 1982). This theory and research suggest a third hypothesis, that openness to experience is positively related to political tolerance.

Finally, when we designed the experiments described in Chapter 4, we thought that the instruction to pay attention to thoughts or feelings would play a central role in our analysis. We expected that when people were more thoughtful, they would also be more tolerant. It was logical to assume, therefore, that differences in predispositions to be thoughtful, or to be more impulsive and intuitive, would affect preexisting levels of tolerance. We reasoned that individuals who are naturally more thoughtful without prompting – those who are more intellectual in their general approach to life – would be more tolerant than people who are less comfortable with reflective deliberation.

If this argument is correct, then citizens who are high in "need for cognition" (Cacioppo & Petty, 1982) should be more tolerant before they experience our experimental conditions than those who are lower in need for cognition. Cacioppo and Petty see this construct as the tendency for an individual to engage in and enjoy thinking. They do not, however, argue that need for cognition is an invariant trait or personality characteristic that influences general behavior across all situations. It is not isomorphic to any of the more general, basic dimensions of personality we have discussed in this chapter. Cacioppo and Petty do, however, suggest that need for cognition is a predisposition that can affect some behaviors depending on the specific situation. Tolerance judgments are likely to provide such a situation, because individuals who take a "sober second thought" respond differently from those who rely more on intuition or instinct. The fourth hypothesis, then, is that individuals high in need for cognition will be more tolerant than those who express less interest in a cognitive approach to life.

In summary, to analyze the effects on tolerance judgments of individual differences in personality, we have drawn on Gray's three-dimensional trait model and on Cacioppo and Petty's work on cognitive orientations. At a general level, we expect that personality factors will have an impact on political tolerance judgments. We expect that tolerance judgments will be negatively related to neuroticism and positively related to openness to experience and need for cognition; our expectations are uncertain about their relationship with extraversion. The second general hypothesis is that standing decisions largely mediate the effects of personality characteristics on political tolerance judgments. In the next section, we will test these hypotheses using the data sets described in earlier chapters.

The Encapsulating Effects of Standing Decisions

In Chapter 4, we assumed that controls for pretest tolerance scores, democratic norms, and gender would hold constant most of the effects of predispositions and other standing decisions. To examine these assumptions, we test the hypotheses about the effects of personality on current tolerance judgments in two ways.

We will first analyze the impact of personality factors on posttest tolerance scores without controlling for measures of standing decisions. We then present the results with explicit controls for these decisions. If measures of personality dimensions have significant effects on current tolerance judgments without these controls, but few effects when these variables are statistically controlled, then we can conclude that the effects of personality are encapsulated in standing decisions. Under these circumstances personality characteristics would influence both the extent to which an individual internalizes democratic norms and the extent to which the individual is tolerant going into the experimental setting.[4]

PERSONALITY AND POLITICAL TOLERANCE

In the first study we conducted with Nebraska students (the first of the three basic experiments described in Chapter 4) and in the democratic-norms experiment with Minnesota students (described in Chapter 6), we measured the basic dimensions of personality using Watson, Clark, and Tellegen's inventory (Watson, 1988b; Watson et al., 1988). Unfortunately, the reliabilities of these scales were low, and a factor analysis did not reveal the required factor structure. As a result, we turned in later studies (the Nebraska adult study described in Chapter 4 and the Texas student study described in Chapter 7) to measures developed by Costa and McCrae (1985). Item analysis revealed much higher reliabilities and a factor structure appropriate to the measurement theory (see Appendix B). In addition, Costa and McCrae (1985) developed their measures based in part on Gray's work, and they validated their measures in several studies. Their three basic dimensions are neuroticism, extraversion, and openness to experience. As a result of these considerations, as well as the greater degree of generalizability provided, we will focus on the results from the adult study. We will summarize the results from the other studies where appropriate.

Costa and McCrae (1985) have shown that high scorers on the neuroticism scale are particularly worrying, nervous, emotional, and insecure individuals who tend to feel inadequate. This is the personality trait related to the state dimension Gray calls negative affect. As noted in Figure 8.2, people high in negative affect have hostile, fearful, nervous, and distressed reactions. High scorers on the extraversion scale are particularly sociable, active, talkative, person-oriented, optimistic, fun-loving, and affectionate. In Gray's state terms, these tend to be people with high positive affect – in Figure 8.2, individuals who tend to have elated, enthusiastic, excited, happy, and active reactions. Finally, high scorers on the openness to experience scale tend to be curious, creative, original, imaginative, nontraditional, and have broad interests (Costa & McCrae, 1985).

Table 8.1 presents the results of analyses using the adult data with and without controls for pretest tolerance scores, democratic norms, and gender.

Table 8.1. *Personality as predisposition – the impact of personality on current tolerance judgments with and without controls for tolerance standing decisions (adult data)*

A. *Without Controls for Standing Decisions (N = 341)*

Variables	Unstandardized regression coefficient	F	p
Antecedent considerations (covariates)			
Neuroticism	−.24	9.9	<.01
Extraversion	−.15	3.3	.07
Openness to experience	.51	45.3	<.01
Contemporary influences (main effects)			
Thoughts/feelings cue		3.1	.08
Normative violations		3.6	.06
Probability		8.2	<.01
Order		0.4	.55

B. *With Controls for Standing Decisions (N = 306)*

Variables	Unstandardized regression coefficient	F	p
Antecedent considerations (covariates)			
Pretest tolerance	.42	92.2	<.01
Democratic norms	.30	15.7	<.01
Gender	.00	0.1	.76
Neuroticism	−.15	5.4	.02
Extraversion	−.08	1.2	.28
Openness to experience	.04	0.2	.66
Contemporary influences (main effects)			
Thoughts/feelings cue		8.4	<.01
Normative violations		6.1	.01
Probability		1.8	.18
Order		0.2	.64

All three personality dimensions have an effect on contemporary tolerance judgments.[5] The results show that, as expected, neuroticism has a moderately strong negative relationship with contemporary tolerance judgments (−.24), while openness to experience has a very strong positive relationship with tolerance (.51). Our expectations with regard to extraversion were mixed. The results suggest that the greater enthusiasm of less tolerant respondents (see Chapter 9) is manifested by a negative relationship between extraversion and tolerance judgments (−.15, a weak but significant relationship).

As Table 8.1B shows, once standing decisions are added to the equation as covariates, only neuroticism continues to have a significant direct effect on tolerance judgments, although its regression coefficient is reduced from −.24 to −.15. The effects of extraversion and openness to experience are fully encapsulated in standing decisions despite the strength of the latter's regression coefficient before controlling for standing decisions. This suggests that individuals' standing decisions incorporate most of the effects of personality. People high on extraversion or low on openness are predisposed toward greater intolerance, and they carry that predisposition with them into the experimental situation, which provides them with additional, contemporary information. They do this in the form of a standing decision to be intolerant of their least-liked group. People low on extraversion or high on openness have a greater predisposition to be tolerant, which they also carry with them into the experimental setting. Finally, however, individuals high in neuroticism − people who are constitutionally nervous, anxious, and worried − are not only less tolerant going into the experiment, but even controlling for this difference, they react more intolerantly after being given contemporary information and being asked to make a current judgment.

Finally, Table 8.1 shows that after controlling for predispositions and standing decisions, the experimental manipulations have the same effects as reported in Chapter 4. Despite the great analytic power of predispositions and standing decisions, contemporary information continues to play a significant role in shaping current tolerance judgments.

These results are replicated in the Texas data originally reported in Chapter 7. We also included Cacioppo and Petty's (1982) need for cognition scale in the Texas study, and the results are reported in Table 8.2. Again, without controls for standing decisions, all of the personality variables have significant relationships with tolerance judgments. And, also once again, neuroticism and extraversion have negative relationships[6] with tolerance judgments, whereas openness to experience has a positive relationship. Need for cognition also has a positive relationship with political tolerance, as suggested by the results of our thoughts-versus-feelings cue as well as previous research.[7]

When controls for standing decisions are added to the equation in Table 8.2, the personality variables no longer have a significant impact on tolerance judgments. As in Table 8.1, the impact of the experimental manipulations is unaffected by examining the direct effects of predispositions and standing decisions.

Table 8.2. *Personality as predisposition – the impact of personality on current tolerance judgments with and without controls for tolerance standing decisions (Texas data)*

A. *Without Controls for Standing Decisions* (N = 738)

Variables	Unstandardized regression coefficient	F	p
Antecedent considerations (covariates)			
Neuroticism	−.20	16.3	<.01
Extraversion	−.20	9.9	<.01
Openness to experience	.16	5.4	.02
Need for cognition	.17	5.3	.02
Contemporary influences (main effects)			
Thoughts/feelings cue		8.2	<.01
Normative violations		11.1	<.01
Democratic norms manipulation		21.0	<.01
Order		0.1	.78
Source		0.1	.77
Racist target group		59.9	<.01

B. *With Controls for Standing Decisions* (N = 728)

Variables	Unstandardized regression coefficient	F	p
Antecedent considerations (covariates)			
Pretest tolerance	.43	136.9	<.01
Democratic norms	.16	9.7	<.01
Gender	−.05	12.3	<.01
Expertise*	.17	20.8	<.01
Neuroticism	−.10	1.1	.31
Extraversion	.04	0.4	.51
Openness to experience	−.06	0.8	.36
Need for cognition	.02	0.1	.81
Contemporary influences (main effects)			
Thoughts/feelings cue		7.8	<.01
Normative violations		10.5	<.01
Democratic norms manipulation		38.5	<.01
Order		0.1	.69
Source		0.0	.96
Racist target group		36.2	<.01

*The results are the same when expertise is excluded. We include it here because, as shown in Chapter 7, it is an important determinant of political tolerance judgments.

In summary, in both the adult and Texas studies, there is consistent evidence that most of the effects of personality differences are summarized by standing decisions. Neuroticism seems to be an exception, an understandable one given that our experiments demonstrate the key role of threat and anxiety in decreasing tolerance. It is not surprising that individual differences in anxiety and nervousness would affect contemporary tolerance judgments directly.

PERSONALITY AND THE TOLERANCE EXPERIMENTS: EFFECTS ON INFORMATION PROCESSING

In Chapter 5, we found that people who are predisposed to be highly threatened are more responsive to contemporary information about normative violations. In Chapter 6, we showed that individuals who enter our survey-experiments with a high level of support for democratic principles are less affected by contemporary information about how to apply these principles than those whose support is weaker. And, in Chapter 7, we demonstrated that experts are less affected than novices by contemporary information about normative violations. In this section, we examine whether individuals with certain personality characteristics are more or less open to contemporary information than other individuals. Specifically, we might expect people who have a high need for cognition to pay particular attention to cognitive cues in the environment since they are especially open to this kind of information. Those low in need for cognition, on the other hand, may be especially unresponsive to this information. In this section, then, we will explore whether certain types of individuals are more responsive to the kind of contemporary information we provided to them in our survey-experiments.

The Need for Cognition

Cacioppo and Petty's (1982) work on cognition suggests one type of individual who will be more responsive to particular kinds of information. Key to their argument is the expectation that some people experience the world more intellectually and cognitively, while others are more affectively and intuitively oriented. People high in "need for cognition" – those who adopt a more intellectual approach to life – will be more thoughtful and reflective in their everyday lives. They are likely to pay attention to, and to think through, many important personal and political issues. They are particularly attentive to certain types of information provided by their environment – they enjoy thinking things through and they pay attention to information that stimulates cogitation. As Fiske and Taylor (1991) note, "People high on the need for cognition generate more cognitive responses, both pro and con, to persuasive communications, and are consequently likely to be more or less persuaded depending on the message" (p. 489).

Although people high in need for cognition may be attentive to hard information about the world, current information is less likely to affect their contemporary judgments. These people have already considered many important issues and arrived at a firm standing decision. They will also generate more thoughts, including counter-arguments that maintain their standing decision, in response to new information. Consistent with this line of argument, Zaller (1992: p. 37) argued that people who are more politically aware – as those high in need for cognition are likely to be – are more selective in the kind of information they internalize. They are, he argued, more likely to reject information and ideas that are inconsistent with their values.[8]

We expect, then, that if people high in need for cognition do respond to the kind of contemporary information we provide, they are likely to respond to cognitive, not affective, information. They seek information to decide whether to alter their standing decision, which is intellectually grounded. They will, therefore, respond to information about the target group's impending power rather than one particular unruly incident.

Individuals who make less-cognitive and more-intuitive judgments tend to handle problems more or less automatically and "on-line" as they arise. They do not think systematically about such issues (Fiske & Taylor, 1991). Individuals who are lower in need for cognition, therefore, may be relatively oblivious to particular types of information from their environment. When required to make judgments, however, they may be sensitive to the kind of information that is processed more instinctively and emotionally (automatically) than that which requires conscious thought (controlled processing).

Since we did not include the need-for-cognition scale in the adult data set, we will examine its influence in the Texas data and in the original Nebraska student survey. In keeping with our previous procedures, we divided the samples into two groups – the approximately top quarter on need for cognition and those in the bottom three-fourths. We then examined the main effects of need for cognition as a dichotomy, and, more particularly, determined whether it had any interactive effects on the treatment variables.[9]

Looking first at the Texas data set, there was one significant interaction between need for cognition and a treatment variable – the

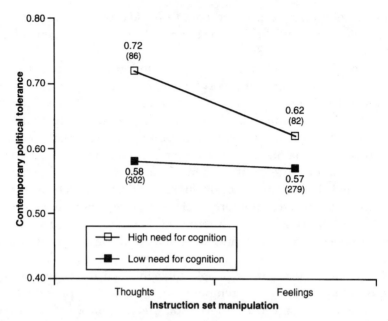

Figure 8.3. *Interaction between need for cognition and instruction set (Texas Data Set — N's are in parentheses)*

thoughts/feelings cue ($p < .10$). As Figure 8.3 shows, one group stands out: those high in need for cognition who were told to pay attention to their thoughts were far more tolerant (.72) than the other three groups (.57 to .62). From these differences, we might conclude that if the need for cognition is low, paying attention to thoughts does *not* enhance tolerance. If people are not comfortable with thinking hard about something, they will not be affected much by whatever thought they do engage in. On the other hand, consistent with Devine's (1989) work on racism and controlled processing, people who like to think about things are affected by their thoughts. In this case, their thoughts lead them to be considerably more tolerant than when they are paying attention to their feelings (.72 versus .62).[10]

Figure 8.4 presents the results for the Nebraska student sample. Need for cognition is not significant as a main effect, but there is a significant interaction between it and normative violations ($p < .02$). In this instance, people with a lower need for cognition are more responsive to threatening information about a noxious group. Once again, one group stands out. People who are low in need for cognition and who read the threatening paragraph are much less tol-

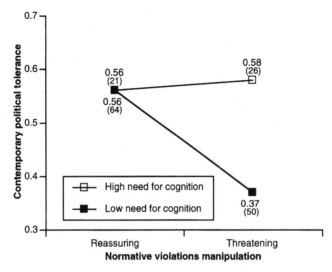

Figure 8.4. *Interaction between need for cognition and normative violations (Nebraska student data – N's are in parentheses)*

erant (.37) than the other three groups (.56 to .58). In this instance, people high in need for cognition were oblivious to whether the normative violations information threatened or reassured them – they were unresponsive to the more emotionally charged information, remaining as tolerant when threatened as when reassured. In fact, those high in need for cognition who were threatened were slightly more tolerant (.58) than those low in it who were reassured (.56)! This confirms the argument that when the need for cognition is low, people respond to more affective, intuitive information. When the need for cognition is high, people respond more to their own thoughts, which in turn make them more tolerant.[11]

SUMMARY AND CONCLUSION

In this chapter, we have developed and tested a number of hypotheses about how personality influences tolerance judgments and about how it modifies the effects of our experimental manipulations. People high in extraversion and neuroticism are less tolerant, while those high in openness to experience and need for cognition are more tolerant. These findings reinforce other research showing that personality differences are important sources of variation in tolerance (Sniderman, 1975; Sullivan et al., 1982). Fundamental and enduring traits therefore play a continuing role in civil liberties judgments, and since they are so central in defining who we are, they provide a stable basis for developing abiding standing decisions. In fact, we found that most – but not all – of the effects of personality are encapsulated in standing decisions.

This analysis demonstrates the important role of what we bring with us as individuals to current political situations. Our judgments are very much continuing ones, reflecting the summation of who we are and the life experiences we have had. We do not reinvent the world each day, even in the political sphere, as some early attitude (or nonattitude) models suggested (Converse, 1964). Our standing decisions – here including attitudes toward democratic principles and preexisting inclinations to support civil liberties concerns in varying degrees – reflect and encapsulate stable predispositions, and also have a strong impact on contemporary decision making. It is also noteworthy that incorporating predispositions into the analysis did not alter the basic results of the survey-experiments reported in Chapter 4.

We also found that certain types of individuals are more affected than others by information about their least-liked group and its behavior. In particular, people who are high in need for cognition are more responsive to the instruction-set cues and less responsive to the normative violations conditions.

Personality affects contemporary tolerance judgments, then, in two ways. First, it influences standing decisions, which in turn have a powerful effect on people's current civil liberties judgments. Second, it has the potential to condition how people process information and attend to their information environment. Not all individuals process and respond to contemporary information in the same way. This serves as a warning that we must not focus exclusively on modal or typical responses to experimental treatments, such as the overall mean differences reported in Chapter 4. The individual differences reported in this chapter (and in Chapters 5, 6, and 7) provide considerable insight into how tolerance judgments are actually made by a diverse electorate, which cannot easily be characterized as engaged in one uniform decision-making process.

In Chapters 5 through 8, we have examined individual differences in how people process and react to the information provided in these experiments. Our focus has been on attitudes and tolerance judgments. While we could not manipulate respondents' behavior, we did ask respondents several questions about their behavioral intentions. In the next chapter, we analyze whether the experimental factors had any effect on the kinds of actions people say they would take if the government undertook actions toward their least-liked group that conflicted with their preferences. We explore the implications of this analysis for understanding real-world behaviors that relate to political tolerance.

PART IV

Implications and Conclusions

T HE FINAL SECTION TRACES the broader implications of our model of tolerance judgments. Our previous sections have largely focused on tolerance attitudes. While these attitudes are obviously important, it is also essential to tie our study to the wider world of politics and political action.

Chapter 9 focuses on behavior. Because we could not directly measure behavior, we instead rely on behavioral intentions. Many people subscribe to the widespread argument that those who are politically unaware will be passive. A related argument suggests that those who are marginalized, who are less aware, will also be more intolerant. However, we hypothesize that the intolerant who expressed the strongest intention of future action would indeed be most likely to act. We examine who is most likely to act to defend their judgments.

Chapter 10, our conclusion, summarizes and extends our findings and raises several implications of our model. First, our research shows that predispositions, standing decisions, and contemporary information all affect tolerance decisions. Several antecedent considerations make a difference: threat predispositions, neuroticism, gender, expertise, democratic norms, and preexisting tolerance attitudes. Contemporary information also contributes to tolerance judgments, including state of mind, democratic norms, and normative violations. We emphasize the encapsulation effect of democratic norms and tolerance as a standing decision on many other antecedent conditions such as personality and least-liked group threat. Finally, we return to the effect of emotion on decision making and suggest that cognition is not the whole story. While emotional appeals can lead to less tolerance, they can also lead to more. In practical political terms this may mean that provocative groups will want to make emotionally reassuring appeals to retain their rights.

CHAPTER 9

Intensity, Motivations, and Behavioral Intentions

> Democratic viability is, to begin with, saved by the fact that
> those who are most confused about democratic ideas are
> also likely to be politically apathetic and without signifi-
> cant influence. Their role in the nation's decision process
> is so small that their "misguided" opinions or non-
> opinions have little practical consequence for stability. If
> they contribute little to the vitality of the system, neither
> are they likely to do much harm.
>
> Herbert McClosky, "Consensus and
> Ideology in American Politics"

Nonprejudiced attitudes, according to Devine (1989), require conscious, controlled processing to override the automatic, nonconscious response of stereotyping. Staub (1989) makes a similar
argument that devaluation and scapegoating are also often automatic. Many people respond to outgroups by devaluing their members and using them as scapegoats when they are forced to live
under difficult conditions, but others consciously inhibit these automatic responses. The latter have a developed sense of individual
responsibility (Staub, 1989) and internalized values (Devine, 1989;
Kelman & Hamilton, 1989). They evaluate their psychological reactions in light of their personal goals, values, and beliefs, and often
set their instinctive reactions aside. This controlled processing, however, is often difficult.

Political tolerance fits into this genre of attitudes that are difficult
to hold: the tolerant find a group to be noxious and its espoused
ideas offensive, yet they are willing to give the members of this group

freedom of speech and of assembly, and the right to be a vocal part of the democratic political system. As McClosky and Brill (1983) note, "Intolerance rather than tolerance may be the easier and more natural posture for most people to assume" (p. 13). Our natural response may be an intolerant one, but we can overcome this automatic response.

Yet is attitudinal tolerance enough? Should we also expect people to *act* on behalf of their tolerance? Mendus (1989) asks just such a question: "We may ask what are the *requirements* of toleration. Does it require forbearance only, or is there an obligation to protect and preserve [basic civil liberties]?" (p. 17). We can similarly ask about intolerance. While we may not wish to encourage the intolerant to act, should we expect them to be passive?

Early research on political tolerance implicitly acknowledged the behavioral implications of tolerance, often making normative judgments about who should and should not be politically involved. According to this research, the tolerant should be highly active, contributing heavily to the ranks of political leaders and elites, whereas the intolerant should be politically apathetic to maintain a democratic political system (see, e.g., McClosky, 1964).

Prothro and Grigg (1960) argued this point well when they deliberated on "the functional nature of apathy for the democratic system" (p. 293):

Many people express undemocratic principles in response to questioning but are too apathetic to act on their undemocratic opinions in concrete situations. And in most cases, fortunately for the democratic system, those with the most undemocratic principles are also those who are least likely to act. (pp. 293–94)

Prothro and Grigg also, however, distinguished between what people *say* and what they *do*. They found that while 42 percent of their Tallahassee respondents said that "a Negro should not be allowed to run for mayor of this city," no effort was made to obstruct the candidacy of an African-American who campaigned for mayor a few months prior to the survey. Prothro and Grigg concluded, "In this case, the behavior was more democratic than the verbal expressions" (p. 294). Thus, the intolerant have antidemocratic attitudes, but by not participating in the political system in an intolerant way, their apathy supports democracy.

But what does it mean to be behaviorally tolerant or intolerant? A tolerant person who acts on his or her tolerance behaves in a way that supports the noxious group's civil liberties. For example, as Gibson and Bingham (1985) found, the most frequent tolerant behavior of ACLU and Common Cause members, in response to the Nazis' proposed march in Skokie, was to increase donations to a group that supported the Nazis' right to march. Tolerant behaviors could include other activities such as writing to the editor of a local newspaper or appearing before the city council to argue for the rights of a noxious group to hold a rally in a city park. An intolerant person, on the other hand, is more likely to try to inhibit the group from exercising its rights. Again, turning to Gibson and Bingham, the most frequent intolerant behaviors included increasing donations to a group opposing the right of the Nazis to march and contacting a government official to express opposition to the proposed march. Other intolerant behaviors could, for example, include joining a counterdemonstration opposed to the group or signing a petition to keep the group from holding its rally. In this way, both the tolerant and intolerant can act on behalf of their attitudes, thereby infusing the concept of tolerance with behavioral consequences.

The behavioral consequences of tolerance have broad implications for a democratic political system. If the tolerant are highly involved in the political system, we will likely see political decisions and policy outcomes that reflect their tolerant beliefs. On the other hand, if the intolerant are highly involved, incursions on civil liberties will be more likely. Yet this argument assumes that attitudes and behavior are strongly related, an assumption that has been questioned by numerous psychologists. In the early years of attitude studies, scholars emphasized the idea that attitudes caused behavior and therefore should correlate highly with relevant behaviors (e.g., Bogardus, 1925). Over the years, however, the evidence did not confirm this simple relationship. For example, LaPiere (1934), in his study of racial prejudice, first ascertained whether the proprietors at various restaurants, hotels, and other public establishments would provide a Chinese couple with service or accommodations. He and a Chinese couple went to 251 different establishments and were refused service at only one. LaPiere later sent a questionnaire to each establishment asking if it would serve members of the Chinese race. He received replies from 128 establishments, and of these 92 said they would not serve Chinese people, while the other 36 said they were uncertain. LaPiere concluded that attitudes in this area were not related to behavior.

In 1969, Wicker published a review of the attitude–behavior literature that also questioned whether such a relationship existed. He found little consistent evidence that attitudes are related directly to behavior. Numerous studies demonstrated that while attitudes would lead one to expect certain behaviors, these predictions were often wrong (e.g., Wrightsman, 1969). Wicker (1969) concluded that there was "little evidence to support the postulated existence of stable, underlying attitudes within the individual which influence both his verbal expressions and his actions" (p. 75). If the importance of attitude research lay predominantly in linking attitudes with behavior, which many scholars contended, then Wicker's review was devastating.

Wicker's criticisms led to a rethinking of the attitude–behavior relationship throughout the 1970s and 1980s. First, researchers began to investigate the conditions under which attitudes and behavior are likely to covary (Weigel & Newman, 1976). The conditions most studied included:

- *The stability of the general attitude base.* Specific attitudes drawn from a stable pool of general attitudes can better predict related behaviors than specific attitudes drawn from an unstable pool (Schwartz, 1978).
- *Direct versus indirect experience with the attitude object.* Individuals whose attitudes about an object are based on direct experience are more likely to behave consistently with their attitude than individuals who have not had any direct experience (Fazio & Zanna, 1981).
- *Self-interest.* Attitudes that involve self-interest are more consistently related to behavior than those that do not, especially if the attitude is important to the person (Sivacek & Crano, 1982; Young, Borgida, Sullivan, & Aldrich, 1987).
- *The norms influencing the behavior.* When social norms are part of the context within which the behavior occurs, the norms strongly influence – and attitudes weakly influence – behavior, but where clear norms are not apparent, attitudes better predict behavior (Ajzen & Fishbein, 1970).
- *Amount of information associated with the attitude.* Attitudes that include a greater amount of information are more related to behavior than those that involve less information (Davidson, Yantis, Norwood, & Montano, 1985).
- *Ease of attitude accessibility.* The more easily accessed an attitude,

the more likely it is that the attitude will be related to behavior (Fazio & Williams, 1986; Kallgren & Wood, 1986; Kiesler, Nisbett, & Zanna, 1969).

Second, psychologists also reexamined the measurement of attitudes and behaviors. For example, studies showed that better prediction of a specific behavior could be made when a specific attitude measure was used (Davidson & Jaccard, 1979; Herblein & Black, 1976). Scholars have also found that general attitude measures were better predictors of general patterns of behavior (Ajzen & Fishbein, 1977; Weigel & Newman, 1976). Thus, it is imperative that researchers measure attitudes and behaviors at the same level of specificity if they expect to find attitude–behavior consistency.

Psychologists have now reached the conclusion that, under certain circumstances, attitudes are strongly related to behavior. At the very least, attitudes reflect a propensity to behave in a certain way. As Gibson and Bingham (1985) argue, "Attitudes do not necessarily produce behavior, but rather they represent a tendency to behave in a certain fashion" (p. 162). Therefore, intolerant attitudes reflect a propensity to act intolerantly and tolerant attitudes reflect a propensity to act tolerantly.[1]

Yet, as we discussed in Chapter 3, Gray adds an interesting dynamic to the attitude–behavior relationship. According to Gray, the behavioral approach system (BAS) controls a dimension of mood that varies from depression and despair to enthusiasm and hope. Variations along this dimension are highly predictive of previously learned behaviors. If someone is feeling enthusiastic, he or she is more likely to become involved in recalled successful actions than someone who is feeling depressed. In essence, enthusiasm strengthens the motivation to take action and depression weakens that motivation.

Gray's account of the BAS suggests to us the importance of the intermediary role of enthusiasm in predicting behavior and therefore can guide us in our study of behavioral tolerance and intolerance. Rather than assuming a direct link between attitudes and behavior, Gray's theory argues that motivation acts as an intermediary variable. People hold certain attitudes about tolerance and they can draw on a political action repertoire when confronted with a situation calling for action. But the motivating link, modulated by the BAS, is enthusiasm. If people feel enthusiastic, they are likely to act on their tolerance or intolerance. We must therefore take into account enthusiasm to gain greater purchase on the relationship between tolerant attitudes and behaviors.

We focus on intensity of attitudes as a measure of enthusiasm. The more enthusiastic people are about a certain attitude (such as support for democratic principles), and hence the more intensely they hold that attitude, the more likely they are to be motivated to engage in actions that are part of their learned action repertoire. When people are closer to the depression end of the mood dimension, they have a weaker motivation to take action. This lack of motivation can be measured by lack of attitudinal intensity.

We therefore examine the behavioral implications of tolerance and intolerance in this chapter, inspired by Gray's formulation of the BAS. We begin with an overview of previous research on political behavior and tolerance, and briefly consider the use of behavioral intentions as a measure of behavior. We then discuss the results of our data analysis, and conclude the chapter with an assessment of the behavioral implications of tolerant and intolerant attitudes.

TOLERANCE AND POLITICAL BEHAVIOR

According to McClosky as well as Prothro and Grigg, the tolerant should be active and the intolerant inactive. Are the tolerant in fact more politically active than the intolerant? As we briefly mentioned in Chapter 2, prior research finds a significant relationship between tolerance and political involvement. The more politically involved people are, the more likely they are to be tolerant. A debate exists, however, over whether political activism directly affects tolerance (i.e., whether activism in and of itself increases tolerance) or whether the politically active simply share certain characteristics related to tolerance (see, e.g., Jackman, 1972; Nunn et al., 1978; Sullivan et al., 1982).

Research has relied on two different methods for examining the relationship between activism and tolerance. Most studies have compared the attitudes of politically active elites with the general public. These studies administered surveys to people in the mass public and people who make up the political elite, whether they are community leaders, public officials, legal elites, or political activists (McClosky, 1964; McClosky & Brill, 1983; Nunn et al., 1978; Stouffer, 1955; Sullivan et al., 1993). Results showed that the political elite were more tolerant than the general public. Other studies have used surveys of the general public to compare the politically involved with the politically uninvolved on measures of tolerance, political knowledge, political interest, and general propensity to participate in politics. These studies also found a relationship between involvement and tolerance, although further analysis showed this relationship was spurious and was based on activists' other characteristics (Sullivan et al., 1982).

Why might the politically active be more tolerant? A number of arguments have been proffered to explain this relationship. Stouffer (1955) held that "responsible community leaders are more likely than the rank and file to give the sober second thought to the civil rights of the nonconformists or suspected nonconformists" (p. 57). McClosky (1964) attributed the greater tolerance of political elites to their greater intellectual ability and political sophistication. Jackman (1972) argued that the higher education levels of the politically involved explain their higher tolerance, while Sullivan, Piereson, and Marcus (1982) also included personality as an important characteristic of political activists. Sullivan et al. (1993) contended that these characteristics of political elites were only part of the story. The adult political socialization of elites leads them to be more tolerant than the general public, even when demographic, personality, and attitudinal variables are taken into account. The debate over the reasons behind the relationship between political activism and tolerance obviously continues, but research shows that the politically active, for various reasons, are more tolerant than the inactive.[2]

This past research has been primarily concerned with the effects of political involvement on tolerance, not the impact of tolerance on behavior. Gibson (1987), however, has specifically addressed the behavioral consequences of tolerance, although Gibson and Bingham (1985) admitted that "the behavioral and policy consequences of attitudes toward democracy are far from obvious, simple, and direct" (p. 161).

In his study of homosexuals and the Ku Klux Klan, Gibson (1987) asked the former about the types of action they took in response to a planned demonstration by the KKK. Only 10 (of 235) subjects, about 4 percent, took any action to support the KKK's right to demonstrate. Gibson suggests that this low rate occurred because the tolerant course of action was to do nothing. In essence, the tolerant would not do anything to *inhibit* the rights of the KKK, but this does not mean that they would act to *support* those rights. A higher percentage of people took action on behalf of their intolerance; 16 percent tried to stop the KKK's demonstration by donating money to opposing groups, contacting public officials, organizing anti-Klan groups, or participating in demonstrations opposing the Klan. Gibson found that the salience of the issue (as measured by knowledge of the dispute), a general propensity toward political activism, and expectation of violence occurring at the demonstration explained behavior. These results highlight the possible importance of intensity in understanding tolerant and intolerant behavior.

BEHAVIORAL INTENTIONS

Gibson used activist samples to identify the behavioral consequences of tolerance and intolerance in specific situations. He studied a homosexual group in Houston confronted with a KKK rally (Gibson, 1987), and ACLU and Common Cause members confronted with Nazis marching in Skokie (Gibson & Bingham, 1985). He was therefore able to obtain behavioral data within the context of a specific situation that demanded a tolerant or intolerant response. While these samples are highly appropriate for his purposes, one concern is that the respondents may be unrepresentative of the general public because they are activists. The samples consisted of people who were already active in the sense that they had joined a politically active group, which may have influenced the behavioral consequences of their tolerance or intolerance. It remains an open question whether the generally inactive public would act on behalf of its tolerance or intolerance.

One way to obtain behaviorally oriented data from a sample of the general public is to measure behavioral intentions rather than actual behavior. Political science research has only rarely examined behavioral intentions, and this work has primarily focused on voting intentions (see, e.g., Berelson, Lazarsfeld, & McPhee, 1954; Fishbein, Ajzen, & Hinkle, 1980; Fishbein & Coombs, 1974; Granberg & Holmberg, 1988; Kelley & Mirer, 1974; Lazarsfeld, Berelson, & Gaudet, 1944). Social psychologists have put significantly greater effort into the study of behavioral intentions and their relationship to behavior (see, e.g., Ajzen & Fishbein, 1969, 1980; Ajzen & Madden, 1986; Bagozzi, 1981; Davidson & Jaccard, 1975, 1979; Saltzer, 1981; Warshaw & Davis, 1985).

The most well-known research on behavioral intentions stems from Fishbein and Ajzen's "theory of reasoned action" (Ajzen &

Fishbein, 1969, 1980; Fishbein & Ajzen, 1975; Fishbein et al., 1980). According to Fishbein and Ajzen, behavioral intentions are the immediate precursor to action. The behavioral intentions–behavior link is affected by several factors, including the level of specificity of the behavioral intentions and behavior measures, the amount of time elapsed between the two measures, personality characteristics, and so on. The correlation between behavioral intentions and behavior was usually quite high, ranging from about .5 to .9 (see, e.g., Bagozzi, 1981; Davidson & Jaccard, 1979; Fishbein & Coombs, 1974). Behavioral intentions are therefore often good predictors of behavior.

Fishbein and Ajzen were also concerned with what *explains* behavioral intentions. They argued that behavioral intentions result from both a person's attitude toward the intended action and from social norms. Attitude toward an action is affected by people's beliefs about the likely outcome of the behavior and an evaluation of whether that outcome is desirable or undesirable. It is important to emphasize that the attitude concerns the act itself, not the attitude object. Fishbein and Ajzen argued that social norms result from two considerations. First, when deciding whether to act or not, people take into account whether reference group members would approve or disapprove of the act. The reference group depends on whose opinion is relevant given the situation at hand. For example, a decision about what to cook for dinner calls to mind a different reference group (family members) from a decision about the journal to which a manuscript will be sent (colleagues). The second consideration is the extent to which a person feels motivated to comply with the reference group.

Behavioral Intentions and the Survey-Experiments

While the theory of reasoned action has proven useful in psychology, our concern, along with Gibson's, is with the behavioral consequences of tolerance. Unlike Gibson, however, we rely on behavioral intentions rather than reported behavior. Our main reason for using behavioral intentions rather than actual behavior is that the subjects in our three basic survey-experiments were not activists, whereas Gibson's respondents were, and our subjects were confronted with a hypothetical rather than a real situation. Therefore, we could not obtain actual behavior measures. Behavioral intentions measures, however, are useful for our purposes.

In all three of the basic survey-experiments described in Chapter 4, we included measures of behavioral intentions (see Appendix B for a full description of the behavioral intentions scales). Recall that in the posttest of these basic experiments, subjects read a scenario about a hypothetical group and then responded to the tolerance statements. To obtain the behavioral intentions data, we then instructed subjects to answer one of two sets of behavioral intentions questions, depending on their answer to the last tolerance statement ("The group [hypothetical group name] should be allowed to hold public rallies"). There were 375 subjects (57%) in the combined weighted data set who gave a *tolerant* response (agree or strongly agree) to this statement. We asked them to turn to another page, at the top of which was the instruction: "Suppose a local judge issued an order forbidding that group to hold a public rally in your community. How likely do you think you would be to do each of the following?" The subjects were then given the following behavioral intention statements with four possible response options (definitely would not, probably would not, probably would, and definitely would):

1. I would vote against that judge in the next election.
2. I would join a peaceful demonstration supporting their right to hold a public rally.
3. I would join an effort to appeal that decision to try to reverse it.
4. I would sign a petition objecting to the judge's decision not to allow them to hold a public rally.

We created the tolerant behavioral intentions scale by summing responses to these statements.

There were 156 subjects (24%) who gave an *intolerant* response (disagree or strongly disagree) to the public rally statement. They were instructed to turn to a different page. The top of this page contained a somewhat different instruction: "Suppose a local judge issued an order allowing that group to hold a public rally in your community. How likely do you think you would be to do each of the following?" The behavioral intentions statements were identical to those already listed, with the same response options (ranging from "definitely would not" to "definitely would"):

1. I would vote against that judge in the next election.
2. I would join a peaceful demonstration against allowing them to hold a public rally.

3. I would join an effort to appeal that decision to try to reverse it.
4. I would sign a petition objecting to the judge's decision allowing them to hold a public rally.

The intolerant behavioral intentions scale was created by summing responses to these statements.[3]

Some subjects gave a *neutral* (118 subjects, 18%) or "don't know" (9 subjects, 1%) response to the public rally statement. These subjects were not asked the behavioral intentions questions for two reasons. First, at a practical level, it was unclear given their response if they would care whether the judge gave an order stopping or allowing the rally. We were therefore uncertain which set of behavioral intentions questions they should answer. Second, people are unlikely to act on nonattitudes or ambivalent attitudes. The people who responded with "don't know" presumably have a nonattitude on the rally statement. The neutral respondents may be completely neutral on the statement or may weigh equally the positive and negative aspects of the group holding a rally, and therefore situate themselves at the neutral response because of this ambivalence. In either case, it is unlikely that they would act on these attitudes.

We conducted the following analyses using the standardized 0–1 range variables and the combined weighted sample of the basic experiments described in Chapter 4. Because our basic experiments utilized three different samples at three time periods, we have a robust test of behavioral intentions.

BEHAVIORAL INTENTIONS AND TOLERANCE

Which group – the tolerant or the intolerant – is more likely to indicate that it would take action against the judge's decision? A simple comparison of means of the intolerant and tolerant behavioral intentions scales tells a dramatic story. The mean behavioral intentions score for the tolerant respondents is .39, whereas the mean score for the intolerant respondents is .67 (the difference is statistically significant, $p < .01$). With the midpoint of the scales at .50, these results place the tolerant on the inactive side of the scale and the intolerant on the active side. The implication of this finding for democratic theory is obvious. The intolerant are significantly more likely to claim they would act on their attitudes than are the tolerant. The intolerant do not indicate the desired passivity that McClosky (1964) argued they would.[4]

But this basic finding also raises a real paradox. Since past research has found the intolerant to be less politically active and the tolerant more active, why would the intolerant indicate a greater intent to participate actively? What explains the difference in mean scale scores? To answer these questions, we can turn to the model we tested in Chapter 4.

Contemporary tolerance judgments, we argued, result from both antecedent considerations and the use of contemporary information. We found that people rely on their predispositions and standing decisions when confronted with a situation requiring a contemporary tolerance judgment. But we also found two of our experimental manipulations to be significant: normative violations and instruction set. When subjects confronted threatening contemporary information about a group's belligerence and treachery, they reacted with greater intolerance than when they were given reassuring information about the group's orderliness and trustworthiness. We also found that subjects who were asked to pay attention to their feelings were significantly more intolerant than subjects who were asked to attend to their thoughts.

We expect to find that contemporary information and standing decisions also affect behavioral intentions. People's behavior may be influenced by information available in the immediate environment, and people may also hold certain standing decisions that predispose them to intend action or inaction.

Looking first at contemporary information, we can analyze the experimental manipulations to determine their impact on behavioral intentions.[5] Since the probability of power manipulation was not related to tolerance because people did not feel threatened by this information, it is unlikely that probability would have an impact on behavioral intentions.

We can, however, expect normative violations to be related to behavioral intentions. First, Gibson (1987) found that the expectation of violence occurring at the KKK rally was related to intolerant behavior. The threatening normative violations paragraph, while not explicitly stating that the hypothetical group used violence, does show that violence did occur and that the group was untrustworthy. Such information might increase the likelihood that subjects would want to take action against the hypothetical group. Second, according to Gray, normative violations increase people's feelings of threat, which then affects further monitoring of the environment. When people perceive threat from a noxious group violating the norms of proper, orderly behavior, they may feel a stronger need to take action against the judge's decision. When reassured, however, they might become less attentive to the immediate environment, more complacent, and consequently less likely to act.

We might also expect similar effects with the instruction-set manipulation. In Chapter 4, we discussed the reason-and-passion debate and the literature on mood accessibility. When we asked people to pay attention to their feelings, they were less tolerant than when they were asked to pay attention to their thoughts. We argued that when people are in a certain mood, they often retrieve memories congruent with that mood. Therefore, if people feel threatened by a certain noxious group, they will recall memories that lead them to be more intolerant toward the group. When people focus on their thoughts, they presumably think about the benefits of their tolerance and therefore demonstrate greater forbearance.

Behavioral intentions may be similarly affected by instruction set. Recall our discussion of Wilson's (1989) research from Chapter 1. Wilson argues that the attitude–behavior relationship is weakened when people think about the reasons for their choices, and that it is strengthened when people rely on their feelings. Thus, when people pay attention to their feelings, they may be more likely to follow their attitudes and take action against the judge's decision. When people pay attention to their thoughts, on the other hand, they may be less inclined to take action as they think about the ramifications of their tolerance judgments and behavioral intentions. However, focusing on feelings or thoughts is an introspective activity, turning people's attention inward. Such introspection may actually divert people from taking action. We therefore expect, given these contradictory arguments, that while instruction set is related to tolerance judgments, it may not be related to behavioral intentions.

To test these hypotheses, we ran an analysis of variance on behavioral intentions by the probability of power, normative violations, and instruction-set manipulations. The results are shown in Table 9.1. It is immediately clear that for both the tolerant and the intolerant these manipulations are unrelated to behavioral intentions. None of the differences is statistically significant. Whether people read the high- or low-probability paragraph, the threatening or reassuring normative violations paragraph, or were asked to attend to their thoughts or to their feelings, they did not significantly differ in their intention to take action against the judge's order.

Table 9.1. *Analysis of variance for behavioral intentions and the experimental manipulations (basic combined weighted data set)*

Experimental Manipulation	Tolerant				Intolerant			
	Behavioral Intensity Mean	N	F	p	Behavioral Intensity Mean	N	F	p
Probability of power								
Low probability	.39	190			.65	69		
			.04	.84			.04	.32
High probability	.39	175			.68	69		
Normative violations								
Reassuring	.40	202			.65	61		
			.88	.35			.89	.35
Threatening	.38	163			.65	77		
Instruction set								
Thoughts	.39	202			.67	57		
			.09	.77			.09	.76
Feelings	.39	162			.66	82		

INTENSITY AND BEHAVIORAL INTENTIONS

We still do not know what explains behavioral intentions. Apparently, contemporary information does not have a direct effect on intention to act. We therefore turn to antecedent considerations. Are there certain antecedent considerations that might be related to behavioral intentions? Key (1961) has argued that an important feature of attitudes related to behavior is intensity. The more intense people's opinions, the more likely it is that they will act on them.

The distribution of intensities within the population may be related to political action. The presumption, subject to verification, is that persons with opinions of high intensity are more disposed to act, to throw their weight around, than are persons whose opinions approach zero intensity. (p. 208)

And,

From our daily impressions of politics we feel that persons who have opinions of high intensity are likely to seek energetically to achieve the ends in which they believe. . . . Little bands of dedicated souls leave their clear imprint on public policy. (p. 229)

Psychologists have also examined in depth the differential effects of important or central attitudes and unimportant or marginal attitudes (see, e.g., Festinger, 1957; Sherif, 1980; Sherif & Cantril,

1947; Smith, Bruner, & White, 1956). For example, Krosnick (1989, 1990) has found that citizens who are passionately concerned about a policy issue think more frequently about that attitude, perceive candidates to be more polarized on the issue, form candidate preferences based on that attitude, and are more resistent to attitude change. Intense attitudes are also strongly related to behavior (see, e.g., Kelman, 1974).

We examine three variables that can be considered standing decisions of intensity: the intensity of malice people feel toward left-wing or right-wing groups, the intensity with which people hold abstract democratic principles, and the intensity of people's tolerance or intolerance of the noxious group. We also analyze two threat variables that may be related to behavioral intentions: threat as a standing decision and threat as a predisposition (see Chapter 5).

Measurement of Intensity and Threat

INTENSITY: People can hold a broad range of intense attitudes. We focus on three intensity measures because of their likely relationship with behavioral intentions. Using three measures of intensity also gives us a multivariate test of the relationship between intensity and behavioral intentions.

First, the more people intensely dislike noxious groups on the right or on the left, the more likely they are to take action to inhibit the rights of a particular group with a certain ideological leaning. We test this hypothesis using the like/dislike questions from the pretest survey (see Appendix B). Subjects were asked about the degree of dislike they felt for eleven noxious groups, and were further asked which group was their most disliked. People who chose a left-wing group as their most disliked were assigned a global dislike intensity score that was the sum of their dislike scores on five left-wing groups (excluding socialists). People who chose a right-wing group similarly were assigned a global dislike intensity score that was a sum of the five right-wing group scores. The global dislike intensity scale was transformed to range from 0 to 1, with higher scores indicating greater dislike of left-wing or right-wing groups.

Second, it is likely that if people hold intensely democratic or antidemocratic principles, they will take action against the judge's order. People intensely committed to democratic principles may be more likely to act on behalf of their tolerance than those who only weakly believe in these principles. Similarly, people who are in-

tensely antidemocratic, meaning that they strongly oppose giving
people their basic civil liberties, may be more likely to act on behalf
of their intolerance than those who are only weakly opposed. To
test this hypothesis, we used the seven democratic principles statements from the pretest survey to create a democratic principles intensity scale by folding subjects' answers to these questions at the
neutral point (3 on a five-point scale, coefficient alpha = .70). Responses thus reflected intensity rather than direction: neutral, agree
or disagree, and strongly agree or strongly disagree.

We expect that intensely held standing decisions are positively
related to behavioral intentions. In essence, if people are predisposed to want intensely to keep a noxious group from taking advantage of its basic rights, they are more likely to take action against
the group. For the tolerant, a predisposition of intensely supporting
the noxious group's basic rights will lead to action designed to support those rights. We therefore created a tolerance intensity scale
using the six tolerance statements in the pretest, ensuring that this
intensity scale reflected a standing decision (coefficient alpha =
.57). We again folded the responses at the neutral point to create
a measure of intensity.

PERCEIVED THREAT: Two more antecedent considerations may be
related to behavioral intentions, although they are not intensity
measures: perceived threat of the least-liked group and perceived
global threat to one's country (Chapter 5). First, the extent to which
people have a standing decision to perceive a noxious group to be
threatening may be related to their intention to take action. In the
pretest, we asked subjects to assess their least-liked group on five
semantic differential items. Scores on these semantic differentials
were added together to form a threat standing decision scale.

A second potentially important threat measure is the extent to
which subjects have a predisposition to perceive noxious groups as
generally threatening. In the pretest, we asked subjects to indicate
on an eleven-point scale, ranging from "not at all threatening to
the country" to "very threatening to the country," their perception
of each of the ten groups, excluding socialists. We created a threat
predisposition scale from these responses (see Chapter 5).

Intensity and Threat – Bivariate Analyses

In this section, we examine the differences between the tolerant and
intolerant respondents on the intensity and threat measures using

difference-of-means tests and correlations. In the next section, we run separate multivariate analyses on tolerant and intolerant behavioral intentions.

INTENSITY: First, do intolerant people dislike more intensely various left-wing or right-wing groups than tolerant people, and is this greater intensity related to behavioral intentions? We first ran a difference-of-means test with amount of dislike felt toward left-wing or right-wing groups. The intolerant respondents had a mean dislike score of .77 whereas the tolerant respondents had a mean score of .79. The small difference shows that the tolerant respondents actually dislike a variety of left-wing or right-wing groups slightly more than the intolerant ($p = .05$). Since the scale ranges from 0 to 1 with a .50 midpoint, it is obvious that both sets of subjects strongly dislike certain unpopular groups.

When this global dislike intensity scale is correlated with tolerant or intolerant behavioral intentions, the results are interesting. The intensity of dislike for certain groups is not related to behavioral intentions among the tolerant ($r = .02$), but is among the intolerant ($r = .20$; $p < .05$). Thus, a standing decision to dislike intensely left-wing or right-wing groups is related to intolerant behavior but not tolerant behavior, even though the tolerant dislike the groups slightly more than the intolerant.[6]

Second, when we ran a difference-of-means test on the democratic principles intensity scale, we found that the intolerant respondents had a mean score of .53 whereas the tolerant respondents had a mean score of .63 ($p < .01$). Therefore, tolerant respondents held their democratic principles more intensely than intolerant respondents. Whereas most people support democratic principles in the abstract, those who are intolerant are less committed to them.[7]

But is democratic principles intensity related to behavioral intentions? It is, for both the tolerant and the intolerant. The correlation between the democratic principles intensity scale and behavioral intentions among tolerant respondents is .19 ($p < .01$) and among intolerant respondents it is .22 ($p < .01$). Therefore, while the tolerant respondents hold their commitment to democratic principles more intensely than the intolerant, both types of respondents are more likely to take action when they hold their principles intensely than when they feel more neutral toward the principles. For the tolerant respondents, these intensely held democratic principles make them more likely to act on behalf of their tolerance.

For the intolerant respondents, a nonobvious interpretation can be drawn from these results. Subjects can hold prodemocratic principles (that is, they can support basic civil libertarian values), or they can hold antidemocratic principles (that is, they oppose freedom of speech, freedom of assembly, and so on). Among the intolerant subjects, 24 percent fell below the midpoint on the democratic principles scale and can therefore be considered antidemocratic. The more intensely these subjects held their antidemocratic principles, the more likely they were to take action against the judge's order to allow the rally. But 76 percent of the intolerant subjects held prodemocratic principles. The more intensely they were committed to democratic principles, the more likely they were to take action against the judge's order to allow the rally. How can this be?

The answer may lie in the democratic beliefs that the intolerant support in this particular circumstance. Recall from Chapter 6 our discussion of competing democratic values. Some people who believe strongly in freedom of speech and assembly can be persuaded that they are not required to give a noxious group its rights if that group would abridge those rights once in power. Given the hypothetical group's behavior in the scenarios, these people may weigh the competing values and come down on the side of intolerance. Sullivan et al. (1993: pp. 66–67) found this relationship between democratic norms and tolerance among members of the Knesset in Israel. Members of the Knesset who believed a certain group "represented a genuine and potentially very powerful threat to democracy itself" refused to apply democratic principles to that group because of its fundamentally undemocratic nature. Thus, the intolerant subjects who were intensely committed to democratic principles were perhaps more likely to indicate an intention to take action in an attempt to protect democratic values, that is, to keep the undemocratic group from coming to power and taking those rights away from others.

The final intensity measure we consider is tolerance intensity. Is there a difference in tolerance intensity as a standing decision between the tolerant and the intolerant? If tolerance intensity can explain the higher behavioral intentions of intolerant respondents, then intolerant people should be more intensely intolerant than the tolerant people should be intensely tolerant. In fact there is a small but statistically significant difference. The mean tolerance intensity score for the intolerant respondents is .95, while the mean for the tolerant respondents is .90 ($p < .01$).[8]

Is tolerance intensity related to behavioral intentions? The correlation of tolerance intensity with intolerant behavioral intentions is .14 (p < .10), and with tolerant behavioral intentions it is .13 (p < .05). Apparently there is a greater tendency for the tolerant to intend to take action when they hold their standing tolerance decisions strongly than when they hold them more weakly. The intolerant hold their intolerance more intensely than the tolerant hold their tolerance, but the relationship between intensity and action is slightly less significant.

PERCEIVED THREAT: Threat as a standing decision is also related to tolerant and intolerant behavioral intentions. First, intolerant respondents had a threat mean score of .87, tolerant respondents had a score of .80 (p < .01). Second, perceptions of threat are correlated with behavioral intentions. Among the intolerant, greater perceived threat was related to an intention to take action against the judge's order (r = .17; p < .05). Among the tolerant, greater perceived threat was related to *inaction* (r = −.11; p < .05). Thus, threat as a standing decision makes the intolerant *more* likely to act on their intolerance and the tolerant *less* likely to act on their tolerance.

The threat predisposition measure is also related to behavioral intentions. The intolerant feel more globally threatened than the tolerant. The mean predisposition threat score for the intolerant was .51, whereas for the tolerant it was .47 (p < .01). The intolerant are more predisposed to feel threat than the tolerant. However, neither the intolerant nor the tolerant are more likely to take action against the judge's order when they are predisposed to see threat (r = .04 for the intolerant and r = −.04 for the tolerant).

SUMMARY: These results begin to clarify the different behavioral intentions of the tolerant and intolerant respondents. First, attitudinal intensity tends to be significantly related to behavioral intentions. The more intensely the tolerant and the intolerant hold democratic principles and their standing tolerance decision, the more likely they are to indicate an intention to act. Only among the intolerant respondents, however, is intensity of global dislike related to behavior: the more they dislike certain left-wing or right-wing groups, the more likely they are to act.

Second, the two threat measures, one a predisposition and the other a standing decision, also provide important clues for understanding behavioral intentions. Having a standing decision to perceive one's least-liked group as threatening *increases* the likelihood that the intolerant will act but *decreases* the likelihood that the tolerant will act. Having a predisposition to view the world as full of threatening groups is not related to behavioral intentions for either the tolerant or the intolerant.

Thus, attitudinal intensity and threat as a standing decision are significantly related to behavioral intentions. However, these bivariate analyses may exaggerate the impact of intensity and threat on behavioral intentions. We therefore need to explore a multivariate model to determine which variables remain significant when the other variables are controlled. We test such a model in the following section.

Multivariate Analysis

We are now in a position to create a model to explain behavioral intentions. In order to examine the direct and indirect effects of antecedent considerations and contemporary information, we must use a multivariate analysis. The analysis of covariance models discussed below examine the effects of antecedent considerations and contemporary information on tolerant and intolerant behavioral intentions.

The antecedent considerations are the standing decisions of global dislike intensity of left-wing or right-wing groups, intensity of commitment to democratic principles, intensity of tolerance as a standing decision, perceived threat of the least-liked group, and, as a predisposition, perceived global threat. Current tolerance intensity is also included in the model and is likely to be most strongly related to behavioral intentions because of the proximity of its measurement to the behavioral intentions measure.[9] Any significant elapsed time between the measurement of attitudes and behavior could allow changes in attitudes or the environment that undermine the attitude–behavior relationship (see, e.g., Davidson & Jaccard, 1979; Schwartz, 1978; Wilson et al., 1989). Both current tolerance intensity and behavioral intentions were measured in the posttest, whereas standing decision intensity and perceived threat were measured in the pretest.

Contemporary information consists of three experimental manipulations: normative violations, probability of the group coming to power, and instruction set. We had expected normative violations to be significantly related to behavioral intentions in the bivariate analyses, but found the relationship to be insignificant. Feeling

Table 9.2. *Tolerant respondents – analysis of covariance of behavioral intentions with standing decisions and contemporary information (basic combined weighted data set)*

Variables	Unstandardized regression coefficient	F	p
Antecedent considerations (covariates)			
Current tolerance intensity	.22	11.1	<.01
Pretest tolerance intensity	−.02	0.1	.76
Democratic principles intensity	.12	3.5	.06
Global dislike of groups	−.07	0.5	.46
Standing decision threat	−.14	4.0	.05
Predisposition threat	−.02	0.1	.79
Contemporary influences (main effects)			
Normative violations		1.1	.30
Probability of power		0.2	.65
Instruction set		0.1	.72
Total weighted N (excluding cases with missing data) = 338			

threatened or reassured, however, may be related to the intensity with which people hold their current tolerance judgments, a possibility we explore below.

BEHAVIORAL INTENTIONS AND THE TOLERANT: In this section, we will focus on the tolerant respondents and their behavioral intentions, examining the effects of standing decision intensity, perceived threat, and contemporary information. The following section provides a similar analysis for the intolerant respondents.

We conducted an analysis of covariance with tolerant behavioral intentions as the dependent variable. The results are presented in Table 9.2. It is immediately clear that current tolerance intensity is strongly and significantly related to behavioral intentions. The more intensely people hold their current tolerance judgment, the more likely they are to take action against the judge's order to protect the rights of the noxious group.

We also find that democratic principles intensity ($p = .06$) and perceived threat of the least-liked group ($p = .05$) are related to behavioral intentions. The intensity with which tolerant respondents hold democratic principles contributes to their intention to take action to protect the rights of the group. Perceived threat has the opposite effect, decreasing the likelihood that tolerant people will take action. The intensity of the standing tolerance decision,

Table 9.3. *Tolerant respondents – analysis of covariance of current tolerance intensity (basic combined weighted data set)*

Variables	Unstandardized regression coefficient	F	p
Antecedent considerations (covariates)			
Pretest tolerance intensity	.46	107.1	<.01
Contemporary influences (main effects)			
Normative violations		3.8	.05
Probability of power		0.9	.34
Instruction set		1.3	.26
Total weighted N (excluding cases with missing data) = 366			

amount of dislike for groups, and global threat as a predisposition are unrelated to behavioral intentions.

The results also demonstrate that none of the manipulated variables is significantly related to tolerant behavioral intentions, which indicates that intention to take action is not directly related to information about the group available in the immediate environment.

We can examine the possibility, however, that contemporary information is related to current tolerance intensity. In a second analysis of covariance, current tolerance intensity was the dependent variable, intensity of the standing tolerance decision was a covariate, and normative violations, probability of power, and instruction set were the main effects.

The intensity of people's standing tolerance decision is significantly related to current tolerance intensity, which means that current intensity level is in part affected by a predisposition to hold tolerant beliefs intensely or weakly (Table 9.3). But current tolerance intensity is also related to the normative violations manipulation (p = .05), that is, the threatening or reassuring information available in the current environment. Probability information and paying attention to thoughts or feelings do not affect current tolerance intensity.

The data show that tolerant behavioral intentions can in part be explained by the intensity with which people hold democratic principles and perceived threat of the least-liked group. Most significant, however, is the intensity of current tolerance judgments, which is strongly related to the standing decision to hold tolerance beliefs intensely. But contemporary information also matters. Contempo-

Table 9.4. *Intolerant respondents – analysis of covariance of behavioral intentions with standing decisions and contemporary information (basic combined weighted data set)*

Variables	Unstandardized regression coefficient	F	p
Antecedent considerations (covariates)			
Current tolerance intensity	.34	16.6	<.01
Pretest tolerance intensity	−.01	0.0	.90
Democratic principles intensity	.16	2.8	.10
Global dislike of groups	.19	1.6	.21
Standing decision threat	.11	0.5	.49
Predisposition threat	−.11	0.7	.40
Contemporary influences (main effects)			
Normative violations		0.0	.87
Probability of power		1.6	.20
Instruction set		0.3	.56
Total weighted N (excluding cases with missing data) = 130			

rary information about normative violations has a significant effect on the intensity with which tolerant subjects hold their current tolerance judgments, and this intensity is then related to behavioral intentions. Normative violations information has an indirect effect on tolerant behavioral intentions through current tolerance intensity.

BEHAVIORAL INTENTIONS AND THE INTOLERANT: We conducted the same analyses for the intolerant. While some of the results mimic the findings on the tolerant, the differences are revealing.

The results from the analysis of covariance, displayed in Table 9.4, show that only one covariate is significantly related to intolerant behavioral intentions: current tolerance intensity. The behavior of the intolerant respondents is intended to keep the noxious group from exercising its basic civil liberties, and the intensity with which they currently feel intolerant explains this intention to behave. Again, none of the experimental manipulations is related to behavioral intentions among the intolerant.

In the second analysis of covariance, with current tolerance intensity as the dependent variable, we find an interesting result that differs from the analysis of the tolerant (Table 9.5). The only variable significantly related to current tolerance intensity of the intolerant respondents is pretest tolerance intensity, a standing decision.

Table 9.5. *Intolerant respondents – analysis of covariance of current tolerance intensity (basic combined weighted data set)*

Variables	Unstandardized regression coefficient	F	p
Antecedent considerations (covariates)			
Pretest tolerance intensity	.34	18.8	<.01
Contemporary influences (main effects)			
Normative violations		1.9	.17
Probability of power		0.0	.85
Instruction set		0.8	.39
Total weighted N (excluding cases with missing data) = 146			

None of the contemporary information manipulations, including normative violations, is significantly related to current tolerance intensity. The intolerant respondents are apparently less open to the influence of contemporary information than the tolerant, relying instead on a standing decision to hold their tolerance judgments intensely.

SUMMARY: At first blush, it is obvious that the analyses of the tolerant and intolerant are quite similar. For example, the intensity with which people hold their standing decision to be tolerant or intolerant is not significantly related to either tolerant or intolerant behavioral intentions. Since the temporal proximity of attitude and behavior measures is important, too much time elapsed between the measurement of tolerance intensity in the pretest and of behavioral intentions in the posttest (two weeks) for there to be a significant relationship. Posttest tolerance intensity, measured immediately before behavioral intentions, is highly significant for both the tolerant and intolerant.

We also found important differences between the tolerant and the intolerant.[10] Figures 9.1 and 9.2 depict these differences. Among the tolerant, contemporary information on normative violations is not directly related to behavioral intentions, but does have an indirect effect through its impact on current tolerance intensity. Thus, for the tolerant, reassuring information about the normative violations of the group prompts greater tolerance intensity which then increases the likelihood that action will be taken. The intol-

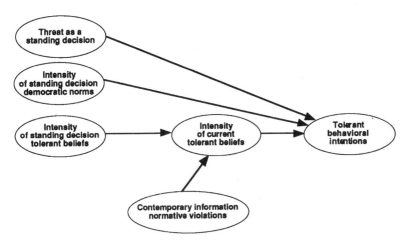

Figure 9.1. *Schematic model for tolerant behavioral intentions*

erant, on the other hand, apparently do not respond to this current information.

Furthermore, whereas the intolerant are prompted to action *only* when they hold their current intolerance intensely, the tolerant are affected by a broader range of considerations. The tolerant are more likely to act when they are intensely tolerant, when they hold their democratic principles intensely, and when they do not perceive the noxious group as threatening. When the tolerant perceive their least-liked group as threatening, they are *less* likely to take action, all else equal.

CONCLUSIONS

Political theorists have only touched on the behavioral requirements of tolerance, perhaps because of the elusive nature of such requirements. Intuitively, it seems that if people hold malice toward a group and its ideas and feel threatened by the group's activities, they will act to limit or restrain the group's rights. In essence, people hate the group, do not want it to spread its message, so do what they can to keep the group from espousing its hated doctrine.

Tolerance, however, is different. The behavioral component in tolerance is often considered inherently passive: we will not take steps to prevent the group from doing what it is legally allowed to do. As Lord Scarman (1987) says,

Figure 9.2. *Schematic model for intolerant behavioral intentions*

Toleration in a legal sense has only a negative content: it is at best a negative virtue. If you were to ask the ordinary man, "What is toleration?" I think he would reply, "Live and let live.". . . toleration, in its negative aspect of not interfering with other people, is really a fairly low-scale value. (p. 49)

How can we expect someone to act on behalf of tolerance, however, when such action entails protecting the activities and ideas of a noxious group?

Early students of tolerance argued that we need tolerant citizens to be active and intolerant citizens to be inactive (McClosky, 1964; Prothro & Grigg, 1960). If the intolerant are actively involved in the political system, their intolerant values will undermine democratic stability. The tolerant, the proponents of civil liberties, should be active to enhance the democratic state. Fortunately for this argument, empirical studies found that the tolerant tended to be more politically involved than the intolerant; hence, the democratic system was in safe hands.

Yet this research did not specifically address the behavioral consequences of tolerance and intolerance. The tolerant may be more politically involved than the intolerant, but are they active on behalf of their tolerance? Are they willing to participate to protect the rights of noxious groups, particularly in specific situations? If the intolerant are more willing to act on their intolerance, while the tolerant simply do nothing to inhibit the noxious group's rights, policymakers will, on occasion, be more responsive to the actively intolerant than to the passively tolerant. A good example of this dynamic is McCarthyism. During the McCarthy era, many of the intolerant were outspoken and active, and policymakers responded. The tolerant, on the other hand, were largely silent and impotent. The behavioral consequences of tolerant attitudes therefore potentially can have an important effect on policy outcomes.

We can find similarly unsettling examples of intolerant activity and tolerant passivity in current times. Indeed, the behavioral consequences of tolerance and intolerance are not just historical concerns, they are relevant to our lives today. For example, people on the religious right are active on behalf of their intolerance in a number of different ways: through elections to local school boards, where they can then influence the choice of curricula and books; through initiatives and referenda, such as the proposed legislation to curtail the rights of homosexuals in Oregon and Colorado; through actively opposing the right to an abortion by pushing for legislation at the state level and blocking entrances to abortion clinics at the local level; through actively calling into question government funding via the National Endowment for the Arts for controversial arts projects. The list could go on. In what activities are tolerant people engaged to counteract the consequences of intolerant behavior? We rarely hear more than grumblings about incursions on civil liberties, and see even less action taken on behalf of tolerance.

The research discussed in this chapter provides preliminary evidence that these concerns about tolerant and intolerant behavior are warranted. The intolerant subjects in our survey-experiments were significantly more likely to indicate an intention to act against the judge's order than the tolerant. The significant difference in the mean behavioral intention scores between the tolerant and intolerant showed that the intolerant were definitely on the active side of the scale and the tolerant on the inactive side. The intolerant may overall be politically inactive, but when they are faced with a noxious group trying to exercise its civil liberties, they are more than willing to express an intention to do something to keep the group from holding its rally. Indeed, a desire to stop the group may be what motivates the intolerant to become involved in politics. The tolerant, who may tend to be more politically involved overall, are generally unwilling to indicate an intention to do what is necessary to protect a noxious group's civil liberties.

What explains behavioral intentions? Using Gray's BAS as a guide, we argued that the motivating link between attitudes and behavior may be enthusiasm, or what Key (1961) calls intensity. In particular, our analyses show that the intensity with which people hold their current tolerance judgments is strongly related to their behavioral intentions, and that this current tolerance intensity is affected by a standing decision on tolerance intensity.

Yet for the tolerant subjects, current tolerance intensity is also affected by the extent to which a noxious group violates norms of proper, orderly behavior; it is also supplemented with democratic principles intensity, and threat as a standing decision, to produce tolerant behavioral intentions. The more intensely people hold their current tolerance judgments and their standing democratic princi- ples, and the more they feel threatened by their least-liked group, the more likely they are to indicate an intention to take action to protect a group's civil liberties. Therefore, tolerant behavioral inten- tions are the direct and indirect effect of standing decisions and contemporary information. Intolerant behavioral intentions are the result of tolerance intensity.

The results of our analysis have implications for democratic po- litical systems. Many scholars studying opinion intensity have com- mented on the potentially negative effects of intense opinions. When opinions are held too strongly, people become fanatical. If many people hold intense opinions, especially when the opinions conflict, political leaders are faced with the difficult task of trying to find an acceptable solution, and democracy can be weakened by the turmoil (see, e.g., Lane & Sears, 1964).

The analysis described in this chapter adds some nuance and complexity to this picture. The active citizen has generally been found to hold the values of democracy more strongly than has the inactive one. Yet, the people who are usually inactive, the intolerant, are more likely to intend to take action to prevent a group from exercising its rights than the usually active tolerant are to protect the group's rights. The intensity with which the intolerant hold their intolerant beliefs helps to propel them to action. Intensity of beliefs, however, can also lead to positive effects. The intensity with which the tolerant hold their tolerance beliefs and democratic principles propels them to take action as well, but this time in support of a group's rights.

CHAPTER 10

Human Nature and Political Tolerance

The . . . Passions of man, are in themselves no Sin. No
more are the Actions, that proceed from those Passions,
till they know a Law that forbids them . . .

Hobbes, *The Leviathan*

We attempt throughout this book to answer an important question:
how do people go about the task of making tolerance judgments?
Because democratic societies can, and often do, extend considerable
responsibilities to citizens, the answer to this question is fundamental to strengthening political society so that diverse and often antagonistic political interests can contend while secure in the enduring
support for the civil rights of all.[1] Democratic theorists endorse the
importance of public debate, deliberation, and being well-informed.
If citizens rely fully on antecedent considerations, then democracy
may stagnate. If citizens also attend to contemporary circumstances,
then they are better equipped to participate in all of the political
choices that democracy affords. Not only can citizens recognize and
perpetuate the values of their society, they can adapt these principles to new circumstances.[2]

If we could better understand how people make political judgments, we could enter into the debate about citizen competency
with a more substantial basis for assessment and consideration (Marcus & Hanson, 1993; Thompson, 1970). How people make political
tolerance judgments may provide considerable insight about how
they make other political choices. Certainly, the choices citizens
make in the realm of political tolerance are considerably more demanding than other, less complex, political choices. Few other do-

mains of choice ask citizens to balance such a complex variety of legitimate and illegitimate considerations.[3]

In this conclusion we have arranged our discussion into three sections. In the first section, we summarize the import of our principal findings as to how people make civil liberties decisions. In the second section we turn to the broader implications of incorporating feelings into the study of human judgment. In the last section we explore how political tolerance, emotions, and democratic politics are intimately connected.

WHAT WE'VE LEARNED ABOUT POLITICAL TOLERANCE

As we pointed out at the beginning of this book, we do not believe that people make judgments from a neutral stance or a position of ignorance. What we have called antecedent considerations incorporate predispositions and standing decisions that collectively summarize what people bring to any decision-making situation. Our model, then, builds on the role of standing decisions and predispositions in establishing a foundation for decision making.

We can summarize our findings as fitting into three broad patterns. First, people rely upon established beliefs to form the foundation of their civil liberties judgments. Sears (1993) is largely right on that score. Second, contemporary information can influence contemporary tolerance judgments. People have latitude in how they express their established beliefs. Although they begin with what they already know and believe, they rely on current salient argument and evidence when they express their contemporary judgments. Third, people differ in how much they rely on contemporary information and how much on established beliefs. Some people rely almost exclusively on what they bring from past experiences. Others are also influenced by the immediate context.

In Tables 10.1 and 10.2 we summarize the antecedent considerations that seem to form the basis for civil liberties decisions. Table 10.1 summarizes the dispositional influences we have explored and Table 10.2 summarizes the standing decisions we have analyzed. In each of these tables we have included approximate ($\approx$) regression coefficients for each covariate to compare the relative impact of the influential factors. These values should not be taken literally, because in different circumstances slightly different values would be obtained. However, we suspect that the general magnitude is fairly accurate.

Table 10.1. *Summary of dispositional factors and their effects on contemporary political tolerance*

Predispositions that directly influence contemporary political tolerance	Predispositions that do not directly influence contemporary political tolerance
◇ Threat predisposition [≈ −.15] ◇ Neuroticism [≈ −.12] ◇ Gender [≈ −.02]	◇ Openness to experience ◇ Introversion/extraversion ◇ Need for cognition

Predispositions that create individual differences in responsiveness to contemporary information

◇ Threat predispositions (those who generally expect the world to be full of dangerous and treacherous groups are more responsive to normative violations)
◇ Need for cognition (those with higher need for cognition are less responsive to normative violations and to the instruction to pay attention to thoughts or feelings)

We have identified three predispositions that directly influence decisions about civil liberties. People with a greater threat predisposition, those at the high end of the neuroticism personality dimension (i.e., more anxious and fearful), and women tend to respond with greater intolerance. The direct influences of these variables are not very powerful, compared to those of the major standing decisions, and certainly the differences related to gender are most modest indeed. Nonetheless, the first two factors, threat predisposition and neuroticism, tend to stack the deck against tolerance.

Table 10.1 also notes several predispositions that proved not to have significant influences on contemporary political tolerance. As we noted in Chapter 8, most personality factors, except neuroticism, had their effects incorporated by standing decisions. This is not surprising, as attitudes often mediate between personality and our expressions of behavior, thoughts, and feelings.

Table 10.1 also summarizes our findings that demonstrate how predispositions can shape citizens' use of contemporary information. For example, compared to people who are not predisposed to see a broad range of threatening political groups in society, those who are so disposed are more responsive to contemporary information about normative violations. Citizens who have a global sense of threat are, in some sense, "primed" to perceive and respond to certain types of contextual information. Their anxiety leads them to pay particular attention to information that either reassures them and heightens their tolerance, or further increases their sense of anxiety and heightens their intolerance. Citizens without this global sense of threat respond differently to the same information – they tend to ignore it and instead rely on their predispositions and other types of contemporary information.

A second predisposition that conditions responsiveness to contemporary contextual information is the need for cognition. Cacioppo and Petty's (1982) notion that some individuals are more intellectually inclined, and that they are fundamentally different from other individuals, is confirmed in the context of contemporary tolerance judgments. Those who tend toward a cognitive style of interaction with the world, unlike those who do not, pay less attention to contemporary information about the normative violations of the target group. Information about normative violations may heighten or dampen anxiety, but these individuals are less motivated by the desire to alleviate anxiety than by the need to comprehend and communicate about what they see. Respondents high in need for cognition are also less responsive to the instruction to pay attention to their feelings.

Thus the overall effects of predispositions on contemporary tolerance judgments are substantial. Some effects are direct and persist despite the considerable distance from their development earlier in life to their application in the present. Other effects are more subtle, being encapsulated in standing decisions or affecting how different types of individuals respond to contemporary contextual information.

Table 10.2 presents the impact of the foundational beliefs that provide the principal basis for making civil liberties decisions. In general, we have found, as have others (Chong, 1993; Gibson, 1987; McClosky & Brill, 1983; McClosky and Zaller, 1984; Sullivan et al., 1982, 1985), that two specific standing decisions have a pervasive and enduring influence on contemporary tolerance judgments: support for abstract democratic principles and the more concrete yet enduring decision to accord civil liberties to one's most disliked political groups. People have a general attitude toward the principles of freedom of speech and minority rights. Some are more disposed to be supportive, whereas others are more guarded and do not internalize these principles as firmly. People also have specific beliefs about groups they find noxious. Some people are generally inclined toward tolerance of their disliked groups, while others are far less forbearing. As has been previously shown, these two factors are often in contention – belief in and support for democratic principles lead us to support civil liberties while the level of malice we

Table 10.2. *Summary of standing decisions and their effects on contemporary political tolerance*

Standing decisions that directly influence contemporary political tolerance

◊ Standing decision to tolerate the least-liked group [≈ .50]
◊ Standing decision to support democratic principles [≈ .20]
◊ Political knowledge (expertise) [≈ .17]
◊ Standing decision to believe the least-liked group is a threat [≈ −.09]

Standing decisions that create individual differences in responsiveness to contemporary information

◊ Political knowledge (those with greater knowledge are less responsive to normative violations)
◊ Democratic principles (those with greater support for democratic principles are less responsive to the democratic norms manipulation)

feel toward our least-liked groups inclines against supporting civil liberties for such groups. Moreover, as we reported previously, the concrete beliefs we have about a specific group are the more influential of the two (Sullivan et al., 1982, 1985).

To this short list we can now add two additional standing decisions that influence civil liberties judgments. The amount of political knowledge people have about the political system, and the expectation that a particular group is threatening, are both taken into account and shape civil liberties decisions. The politically knowledgeable seem more inclined to apply democratic norms in a positive manner, and all citizens are less inclined to tolerate specific groups they believe to be dangerous and untrustworthy. Although our previous work (Sullivan et al., 1982) suggested that political participation did little to elevate the commitment to tolerance, the finding that knowledge matters gives some corroboration to the hopes of Stouffer and those who endorse participatory democracy that extending the reach of democratic practices can strengthen democracy rather than weaken it (Barber, 1984; Pateman, 1970; Stouffer, 1955). Of course, this depends on enhancing the public's general level of political knowledge and awareness.

Standing decisions form the foundation of salient considerations that people bring to any particular situation demanding a decision about political tolerance. In our study, people's attitudes toward democratic norms and civil liberties issues tend to reflect – or as we called it, to *encapsulate* – their predispositions, such as personality characteristics and a tendency to feel globally threatened. The powerful role of standing decisions across all of our studies reinforces

the importance of enduring attitudes. This point is at the core of the symbolic politics paradigm (Kinder & Sears, 1981; Sears, 1990; Sears, Hensler, & Speer, 1979; Sears, Lau, Tyler, & Allen, 1980). Yet, as powerful as they are, standing decisions do not completely predetermine contemporary judgments. They provide the foundation on which contemporary information builds.

In addition to playing a powerful direct role in contemporary tolerance judgments, standing decisions also shape how people respond to contemporary information. In particular, two types of standing decisions inoculate citizens from responsiveness to contemporary information. First, political expertise functions much like the need for cognition. Citizens who make the decision to engage in significant learning about politics are less responsive than others to information about the target group's normative violations. They are knowledgeable in general, and they apparently use this knowledge when they arrive at standing decisions. As a consequence, their decisions regarding civil liberties are less easily influenced by affect-inducing information about how the target group behaves in the current political context.

Second, citizens who have a strong preexisting commitment to democratic principles are less responsive to contemporary information about how to apply democratic principles. These citizens have already decided to support the civil liberties of unpopular groups, and information designed to influence whether the rights of a particular group in a particular context warrant protection confronts counterargument and a more firm foundation than is the case among other people. Citizens who have not internalized democratic principles as completely engage in less counterargument and, in the end, are more swayed by how environmental cues suggest the principles ought to be applied in a particular context.

Recall that our conceptualization of standing decisions incorporates the idea of latitudes or ranges of potential responses. In essence, a standing decision is not a fixed response point but a range of acceptable responses among which people can choose in a specific situation. The response people make depends on the information available in a particular context.[4] This context includes the nature of the target group, such as its platform, style, behavior in previous situations, proposed actions in the current context, and unstated purposes of the proposed activity. Variations in this context will prompt individuals toward more tolerant or intolerant contem-

Table 10.3. *Summary of contemporary influences and their effects on contemporary political tolerance*

Contemporary factors that directly influence contemporary political tolerance

◊ Normative violations (reassurance increases tolerance, threat increases intolerance)
◊ Arguments about the proper application of democratic principles (arguments that favor the rights of expression increase tolerance, arguments that favor order increase intolerance)
◊ State of mind (attention to thoughts increases tolerance, attention to feelings increases intolerance)

Contemporary factors that do not influence contemporary political tolerance

◊ Probability of power (whether the target group is believed to be growing or declining in strength and influence)

---

porary tolerance judgments, within their range of latitude, as they evaluate contemporary information.

While standing decisions form the foundation of judgment, they are not the entire story. Contemporary information does enter into most people's decision-making. But not all contemporary information influences tolerance judgments. In general, two kinds of contemporary information have an impact on civil liberties decisions. First, information that affects people's perceptions of the belligerence and treachery of the group has a consistent and significant impact on whether they express more or less tolerant attitudes. Information that reassures yields greater tolerance, whereas threatening information evokes greater intolerance. Both our theoretical formulation and our evidence suggest that affective responses lie at the heart of the influence of normative violations. Second, arguments as to how to apply democratic norms, in the particular circumstance, are also influential. Democratic principles appear to be sufficiently elastic that they can be useful to those who would restrict political rights as well as to those who would defend broad applications of these rights. Table 10.3 summarizes the influences of different types of contemporary information.

Consistent across all of our studies has been the failure of the probability manipulation to influence the civil liberties decisions people make. Our validation studies (Appendix 4A) suggest that people notice the difference between potentially weak and powerful groups. However, people do not alter their civil liberties decisions based on that information. Rather, they seem to make decisions that are basically normative – what should be permitted based on what groups do to comply with or violate norms of proper political behavior.

Finally, state of mind has had the most robust effect of all of the contemporary influences. When encouraged to concentrate on their feelings, people offer less tolerant decisions, but when instructed to concentrate on their thoughts, they offer more tolerant decisions. Because the role of affect has been given little rigorous theoretical attention and because our understanding of this finding is at the center of our theoretical approach, we will discuss this aspect of our study in greater detail.

The impact of contemporary influences can be shaped by events or the principal actors in the direction of greater tolerance or of greater intolerance. Moreover, the magnitude of these influences is likely to be shaped by the degree of normative violation and the consistency and quality of arguments expressed in support of, or opposition to, tolerance in the immediate instance. Nonetheless, the combined effect of the three relevant contemporary influences can at times be substantial. Of course, the combined effects are not always mutually reinforcing. For example, an extremist group might take actions that are perceived to be provocative and threatening whereas at the same time opinion leaders may argue for tolerance. Thus, the effect of these actions, increased anxiety and intolerance, may be offset by the effects of arguments counseling forbearance. But if they are mutually reinforcing, so that the principal public discussion and debate is consistent with the message conveyed by the actions of the group (i.e., both effects commending reassurance or encouraging intolerance) then the combined effects of contemporary influences are consequential. Further, the citizens' state of mind adds to the possible swing of public opinion. Taken together, these three effects – normative violations, arguments about how to apply democratic principles, and state of mind – represent a possible swing that is equivalent to moving citizens who are neutral to a tolerant or intolerant position, or the already tolerant or intolerant to a strongly tolerant or strongly intolerant position.[5]

In general, when making contemporary judgments, people bring both predispositions and standing decisions to the current decision-making situation. Standing decisions are themselves fashioned in part by individual differences in predispositions, such as personality traits or a global sense of diffuse threat. Standing decisions, then, fashion a range of possible judgments to be expressed in the absence of fresh information about current circumstances. Within the context of these predispositions and standing decisions, people receive and evaluate information about the present context. If the environment provides relevant information about existing circumstances, most people will take such information into account before rendering a contemporary judgment.

For example, when people make a judgment about the civil liberties of a political group they do not like, many of them will bring to the situation some sort of standing decision, however nascent it may be. Some individuals may have internalized attitudes supporting a liberal interpretation of democratic norms and values. These attitudes encapsulate differences in personality and other predispositions, and they serve as a tentative general decision favoring a tolerant judgment. Other individuals may be generally fearful of certain types of political groups and ideas, and they may develop a standing decision to deprive such groups of their civil liberties. Both types of individuals, then, have a predilection, even if only incipient, before they receive any information about the specific situation and circumstances they are being asked to evaluate and judge.

Civil Liberties Decisions in the Absence of Malice

Some (e.g., Sniderman et al., 1989, 1991a) have argued that tolerance does not require forbearance. Instead they believe that it is unnecessary to establish the presence of an objection when studying civil liberties judgments. The Texas study afforded us the opportunity to determine whether the process of making civil liberties judgments differs between two sets of people – those who are confronted with a group that they strongly dislike and those who hold little or no malice toward that particular group. We discovered that the citizens who held no malice toward the group do not rely much on contemporary information to guide their civil liberties judgments. Instead, they rely solely on antecedent considerations to form a judgment.[6] This is a considerably simplified decision-making process compared to that undertaken by those who have to contend with a group they strongly dislike.

Table 10.4 shows that much of the contemporary information that affects people who are confronted with a strongly disliked group is irrelevant among people confronted with a group that is not especially disliked. In the absence of strong objection to a group and its ideas, these citizens' state of mind does not affect their tolerance judgments, nor does exposure to information identifying

Table 10.4. *Factors affecting civil liberties decisions when the target group is not strongly disliked*

Factors that *do* influence contemporary political tolerance	Factors that do *not* directly influence contemporary political tolerance	Factors that influence contemporary political tolerance differently
◊ Support for democratic principles [≈ .26] ◊ Political knowledge [≈ .23] ◊ Threat predisposition [≈ −.22] ◊ Neuroticism [≈ −.17]	◊ State of mind ◊ Arguments as to how to apply democratic principles	◊ Normative violations

how to apply democratic principles and values to the group's predicament. Information about whether the target group is compliant or threatening, however, does influence them. However, they respond in exactly the opposite way from those with significant malice toward the target group – under the more threatening circumstances, they express a greater level of support ("tolerance") for the group.

These findings demonstrate that we ought not to aggregate those with strong malice toward a group with those who lack strong malice. We would distort the decision-making process underlying civil liberties judgments if we were to do so. In general, we would underestimate the impact of contemporary information on tolerance judgments, since among those lacking malice, antecedent considerations play the stronger role. We would also fail to understand the fundamentally *supportive* nature of the relationship between those lacking malice and the potential target group, a relationship revealed by how these supportive individuals respond to information about the normative violations of the group in question.

Hypothetical Scenarios

The use of hypothetical groups in the survey experiments precludes too great a reliance on these findings to estimate the relative weight of antecedent considerations and contemporary circumstances. We have not offered much discussion of the relative weight of historical influences versus contemporary information. Our studies suggest that such an analysis would favor the importance of the former and the more modest impact of the latter. Because the target groups in the scenarios are depicted as hypothetical, are presented in a semantic fashion, and are clearly not "real," we cannot rely on these findings to generalize directly to real historical events. That we demonstrate any influence suggests that the balance would shift if people were presented with real groups using vivid display of information (e.g., television). How much, and in what direction it would shift, we cannot say.

However, our studies provide a true, though mild, test of the claim that people rely on contemporary information in making political tolerance judgments. Because these scenarios present groups that are new to each subject, none of the subjects could bring to bear contemporary information other than that which we provided for them in the experiments. They could, and indeed did, bring established antecedent considerations into the experiment. The point we wish to emphasize here is that the information contained in the scenarios could not have been supplemented by contemporary news accounts.

One of the ways that Gray's work on emotion can help us understand the importance of more fully grasping the role of passion is, as our epigram to this chapter suggests, by offering some insight into motivation. Emotions, as their very name suggests, are what move us to take action (e-motion: that is, to be in motion). We turn to that topic next.

Behavioral Intentions

One reason political scientists try to understand attitudes is because they are linked to behavior. The attitude–behavior linkage is of special importance when the behavior in question either supports or opposes civil liberties. Two factors appear to be extremely important in determining whether an intention to behave is expressed: intensity and immediacy. These two factors combine to make current tolerance intensity the strongest predictor of people's behavioral intentions. The intensity factor is substantively important because of its asymmetry; it distinguishes between the intolerant and the tolerant. The intolerant are much more intense and hence express stronger behavioral intentions, which is consistent with Gibson's findings (Gibson, 1987; Gibson & Bingham, 1985). For the intolerant, the singular force of current tolerance intensity tells the entire story. Intolerant individuals do not focus on contemporary information or their beliefs about democratic principles to decide whether to act; they rely solely on their preexisting attitudes and standing decisions about civil liberties for their least-liked group.

For the tolerant, the intensity of current tolerance beliefs is also crucial, but three other factors also matter. First, the *more* threatening they believe their least liked group is, the *less* likely they are to intend action. Second, the intensity of democratic principles directly affects their potential to act. Mobilizing the tolerant, then, could be achieved by appealing to their beliefs about democratic principles because they believe so intensely in those values. Third, a particular type of contemporary information indirectly affects the behavioral intentions of the tolerant. Normative violations information affects the intensity of their current tolerance attitude, which in turn has the greatest impact on behavioral intentions.

One rather alarming finding needs to be highlighted. We have noted that the intolerant are far more predisposed to act than the tolerant. In addition, unlike the tolerant, their inclination to act is not influenced by current information or by their intensity about democratic principles. Because the intolerant root their inclination to act in their standing decisions rather than in current information, it is more difficult to moderate their intentions. The intolerant remain closed to some types of information to which the tolerant remain open, making the intolerant more difficult to influence. Given that they profess greater propensity for action, this may cause some anxiety over their impact on the democratic process.

WHAT WE HAVE LEARNED ABOUT THINKING AND FEELING IN MAKING TOLERANCE JUDGMENTS

Much of the current research in social and political psychology is concerned with cognition, particularly with cognitive information processing (Ferejohn & Kuklinski, 1990; Hastie, 1986). Yet this heavy emphasis on cognition misconstrues the full nature of how information is processed. Our survey experiments show time and again that affective information matters. It is therefore imperative in this concluding chapter that we examine at some length the role both cognition *and* affect play when people make tolerance judgments.

In Chapter 3, we reviewed Gray's model of emotionality and, in particular, the two systems most relevant to our study of tolerance: the behavioral inhibition system (BIS) and the behavioral activation system (BAS). We kept this discussion at a fairly abstract level, both because we could not directly test this model with our experimental design and because we intended to use Gray's work as a conceptual template for our research. Gray's work has indeed been invaluable in guiding our thinking about how affect influences tolerance judgments, particularly by identifying the manner in which threat perceptions play a central role in this process. In this section, we will spell out specifically what we think we have learned about the affective and cognitive underpinnings of tolerance judgments, discoveries that have important implications for understanding democratic processes.

Gray's model has been useful because it led us to examine the conditions under which people are responsive to contemporary information. According to his model, the BIS attends to threatening stimuli in the environment. Perceptions of threat, according to Gray, are the key element. If people are confronted with a threat of some sort, they feel more anxious and they are more reactive to contemporary information.

But were the scenarios sufficiently threatening to arouse people's sensitivity to contemporary information? The answer is generally yes. We found that people who strongly dislike a group are responsive to the threatening information we provided – they feel more anxious when confronted with the group acting in an objectionable way, and they feel less anxious when the group acts in a reassuring manner. In turn, people who feel threatened react with greater intolerance, whereas people who feel reassured react with greater tolerance.

If people lack malice toward a group, however, they do not feel threatened by information about that group's improper and disorderly behavior. In essence, threat is not present and they do not respond to threatening contemporary information by becoming less tolerant. Therefore, the threatening normative violations information makes people less tolerant *when they feel threatened*, which they do when they strongly dislike the target group, but it can actually make people more supportive when they do not dislike the group.

These findings concerning the normative violations manipulation show that people respond to contemporary information that arouses affect and that this information influences judgments. The more threatened people feel, the less tolerant they are. We also found, in our instruction-set manipulation, that people who were told to attend to their feelings were significantly less tolerant than people who were told to attend to their thoughts. Focusing on feelings, which may be people's natural inclination (Kuklinski et al., 1987, 1991, 1993), increases intolerance. The evidence therefore strongly supports the conclusion that emotional responses can be strongly intolerant responses.

But this general argument ignores an important nuance. Affect increases intolerance when people feel threatened and when they focus on naturally negative feelings. But affect can also lead to greater tolerance. When people feel reassured about a disliked and potentially threatening group, they react with greater calm to the group's actions and are more tolerant. Affect may usually lead to intolerance, but it can also increase tolerance when people feel reassured.

What about the impact of cognition on tolerance judgments? Our findings strongly suggest that when people are thoughtful and deliberative – when they take a "sober second thought" – they are significantly more tolerant. Several of our findings support this conclusion.

First, people who are asked to pay attention to their thoughts give significantly more tolerant responses than people who are asked to attend to their feelings. This result raises a potential caveat to existing research. According to several scholars, paying attention to thoughts diminishes people's capacity to function well in several ways: in the accurate recall, or prediction, of feelings (Wilson, Laser, & Stone, 1982); in directing behavior (Wilson et al., 1989); and in accurately recovering our "reasons" for doing things (Rahn, Krosnick, & Breuning, 1992). But our research on tolerance adds an interesting twist to this story. When people pay attention to their feelings, they are more intolerant. As McClosky and Brill (1983) argue, intolerance may be the more natural and "easy" position to hold. Focusing on thoughts directs people away from this natural, intolerant reaction. Research may show that people make worse judgments when they focus on their thoughts, but our survey-experiments suggest that in some circumstances thoughtfulness may help people to be more tolerant, bringing their judgments *more* in line with those made by "experts" (McClosky & Brill, 1983).

Second, people who are more knowledgeable about politics, and therefore have more information to draw on when making political judgments, are more tolerant than people who are less knowledgeable. This result corroborates findings from previous research that show that the politically sophisticated have more tolerant standing decisions than the less sophisticated (McClosky & Brill, 1983;

McClosky & Zaller, 1984; Sullivan et al., 1993). But our research also suggests that the processes people use to make tolerance judgments differ depending on their level of expertise. As Zaller (1992) contended, political experts have the information base necessary to counterargue contemporary information. We find that experts are indeed quite unresponsive to information concerning normative violations. Novices, on the other hand, react strongly to contemporary information about the group's belligerence and treachery. Thus, people who are more knowledgeable, thoughtful, and deliberative about politics are initially more tolerant and do not react to information in the immediate environment. Political novices are initially much less tolerant and are reactive to inflammatory contemporary information.

Finally, we can examine the effects of cognition on tolerance by looking at differences between people who have a high need for cognition and those who do not. Similar to our findings on expertise, people with a high need for cognition are significantly more tolerant and less responsive to normative violations information than those with a low need for cognition. They were also less responsive to the instruction to pay attention to their feelings. Those with a low need for cognition are more intolerant, and they react strongly to contemporary information that is threatening.

Our research therefore demonstrates that the degree to which affect and cognition are prevalent in the decision-making process on tolerance makes a big difference. Affect can increase tolerance when people feel reassured, but our other measures of affect demonstrate that affect makes people more intolerant. Indeed, it is not affect that increases expressions of tolerance, it is cognition. People are more tolerant the more they know, the more thoughtful and deliberative they are, and the more willing they are to take a sober second thought. A heavier reliance on cognition, measured in a number of different ways, leads both to higher tolerance generally *and* makes people less likely to react intolerantly when confronted with contemporary information, including threatening normative violations information.

So far we have focused on the impact of affect and cognition on contemporary tolerance judgments, but our research also contributes to a better understanding of what motivates behavior. According to Gray's model, behavior is motivated by the BAS, which carefully monitors the extent to which people feel enthusiastic or depressed about how successfully they are executing their plans.

People who feel enthusiastic are motivated to take action, whereas those who are depressed are less likely to act.

Our findings show that affect is strongly related to behavioral intentions, as Gray's model led us to expect. The enthusiasm, or intensity, with which subjects hold their contemporary tolerance judgments is strongly related to their intention to act on their beliefs. But this is not the whole story. It is the intolerant, rather than the tolerant, who are more likely to say they intend to take action on their tolerance beliefs. Enthusiasm, therefore, is likely to motivate intolerant rather than tolerant behavior. Our finding that extraversion is consistently related to greater intolerance reinforces this conclusion. People who are high in extraversion are more intense and enthusiastic *as people*, and because they are more enthusiastic, they are more likely to act on their intolerance.

We can examine the relationship between affect and behavior further by turning to the research done by Wilson and his colleagues (Wilson et al., 1989; 1991). They show that an instruction set, much like the one we use in our work, operates to strengthen the prior attitude–behavior linkage when subjects are instructed to attend to their feelings, and to weaken the linkage when subjects are instructed to attend to their thoughts. If they are right, we should find that the correlation between tolerance standing decisions and behavioral intentions is stronger among those in the "pay attention to feelings" group and weaker among those in the "pay attention to thoughts" group. Indeed, this proves to be the case.[7] Among those told to attend to their thoughts, the correlation is −.29, whereas among those told to attend to their feelings, the correlation is −.40. Both correlations are statistically significant ($p < .01$), but the affect instruction group's relationship is much stronger. Thus the mere encouragement to focus on thoughts weakens the linkage between an existing impulse and action. Since those who are most intense are most likely to act intolerantly, weakening that specific link between intention and action is often desirable.

Do our conclusions in this section mean that affect is bad for democratic societies? Our answer is no. We think it is essential that people develop a strong baseline of tolerance, including a strong commitment to democratic principles. But people must be open and attentive to contemporary information. Sometimes noxious groups truly are a threat to democratic society and taking action against them may be desirable. What citizens need to develop is the ability to discern serious threat from inflammatory behavior on the part of nonconformist groups and from inflammatory cues designed to obtain partisan advantage, as happened during the McCarthy era. We interpret our findings to suggest that this is what thoughtful, deliberative people do. They attend to threatening information that confronts them, but they have the necessary wherewithal to apply abstract democratic principles and potentially to evaluate and counterargue the threatening information. Both affect and cognition are at work here: affect enhances attention to contemporary information and the readiness to take action, and thoughtfulness helps to discern whether threats posed by the group are realistic. Democracy requires both affectively engaged and thoughtful citizens.

WHAT WE HAVE LEARNED ABOUT POLITICS

Our research suggests that people have a particular range of tolerance attitudes. Within this latitude, their tolerance judgments can be modified by the information they receive. In essence, people pay attention to contemporary information and augment their judgments based on contextual cues. These results have serious ramifications for the behavior of both political elites and activists.

Political elites play a special role in democratic societies. They must follow the wishes of the public but at the same time they must fulfill the crucial responsibility of strong leadership. One area where such leadership is potentially powerful is in the shaping of public opinion. An evolving body of research attempts to demonstrate the connections between elite cue giving and public opinion (Krosnick & Kinder, 1990; Zaller, 1987, 1992). Zaller (1992) and McClosky and Brill (1983), for example, show that if an elite consensus exists, then the public will often go along with elite opinion.

Elites are likely to have an especially strong impact when the issue of political tolerance arises. For most people, principles of tolerance will not be a prominent part of their immediate environment. They will look to political leaders both for information on what is happening and how they should respond to issues of threat and tolerance.[8] This enables political elites to play a special role. Leaders can provide reassurance about the existence of threat and emphasize the importance of applying democratic values in order to sustain civil liberties rather than to undermine such rights. Or, leaders can play on feelings of threat and invoke principles counter to extending civil liberties. It is the responsibility of political elites to provide cues to the general public based on democratic principles and realistic information about any threats to political freedom.

Contemporary events in Europe and other places in the world reveal that elites often draw upon ethnocentric and intolerant appeals to legitimate their authority. Political elites have a tempting but destructive option to secure their career goals at the expense of civil liberties (Fried, 1990). And unhappily, as current events demonstrate, the public is often tempted to respond to jingoist, anti-immigrant, and xenophobic appeals advanced by elites seeking to gain public support by any device. Indeed, a long tradition exists of actions against "outsiders." The temptation for elites to engage in leadership through "scapegoating" has a rich historical tradition, including fascism, Nazism, the Dreyfuss affair, McCarthyism, and (most recently) "ethnic cleansing" and religious intolerance.

The results in the democratic-norms experiment cause some alarm in this respect because statements about democratic principles can be used to decrease tolerance as well as increase it. Given that democratic principles are contested and that leaders may use such principles for individual advantage, our concern may be warranted. However, political elites often speak up in support of democratic values, and these cues may strengthen support for civil liberties, particularly if courts and legal elites agree on the general democratic principles (McClosky & Brill, 1983).

Even so, we remain cautious. Creating and sustaining a tolerant and democratic society requires accounting for the actions and intentions of political elites, as well as for the role of institutions (Hanson, 1993). The actions of elites may not always be directed at securing the common good and ensuring the uniform practice of civil liberties. Elites, even elites who profess dedication to political tolerance, are not sufficient to ensure a politically tolerant society. A democratic society requires as one of its constituent elements good leadership, but it also requires an engaged citizenry. The studies of tolerance we have presented here help us better understand what information people attend to and how they respond to contemporary messages provided by elites and the media.

Our research also raises a concern relevant to political activists. Links between threat, attention, and intolerance suggest an important double bind facing groups trying to gain a place on the national political agenda. On the one hand, the most certain way to gain attention is to be involved in some spectacle of either novel scope or threatening character (Edelman, 1964, 1988; Marcus & Mac-Kuen, 1993). Yet the very strategy that achieves successful attention also generates resistance and hostility. Groups that use threatening actions to gain attention to their cause probably pay a substantial price for that strategy.

So, being provocative gains attention, but provocative actions are those most likely to engender feelings of anxiety and perceptions of threat. Thus, the activist is caught in a dilemma. The actions necessary to gain public attention may provoke intolerance toward the activists and their cause. Activists, if they are persuasive, can offset the negative consequences of their attention-getting actions. This does not guarantee them a receptive or even a neutral audience, but it does offer some purchase on shifting public opinion. However, if activists are not mindful of the need to make a persuasive appeal to a potentially hostile audience, whose hositility is itself somewhat a reaction to the initiatives of the activists themselves, they may well provoke a backlash both against their ideas and against their right to engage in political action. One can see the double bind in operation in such instances as actions by Act-Up to garner greater attention for the problem of AIDS and the need for greater governmental efforts, and actions by prochoice and prolife groups. In both cases, activists are involved in actions designed to capture public attention and to increase public awareness, but they confront the risk of losing public sympathy and alienating their groups from mainstream political discourse.[9]

Finally, there has been a determined effort by many to force a rational cast on the qualities and abilities required of a democratic polity (Downs, 1957; Enelow & Hinich, 1984; Foster, 1984; Kant, 1970; Page & Shapiro, 1992; Paine, 1973). Yet those who have studied democratic politics find that emotions permeate throughout (Blight, 1990; Campbell, Converse, Miller, & Stokes, 1960; Conover & Feldman, 1986; Marcus, 1988b; Marcus & MacKuen, 1993; Masters & Sullivan, 1993; Masters, Frey, & Bentc, 1991; Sullivan & Masters, 1988). Arkes (1993) has posed the question, "Can emotion supply the place of reason?" as part of his defense of the preeminent position of reason. Others, philosophers among them, have begun to reexamine the wisdom of trying to completely supplant the role of passion with reason (de Sousa, 1987; Frank, 1988; Gibbard, 1990; Okin, 1989). There is, however, an older tradition that has understood the inescapable role of emotion in politics (Hobbes, 1968; Hume, 1739–40; Madison, Hamilton, & Jay, 1961).

Democratic politics, in large and diverse societies, encompasses great numbers of strangers. To enable a diverse people to function as a polity requires loyalty and charismatic bonds between and among the people, and shared and deeply held values between citizens and their leaders. Further, a polity should display perseverance in the face of difficulties and obstacles as it attempts to achieve collective goals. These requirements are met not only by the faculties of conscious awareness or reason, but also by our emotional faculties.[10] In order to understand more fully how democratic societies work, we must broaden our understanding beyond the idealized rational democratic citizen.

APPENDIX A

Hypothetical Group Scenarios and Manipulations

NATIONALIST PARTY OF AMERICA (NPA)

Now we would like you to read the following scenario about a hypothetical group that has organized in the United States. While you read the scenario, please think about how you and the people in your social network would react to such a group.

Suppose it is the late 1990s and a new political group has been formed in the United States. It is an extremist group that evolved from a pro-Nazi group of the 1980s. This group – the Nationalist Party of America (NPA) – has pledged to rid the United States of Jewish influence which they believe has grown too great. They believe that Jews control the international monetary system, and ultimately the economy of the United States. Recent evidence of this, they believe, is the farm crisis and the way it has been handled by big government and big business, particularly the Jewish-controlled banks. They believe that American society has lost its small family farms and businesses and blame the Jews for this. They are also beginning to worry more and more about the power and influence of Blacks as well, but have decided to concentrate for now on the Jews.

The NPA has not been very specific about the actions they propose to take, but there are hints that they would like to restrict the economic and political rights of Jews and perhaps even Blacks. They would like to keep Jews out of public office, and have stated that campaign contributions from rich Jews have been used to buy off politicians and help Jews amass a great deal of America's wealth. They would like to restrict these contributions, and have mentioned breaking up the big banks into smaller, home-owned and operated local banks. They have stated that they will not use violence to achieve their aim of limiting Jewish influence in America.

Another part of the NPA program seems to be restricting entry into colleges and universities, largely because they perceive them to be the major training ground for liberals and Jewish intellectuals. These liberals and intellectuals have masterminded the decay of fundamental white Christian values and have assisted in creating and maintaining the Jewish and liberal stranglehold on the economy and the banking system in the United States. The NPA would like to restrict the college experience to small denominational Christian institutions and to do away with the large research universities across the country. They want to ensure that only the physically and intellectually "fit" are allowed to attend college and to become part of the governing classes in the U.S. Although they have not explicitly said so, it appears likely they would institute a screening program to weed out dangerous college professors.

Probability Manipulation

LOW: The NPA has tried raising money for an advertising campaign, but public opinion polls show that few people are paying much attention to them. In fact, many people find their views objectionable, and most people are apathetic about the group and its agenda. The group has grown some in recent years, but most political analysts have classified it as another in a long line of extremist groups in the U.S. that simply do not appeal to the bulk of the moderate American public. Analysts agree that they might indeed do harm to some Jewish groups and individuals but they have little chance of gaining any significant political power.

HIGH: The NPA has already amassed large sums of money for a sophisticated and subtle advertising campaign. Public opinion polls show that although they are not likely to win any major national elections soon, more and more people – particularly young people – are beginning to listen to their message and to find some value in it. Most people do not agree with everything they say, but do find some points appealing. This is evidenced by some electoral gains that the NPA has begun to register in local elections in some parts of the country, particularly Chicago, Southern California, parts of the South, and in a few midwestern farm communities. Some public opinion polls indicate that as much as 10% of the public feels sympathy for the NPA and its point of view, and the percentage appears to be on the rise. Several Jewish groups, including the Anti-Defamation League, are taking the threat very seriously indeed and have begun an urgent campaign to combat the NPA.

Normative Violations Manipulation

REASSURING: The NPA has begun to hold public rallies to generate support for their cause. Before their rallies, they cooperated with the police and local authorities and promised to have peaceful demonstrations according to the conditions of their parade permits. They have marched along the designated routes and did not cause any trouble with counter demonstrators, spectators or the police. At the rallies and demonstrations, leaders of the NPA have asked their supporters to act vigorously but as lawfully as possible to pursue their cause.

THREATENING: The NPA has begun to hold public rallies to generate support for their cause. Before their rallies, they refused to cooperate with the police and local authorities but did promise to have peaceful demonstrations according to the conditions of their parade permits. However, they have not always marched along the designated routes and have gotten enmeshed with counter demonstrators and the police. As a result violence has broken out at some of the rallies. Fist fights and rock throwing have resulted in spectators, demonstrators and some police getting hurt. Members of the NPA have shouted "First get the Jews, then the Blacks" and "The U.S. for Christians only, out with the Jew thieves." At the rallies and demonstrations, leaders of the NPA have asked their supporters to take bold actions to pursue their cause.

NEW MOVEMENT FOR AMERICA (NMA)

Now we would like you to read the following scenario about a hypothetical group that has organized in the United States. While you read the scenario, please think about how you and the people in your social network would react to such a group.

Suppose it is the late 1990s and a new political group has been formed in the United States. It is an extremist left-wing reaction to the conservative policies of the Reagan years. This group – the New

Movement for America (NMA) – has pledged to rid the United
States of the influence of the wealthy and business people which
the NMA believes has grown too great. They believe the economic
system should be changed to make it "fair and egalitarian," and
believe that the upper classes have too much influence in government. Recent evidence of this, the NMA believes, is the cuts in welfare spending and the deregulation of businesses. They believe that
American society has become more economically unequal, and
blame the wealthy and business people for this. They are also beginning to worry more and more about the power and influence of
the Christian Right, but have decided to concentrate for now on
the economic conservatives.

The NMA has not been very specific about the actions they propose to take, but there are hints that they would like the government
to have a great deal of control over the economic system by fully
regulating (and even taking over) businesses in the United States.
They would like to keep the wealthy and business people out of
public office, and have stated that campaign contributions from
wealthy people and businesses have been used to buy off politicians
and help these groups amass a great deal of America's wealth. They
would like to start a steeply progressive tax system where the wealthy
and corporations would be required to pay very high taxes, and have
proposed a very open welfare system. They have stated that they will
not use violence to achieve their aim of limiting the influence of
economic conservatives in America.

Another part of the NMA program seems to be the formation of
a much stronger alliance with leftist countries, especially Cuba, Nicaragua, and the Soviet Union. Student exchanges with communist
countries would be increased, and all schools would be forced to
teach about Marxism and alternative forms of government. The
NMA would like to restrict the college experience to large research
universities and to do away with the small denominational Christian
institutions across the country. Although they have not explicitly said
so, it appears likely they would institute a screening program to weed
out conservative college professors.

Probability Manipulation

LOW: The NMA has tried raising money for an advertising campaign, but public opinion polls show that few people are paying
much attention to them. In fact, many people find their views ob-

jectionable, and most people are apathetic about the group and its agenda. The group has grown some in recent years, but most political analysts have classified it as another in a long line of extremist groups in the U.S. that simply do not appeal to the bulk of the moderate American public. Analysts agree that they might indeed do harm to some groups and individuals but they have little chance of gaining any significant political power.

HIGH: The NMA has already amassed large sums of money for a sophisticated and subtle advertising campaign. Public opinion polls show that although they are not likely to win any major national elections soon, more and more people – particularly young people – are beginning to listen to their message and to find some value in it. Most people do not agree with everything they say, but do find some points appealing. This is evidenced by some electoral gains that the NMA has begun to register in local elections in some parts of the country, particularly in the Northeast and in northern California. Some public opinion polls indicate that as much as 10% of the public feels sympathy for the NMA and its point of view, and the percentage appears to be on the rise. Several conservative groups are taking the threat very seriously indeed and have begun an urgent campaign to combat the NMA.

Normative Violations Manipulation

REASSURING: The NMA has begun to hold public rallies to generate support for their cause. Before their rallies, they cooperated with the police and local authorities and promised to have peaceful demonstrations according to the conditions of their parade permits. They have marched along the designated routes and did not cause any trouble with counter demonstrators, spectators or the police. At the rallies and demonstrations, leaders of the NMA have asked their supporters to act vigorously but as lawfully as possible to pursue their cause.

THREATENING: The NMA has begun to hold public rallies to generate support for their cause. Before their rallies, they refused to cooperate with the police and local authorities but did promise to have peaceful demonstrations according to the conditions of their parade permits. However, they have not always marched along the designated routes and have gotten enmeshed with counter demonstrators and the police. As a result violence has broken out at some of the rallies. Fist fights and rock throwing have resulted in spectators, demonstrators and some police getting hurt. Members of the NMA have shouted "Rob from the rich, give to the poor" and "Greedy capitalist pigs must go." At the rallies and demonstrations, leaders of the NMA have asked their supporters to take bold actions to pursue their cause.

CHRISTIANS IN POLITICS (CP)

Now we would like you to read the following scenario about a hypothetical group that has organized in the United States. While you read the scenario, please think about how you and the people in your social network would react to such a group.

Suppose it is the late 1990s and a new political group has been formed in the United States. It is an extremist group that evolved from the fundamentalist Born-Again Christian movement of the 1980s. This group – the Christians in Politics (CP) – has pledged to rid the United States of atheistic and secular influence which they believe has grown too great. They believe that the separation of Church and state has gone too far and must be put into proper perspective. Recent evidence of this, they believe, is the Supreme Court's decision allowing abortion, the difficulties experienced by many schools over prayer in the classroom, and the acceptance of the theory of evolution by the educational and scientific community. They believe that American society has become too secular and even atheistic, and blame non-believers and various liberal groups for this. They are also beginning to worry more and more about the power and influence of Jews as well, but have decided to concentrate for now on non-believers.

The CP has not been very specific about the actions they propose to take, but there are hints that they would like to restrict the economic and political rights of non-believers and of people who are pro-choice on the abortion issue and perhaps even Jews. They would like to keep atheists and pro-abortionists out of public office, and have stated that campaign contributions from wealthy materialistic humanists have been used to buy off politicians and help maintain an overly secularized and unholy political system in the U.S. They would like to restrict these contributions and have mentioned instituting a screening process involving an examination of Christian and fundamentalist values as the number one criterion. They have stated that they will not use violence to achieve their aim of limiting non-believers' influence in America.

Another part of the CP program seems to be restricting entry into colleges and universities, largely because they perceive them to be the major training ground for atheists and liberals. These atheists and liberals have masterminded the decay of fundamental Christian values and have assisted in creating and maintaining the secular and liberal stranglehold on the political system in the United States. The CP would like to restrict the college experience to small denominational Christian institutions and to do away with the large research universities across the country. They want to ensure that only the morally and intellectually "fit" are allowed to attend college and to become part of the governing classes in the U.S. Although they have not explicitly said so, it appears likely they would institute a screening program to weed out dangerous college professors.

Probability Manipulation

LOW: The CP has tried raising money for an advertising campaign, but public opinion polls show that few people are paying much attention to them. In fact, many people find their views objectionable, and most people are apathetic about the group and its agenda. The group has grown some in recent years, but most political analysts have classified it as another in a long line of extremist groups in the U.S. that simply do not appeal to the bulk of the moderate American public. Analysts agree that they might indeed do harm to some atheist groups and individuals but they have little chance of gaining any significant political power.

HIGH: The CP has already amassed large sums of money for a sophisticated and subtle advertising campaign. Public opinion polls show that although they are not likely to win any major national elections soon, more and more people – particularly young people – are beginning to listen to their message and to find some value in it. Most people do not agree with everything they say, but do find some points appealing. This is evidenced by some electoral gains that the CP has begun to register in local elections in some parts of the country, particularly Southern California and parts of the Midwest and South. Some public opinion polls indicate that as much as 10% of the public feels sympathy for the CP and its point of view, and the percentage appears to be on the rise. Several liberal groups, including some of the more progressive religious denominations, are taking the threat very seriously indeed and have begun an urgent campaign to combat the CP.

Normative Violations Manipulation

REASSURING: The CP has begun to hold public rallies to generate support for their cause. Before their rallies, they cooperated with the police and local authorities and promised to have peaceful demonstrations according to the conditions of their parade permits. They have marched along the designated routes and did not cause any trouble with counter demonstrators, spectators or the police. At the rallies and demonstrations, leaders of the CP have asked their supporters to act vigorously but as lawfully as possible to pursue their cause.

THREATENING: The CP has begun to hold public rallies to generate support for their cause. Before their rallies, they refused to cooperate with the police and local authorities but did promise to have peaceful demonstrations according to the conditions of their parade permits. However, they have not always marched along the designated routes and have gotten enmeshed with counter demonstrators and the police. As a result violence has broken out at some of the rallies. Fist fights and rock throwing have resulted in spectators, demonstrators and some police getting hurt. Members of the CP have shouted "America for Christians only" and "Atheists and Commies must go." At the rallies and demonstrations, leaders of the CP have asked their supporters to take bold actions to pursue their cause.

WOMEN FOR JUSTICE (WJ)

Now we would like you to read the following scenario about a hypothetical group that has organized in the United States. While you read the scenario, please think about how you and the people in your social network would react to such a group.

Suppose it is the late 1990s and a new political group has been formed in the United States. It is an extremist left-wing reaction to the conservative policies of the Reagan years. This group – the Women for Justice (WJ) – has pledged to rid the United States of male dominance. They believe that recent government policies reflect conservative "fundamentalist" values and are ruining the gains made by liberals in the 1960s. Recent evidence of this, they believe, is the cuts in financial aid to mothers on welfare and the growing number of rules affecting abortions. They believe that American society favors Christians and whites, and blame social conservatives and people who are pro-life for this. They are also beginning to worry more and more about the economic system in America, but have decided to concentrate for now on social values.

The WJ has not been very specific about the actions they propose to take, but there are hints that they would like to see the traditional family structure changed, and have argued that the traditional family has kept women in a subordinate position for too long. They would like to keep social conservatives out of public office, and have stated that they would like to screen candidates to make sure they do not support fundamentalist, pro-life programs. They believe that abortions should be made freely available and that birth control clinics should be put in all high schools and many junior high schools so that adolescents can get birth control easily. They have stated that they will not use violence to achieve their aim of limiting the influence of social conservatives in America.

Another part of the WJ program has been to blame beliefs in the Christian religion for the status of women in American society and has argued forcefully that secular humanism should be the official norm of the United States. They have led the fight to not allow prayers (or moments of silence) in schools and want to keep religion out of schools. The WJ would like to restrict the college experience to large research universities and to do away with small denominational Christian institutions across the country. Although they have not explicitly said so, it appears likely they would institute a screening program to weed out conservative college professors.

Probability Manipulation

LOW: The WJ has tried raising money for an advertising campaign, but public opinion polls show that few people are paying much attention to them. In fact, many people find their views objectionable, and most people are apathetic about the group and its agenda. The group has grown some in recent years, but most political analysts have classified it as another in a long line of extremist groups in the U.S. that simply do not appeal to the bulk of the moderate American public. Analysts agree that they might indeed do harm to some male groups and individuals but they have little chance of gaining any significant political power.

HIGH: The WJ has already amassed large sums of money for a sophisticated and subtle advertising campaign. Public opinion polls show that although they are not likely to win any major national elections soon, more and more people – particularly young people – are beginning to listen to their message and to find some value in it. Most people do not agree with everything they say, but do find some points appealing. This is evidenced by some electoral gains that the WJ has begun to register in local elections in some parts of the country, particularly in the Northeast, parts of the Midwest, and in northern California. Some public opinion polls indicate that as much as 10% of the public feels sympathy for the WJ and its point of view, and the percentage appears to be on the rise. Several conservative groups are taking the threat very seriously indeed and have begun an urgent campaign to combat the WJ.

Normative Violations Manipulation

REASSURING: The WJ has begun to hold public rallies to generate support for their cause. Before their rallies, they cooperated with the police and local authorities and promised to have peaceful demonstrations according to the conditions of their parade permits. They have marched along the designated routes and did not cause any trouble with counter demonstrators, spectators or the police. At the rallies and demonstrations, leaders of the WJ have asked their supporters to act vigorously but as lawfully as possible to pursue their cause.

THREATENING: The WJ has begun to hold public rallies to generate support for their cause. Before their rallies, they refused to cooperate with the police and local authorities but did promise to have peaceful demonstrations according to the conditions of their parade permits. However, they have not always marched along the designated routes and have gotten enmeshed with counter demonstrators and the police. As a result violence has broken out at some of the rallies. Fist fights and rock throwing have resulted in spectators, demonstrators and some police getting hurt. Members of the WJ have shouted "Prayer out of school" and "Freedom to choose – get the Christian nuts." At the rallies and demonstrations, leaders of the WJ have asked their supporters to take bold actions to pursue their cause.

AMERICANS AGAINST THE MILITARY (AAM)

Now we would like you to read the following scenario about a hypothetical group that has organized in the United States. While you read the scenario, please think about how you and the people in your social network would react to such a group.

Suppose it is the late 1990s and a new political group has been formed in the United States. It is an extremist left-wing reaction to the Reagan years in America. This group – the Americans Against the Military (AAM) – has pledged to rid the United States of the influence of the military-industrial complex, which they believe has grown too great. They believe that people who are pro-defense have pushed for too much defense spending and are making the world unsafe by increasing the number of nuclear weapons being produced. Recent evidence of this, they believe, is the money being spent on SDI (Star Wars) and the unwillingness of the government to reach an arms control agreement with the Soviet Union. They believe that American society has become too militaristic, and blame pro-defense people for this. They are also beginning to worry more and more about the power and influence of the wealthy and business people, but have decided to concentrate for now on people who are pro-defense.

The AAM has not been very specific about the actions they propose to take, but there are hints that they would like the United States to unilaterally disarm itself of nuclear weapons, cut all defense spending on nuclear weapons, and stop all research into advanced weapons systems. They would like to keep pro-military people out of public office, and have stated that campaign contributions from defense contractors and pro-defense groups have been used to buy off politicians and help maintain an overly militarized political system in the U.S. They believe that concessions should be made to the Soviet Union on defense issues and numerous social exchanges should be set up to aid in creating friendly relations with the Soviets. They have stated that they will not use violence to achieve their aim of limiting the influence of pro-defense people in America.

Another part of the AAM program seems to be the formation of a much stronger alliance with leftist countries, such as Cuba and Nicaragua. They want to dramatically change United States foreign policy by strongly favoring the current Nicaraguan government, opposing the CIA's activities in Nicaragua and other Central American countries, and increasing student exchanges with communist countries. The AAM would like to restrict the college experience to large research universities and do away with small denominational Christian institutions across the country. Although they have not explicitly said so, it appears likely they would institute a screening program to weed out conservative college professors.

Probability Manipulation

LOW: The AAM has tried raising money for an advertising campaign, but public opinion polls show that few people are paying much attention to them. In fact, many people find their views objectionable, and most people are apathetic about the group and its agenda. The group has grown some in recent years, but most political analysts have classified it as another in a long line of extremist groups in the U.S. that simply do not appeal to the bulk of the moderate American public. Analysts agree that they might indeed do harm to some conservative groups and individuals but they have little chance of gaining any significant political power.

HIGH: The AAM has already amassed large sums of money for a sophisticated and subtle advertising campaign. Public opinion polls show that although they are not likely to win any major national elections soon, more and more people – particularly young people – are beginning to listen to their message and to find some value in it. Most people do not agree with everything they say, but do find some points appealing. This is evidenced by some electoral gains that the AAM has begun to register in local elections in some parts of the country, particularly in the Northeast and in northern California. Some public opinion polls indicate that as much as 10% of the public feels sympathy for the AAM and its point of view, and the percentage appears to be on the rise. Several conservative groups are taking the threat very seriously indeed and have begun an urgent campaign to combat the AAM.

Normative Violations Manipulation

REASSURING: The AAM has begun to hold public rallies to generate support for their cause. Before their rallies, they cooperated with the police and local authorities and promised to have peaceful demonstrations according to the conditions of their parade permits. They have marched along the designated routes and did not cause any trouble with counter demonstrators, spectators or the police. At the rallies and demonstrations, leaders of the AAM have asked their supporters to act vigorously but as lawfully as possible to pursue their cause.

THREATENING: The AAM has begun to hold public rallies to generate support for their cause. Before their rallies, they refused to cooperate with the police and local authorities but did promise to have peaceful demonstrations according to the conditions of their parade permits. However, they have not always marched along the designated routes and have gotten enmeshed with counter demonstrators and the police. As a result violence has broken out at some of the rallies. Fist fights and rock throwing have resulted in spectators, demonstrators and some police getting hurt. Members of the AAM have shouted "Down with the military industrial complex – put the killer generals in jail" and "The military is evil and must be abolished." At the rallies and demonstrations, leaders of the AAM have asked their supporters to take bold actions to pursue their cause.

WSF REVISED SCENARIO–FALL 1993 TEXAS STUDY

Now we would like you to read the following scenario about a hypothetical group that has organized in the United States. While you read the scenario, please think about how you and the people in your social network would react to such a group.

Suppose it is early in the twenty-first century and a new political group has been formed in the United States. It is an extremist group that evolved from the Ku Klux Klan of the 1980s and early 1990s. This group, the White Supremacist Faction (WSF), has pledged to rid the United States of Black influence which they believe has grown too great. They believe that Blacks have been favored by liberal government policies and have taken advantage of the system. Recent evidence of this, they believe, is the massive affirmative action efforts of recent decades and the various special job training programs in Black neighborhoods and communities, as well as attempts to integrate schools. They also believe that American society has lowered its standards, and blame Blacks for this. They claim that

Blacks are inferior to White Americans and do not have the same high moral standards or family values as whites. The WSF is also beginning to worry more and more about the power and influence of Jews but has decided for now to concentrate on Blacks.

The WSF has not been very specific about the actions they propose to take, but there are hints that they would like to restrict the economic and political rights of Blacks and perhaps even Jews. They would like to keep Blacks out of public office, and have stated that they also want to screen white candidates to make sure they do not support programs designed to help disadvantaged minorities. They would like to eliminate many job and welfare programs. They have stated that they will not use violence to achieve their aim of limiting Black influence in America.

Another part of the WSF program seems to be restricting entry into colleges and universities, largely because they perceive them to be the major training ground for the Black middle classes and liberal intellectuals. They think that Blacks and white intellectuals have masterminded the decay of white middle-class values and have assisted in creating and maintaining a liberal stranglehold on the political system in the United States. The WSF would like to restrict the college experience to small, denominational, Christian institutions and to do away with large research universities across the country. They want to ensure that only the physically and intellectually "fit" are allowed to attend college and to become part of the governing classes in the U.S. Although they have not explicitly said so, it appears that they want to institute a screening program to weed out dangerous college professors.

Democratic Norms

NEGATIVE: (Low source credibility): The WSF held a rally to generate support for its cause. During rallies of the WSF, television reporters sought the reaction of bystanders. One person said in an interview:

(High source credibility): The WSF held a rally to generate support for its cause. During rallies of the WSF, television reporters sought the reaction of experts. One state judge said in an interview:

While the First Amendment protects freedom of speech, those rights are not absolute. Groups like the WSF shouldn't be allowed to say the things they're saying because the group does not seem to respect the rights of others. In fact, it presents an outright danger to the rights and freedoms of law-abiding citizens in our country. If people like that get into power, they would do away with freedom of speech and persecute those who disagree with them. They would destroy this great democracy and would take away our Constitution and Bill of Rights. People like that should not be given a chance to destroy the very rights that protect them. After all, this is a democracy, and in a democracy the majority sets the rules that everyone has to follow. Those rules mean protecting all of us from extremists in the minority. Furthermore, their ideas can cause political disorder and instability. In order to protect civil liberties for most of us, we need to stop these extremists from misusing freedom of speech.

POSITIVE: (Low source credibility): The WSF held a rally to generate support for its cause. During rallies of the WSF, television reporters sought the reaction of bystanders. One person said in an interview:
(High source credibility): The WSF held a rally to generate support for its cause. During rallies of the WSF, television reporters sought the reaction of experts. One state judge said in an interview:

The First Amendment of the Constitution says that we have freedom of speech, so that members of groups like the WSF can speak their minds freely. Freedom means allowing minority groups like the WSF to persuade people that their views should be the majority view. After all, free speech in our system is supposed to invite dispute. Really, free speech might be at its finest when it creates dissatisfaction or discomfort. A lack of dissent in a society actually indicates weakness, while dissent itself allows a stronger society to develop. One great quality of the United States is that our freedom is far greater than in other countries, like South Africa or China. The Bill of Rights guarantees everyone's right to express their views, so no matter how much I dislike the message of this group, the members should have the freedom to speak out on public issues.

Normative Violation

THREATENING: After the Rodney King verdict, and in wake of the Los Angeles riots that followed, the members of the WSF held additional public rallies to generate support for their cause. Before their rallies, they refused to cooperate with the police and local authorities but did promise to have peaceful demonstrations according to the conditions of their parade permits. However, they have not always marched along the designated routes and have gotten enmeshed with counter demonstrators and the police. The police have suggested that they cannot be trusted and might be dangerous. In fact, at some of the rallies, fist fights and rock throwing have resulted in spectators, demonstrators and some police getting hurt. Members of the WSF have shouted "Whites only, down with Blacks," and "First get the dirty N————, then the Jews." At the rallies and demonstrations, leaders of the WSF have asked their supporters to take bold actions to pursue their cause, that the ends justify the means.

REASSURING: The WSF held more demonstrations. Before their rallies, they cooperated with the police and local authorities and promised to have peaceful demonstrations according to the conditions of their parade permits. The police have suggested that they can be trusted and are not dangerous. The WSF have marched along the designated routes and did not cause any trouble with counter demonstrators, spectators or the police. At the rallies and demonstrations, leaders of the WSF have asked their supporters to act vigorously but as lawfully as possible to pursue their cause.

Methodological Approaches and Scales

We present in this section the scale items and scales used in the reported research. We adopted the following guidelines in selecting scales. First, we relied on published scales where possible in order to use widely known measures. Second, we evaluated all scales for reliability and construct validity, dropping individual items that reduced the scale's reliability or undermined the construct validity. The items we dropped from the final scales are listed below and noted.

Third, in creating scales, missing data often pose a major problem. If a single response is omitted, the scale cannot be built and that case is treated as missing. With many scales the problem of missing data can often truncate a data set by one-fourth or even more. In order to preserve as many cases as possible, we used a mean value for all scales with the important provisos that a mean would be used if and only if the majority of items in a scale had a valid response. For example, if at least four out of six scale items had a valid response, then we used the mean score of the four, five, or six items as the scale value for that case (for seven items we required five valid responses, and so forth). If fewer than four items were valid responses (i.e., not missing) then a missing value was assigned this case. We have rerun our analyses using both the mean scales and scales that delete cases when any item in the scale is a missing value. The results do not differ substantively, though, of course, more cases are retained when the scales are constructed as described. In the expertise study, where we have more than sufficient cases, we do not use mean replacement in our scales.

Fourth, experiments offer the opportunity for replication. Whenever it was feasible, we have repeated our experiments to further corroborate the robustness of the finding. By and large, we have used the same scales to measure key concepts. However, with regard to the personality measures, we departed from this practice. In the adult study, we replaced the Tellegen measures of personality with those developed by Costa and McCrae. We did so to gain more efficient and more reliable personality measures. The short form of the NEO scales offered greater reliability with, on balance, fewer items. Moreover, both personality measures, though adopting different names for the principal dimensions, nonetheless have been shown to be equivalent for these dimensions (Costa & McCrae, 1985).

Finally, we report our results in analysis of covariance models. By doing so, we introduce our scales – as covariates – in ANOVA models. We report the results in the standard fashion, F tests and probability levels. With analysis of covariance we also obtain the regression coefficients of the covariates (b's). Regression coefficients are less readily interpretable because the magnitude of the coefficient is influenced, in part, by the range of the scale. Change the range (typically that involves standardizing to a o-to-1 range) and the coefficient will change. We have chosen to standardize the underlying scales before introducing them into the analysis of covariance. One principal use of standardizing is to make comparisons across different covariates and to facilitate comparison with treatment effects. Since our treatments are arbitrary (that is, we claim that the treatments and the differences they may produce in the experiments are *not* likely to mirror what real-world stimuli produce) we choose to standardize our various scales only to afford greater comparison across the various studies, as well as to enable us to compare the relative impact of the different covariates.

Standing Decision Political Tolerance Scale

Coefficient alpha for the combined basic studies is .81, for the democratic-norms experiment is .76, and is .78 for the 1993 Texas study.

*1. Members of the [subject selected least-liked group] should be banned from running for public office in the U.S.

2. Members of the [subject selected least-liked group] should be allowed to teach in public schools.

*3. The [subject selected least-liked group] should be outlawed.

4. Members of the [subject selected least-liked group] should be allowed to make a public speech.

*5. The [subject selected least-liked group] should have their phones tapped by our government.

6. The [subject selected least-liked group] should be allowed to hold public rallies.

*reversed

Political Tolerance – Contemporary Judgment Scale

Coefficient alpha for the combined basic studies is .86, for the democratic norms experiment is .80, and is .86 for the 1993 Texas study.

*1. Members of the [scenario group presented to subject] should be banned from running for public office in the U.S.

2. Members of the [scenario group presented to subject] should be allowed to teach in public schools.

*3. The [scenario group presented to subject] should be outlawed.

4. Members of the [scenario group presented to subject] should be allowed to make a public speech.

*5. The [scenario group presented to subject] should have their phones tapped by our government.

6. The [scenario group presented to subject] should be allowed to hold public rallies.

*reversed

Standing Decision Democratic Principles Scale

Coefficient alpha for the combined basic studies is .70, for the democratic norms experiment is .73, and is .72 for the 1993 Texas study.

*1. If someone is suspected of treason or other serious crimes, he should not be entitled to be released on bail.

*2. Society shouldn't have to put up with those who have political ideas that are extremely different from the views of the majority.

*3. When the country is in great danger we may have to force people to testify against themselves even if it violates their rights.

4. Free speech ought to be allowed for all political groups even if some of the things these groups believe in are highly insulting and threatening to particular segments of society.

5. No matter what a person's political beliefs are, he is entitled to the same legal rights and protections as anyone else.

6. It is refreshing to hear someone stand up for an unpopular view.

7. I believe in free speech for all no matter what their views might be.

   *reversed

Need-for-Cognition Scale

ITEMS FROM CACIOPPO AND PETTY'S NEED-FOR-COGNITION SCALE: Coefficient alpha is .69 in the basic experiment, .70 in the democratic-norms experiment, and .70 for the 1993 Texas study.

1. I would prefer complex to simple problems.

2. I feel relief rather than satisfaction after completing a task that required a lot of mental effort.

3. I like to have the responsibility of handling a situation that requires a lot of thinking.

4. I find satisfaction in deliberating hard and for long hours.

*****5.** Thinking is not my idea of fun.

*****6.** I only think as hard as I have to.

7. I usually end up deliberating about issues even when they do not affect me personally.

   *reversed

Standing Decision Threat Scale

ITEMS FROM THE PRETEST QUESTIONNAIRE: Coefficient alpha is .68 for the combined basic studies and .71 for the 1993 Texas study.

Now, please read some pairs of adjectives that can be used to describe the group you selected. Taking each pair one at a time, please circle the number that comes closest to describing the group you dislike the most. Just circle a number between 1 and 7 to reflect how you would describe the group with that pair of adjectives. If you don't know, just circle the 8.

1.	Very honest						Very dishonest	Don't know
	1	2	3	4	5	6	7	8
2.	Very trustworthy						Very untrustworthy	Don't know
	1	2	3	4	5	6	7	8
3.	Very dangerous						Very safe	Don't know
	1	2	3	4	5	6	7	8
4.	Very violent						Very non-violent	Don't know
	1	2	3	4	5	6	7	8
5.	Very good						Very bad	Don't know
	1	2	3	4	5	6	7	8

Appendix B

Predisposition Threat Scale

ITEMS FROM THE PRETEST QUESTIONNAIRE: Coefficient alpha is 70 for the combined basic studies and .65 for the Texas study.

Now, keeping these same groups in mind, how threatening do you believe each group is to our country as a whole. On a scale from 1 to 11, suppose 1 means that the group is not at all threatening to the country, 11 means that the group is very threatening to the country, and the middle number – 6 – means that the group is somewhat threatening to the country. Now, let's take religious fundamentalists. On this scale between 1 and 11, circle the number which best describes how threatening you believe each group is to the country as a whole.

	Not at all threatening to the country				Somewhat threatening to the country					Very threatening to the country	
1. Religious fundamentalists	1	2	3	4	5	6	7	8	9	10	11
2. American communists	1	2	3	4	5	6	7	8	9	10	11
3. Ku Klux Klan	1	2	3	4	5	6	7	8	9	10	11
4. American Nazis	1	2	3	4	5	6	7	8	9	10	11
5. Those who are prolife on abortion	1	2	3	4	5	6	7	8	9	10	11
6. Those who are prochoice on abortion	1	2	3	4	5	6	7	8	9	10	11
7. Those who oppose any prayer or religion in the public schools	1	2	3	4	5	6	7	8	9	10	11
8. Feminists	1	2	3	4	5	6	7	8	9	10	11
9. American racists	1	2	3	4	5	6	7	8	9	10	11
10. Socialists	1	2	3	4	5	6	7	8	9	10	11
11. Those who actively oppose nuclear weapons and our foreign policy	1	2	3	4	5	6	7	8	9	10	11

Costa and McCrae's Personality Scales – NEO Dimensions
(short form)

ITEMS FROM NEUROTICISM SCALE: Coefficient alpha is .84 in adult experiment (experiment 3) and .86 for the 1993 Texas study.

   *1. I am not a worrier.
   2. I often feel inferior to others.
   3. When I'm under a great deal of stress, sometimes I feel like I'm going to pieces.
   *4. I rarely feel lonely or blue.
   5. I often feel tense and jittery.
   6. Sometimes I feel completely worthless.
   *7. I rarely feel fearful or anxious.
   8. I often get angry at the way people treat me.
   9. Too often, when things go wrong, I get discouraged and feel like giving up.
   *10. I am seldom sad or depressed.
   11. I often feel helpless and want someone else to solve my problems.
   12. At times I have been so ashamed I just want to hide.

*reversed

ITEMS FROM EXTRAVERSION SCALE: Coefficient alpha is .82 in adult experiment (experiment 3) and .78 for the 1993 Texas study.

   1. I like to have a lot of people around me.
   2. I laugh easily.
   *3. I don't consider myself especially "light-hearted."
   4. I really enjoy talking to people.
   5. I like to be where the action is.
   *6. I usually prefer to do things alone.
   7. I often feel as if I'm bursting with energy.
   8. I am a cheerful, high-spirited person.
   *9. I am not a cheerful optimist.
   10. My life is fast-paced.
   11. I am a very active person.
   *12. I would rather go my own way than be a leader of others.

*reversed

ITEMS FROM OPENNESS SCALE: Coefficient alpha is .80 in adult experiment (experiment 3) and .76 for the 1993 Texas study.

*1. I don't like to waste my time daydreaming.

*2. Once I find the right way to do something, I stick to it.

3. I am intrigued by the patterns I find in art and nature.

*4. I believe letting students hear controversial speakers can only confuse and mislead them.

5. Poetry has little or no effect on me.

6. I often try new and foreign foods.

*7. I seldom notice the moods or feelings that different environments produce.

*8. I believe we should look to our religious authorities for decisions on moral issues.

9. Sometimes when I am reading poetry or looking at a work of art, I feel a chill or wave of excitement.

*10. I have little interest in speculating on the nature of the universe or the human condition.

11. I have a lot of intellectual curiosity.

12. I often enjoy playing with theories or abstract ideas.

*reversed

Political Tolerance Behavioral Intentions Scale

Coefficient alpha for the combined basic studies is .79 for the tolerant and .82 for the intolerant.

Suppose a local judge issued an order [those who gave a tolerant answer on last question in contemporary tolerance judgment scale – *forbidding*; those who gave an intolerant answer on last question in contemporary tolerance judgment scale – *allowing*] that group to hold a public rally in your community. How likely do you think you would be to do each of the following?

Tolerant Behavioral Intentions

	Definitely would	Probably would	Probably would not	Definitely would not
1. I would vote against that judge in the next election.	4	3	2	1
2. I would join a peaceful demonstration supporting their right to hold a public rally.	4	3	2	1
3. I would join an effort to appeal that decision to try to reverse it.	4	3	2	1
4. I would sign a petition objecting to the judge's decision not to allow them to hold a public rally.	4	3	2	1
5. I would accept the decision of the judge and do nothing.	4	3	2	1

Intolerant Behavioral Intentions

	Definitely would	Probably would	Probably would not	Definitely would not
1. I would vote against that judge in the next election.	4	3	2	1
2. I would join a peaceful demonstration against allowing them to hold a public rally.	4	3	2	1
3. I would try to stop them from holding their public rally even if I had to use force.	4	3	2	1
4. I would join an effort to appeal that decision to try to reverse it.	4	3	2	1
5. I would sign a petition objecting to the judge's decision allowing them to hold a public rally.	4	3	2	1
6. I would accept the decision of the judge and do nothing.	4	3	2	1

Political Knowledge (Expertise) Items

Coefficient alpha for the 1993 Texas Study is .80

Finally, here are a few questions about the government in Washington. Many people don't know the answers to these questions, so if there are some you don't know, just check that space and move on.

1. Whose responsibility is it to nominate federal judges?

_____   ___ don't know/not sure

2. What are the first ten amendments called?

_____   ___ don't know/not sure

3. Which party has the most seats in the Senate?

_____   ___ don't know/not sure

4. What position is held by William H. Rehnquist?

_____   ___ don't know/not sure

5. What position is held by Tom Foley?

_____   ___ don't know/not sure

6. How many U.S. senators represent the state of California?

_____   ___ don't know/not sure

7. How many years is the term of a United States Congressman/woman in the House of Representatives?

_____   ___ don't know/not sure

The following questions ask you to categorize a number of contemporary political leaders as politically liberal or conservative. Please read the name carefully and then circle the label that best describes the official.

8. Jack Kemp	liberal	conservative	don't know/not sure
9. Alan Cranston	liberal	conservative	don't know/not sure
10. Robert Dole	liberal	conservative	don't know/not sure
11. Richard Gephart	liberal	conservative	don't know/not sure
12. Ronald Reagan	liberal	conservative	don't know/not sure
13. Michael Dukakis	liberal	conservative	don't know/not sure
14. Jesse Helms	liberal	conservative	don't know/not sure

15. Do you happen to know the job or political office now held by Al Gore?

16. Whose responsibility is it to determine if a law is constitutional or not? Is it the president, the Congress or the Supreme Court?

_____ President

_____ Congress

_____ Supreme Court

17. How much of a majority is required for the U.S. Senate and House to override a presidential veto?

18. Do you happen to know which party has the most members in the House of Representatives?

19. Would you say that one of the parties is more conservative than the other at the national level? Which party is more conservative?

Notes

1: POLITICAL TOLERANCE AND DEMOCRATIC PRACTICE

1. This explanation parallels one offered for the lack of ideological thinking displayed by the American public (Converse, 1964; Neuman, 1986; Smith, 1989). Some have argued that the lack of ideological thinking results from the inability of many to link various policy issues and to organize them according to some more general ideological principle.

2. Spinoza and Kant are representative of the dominant view. Thomas Hobbes and David Hume would support Pascal.

2: ANTECEDENT CONSIDERATIONS AND CONTEMPORARY INFORMATION

1. Although Barber's analysis incorporated factors other than predispositions, in comparison to other approaches he places relatively greater emphasis on predispositions.

2. This conceptualization is similar to that held by Pierce and Rose (1974), who argued that an attitude is a range rather than a discrete point on a scale. Social judgment theory proposes a slightly different conceptualization, holding that attitudes consist of three latitudes: one of acceptance, one of rejection, and one of noncommitment (Sherif & Hovland, 1961; Sherif, Sherif, & Nebergall, 1965).

3. Ajzen (1988) made a similar distinction between personality traits and attitudes. He argued that attitudes are directed at specific targets and are relatively malleable, whereas personality traits are responses in a broader domain and are much less malleable. Ajzen further argued that both traits and attitudes are stable and enduring. These characterizations of personality traits and attitudes reflect our definitions of predispositions and standing decisions, respectively.

4. Sullivan, Pierson, and Marcus (1982) argued that citizens can tolerate only groups they dislike. If they like a group and grant it rights, they are indicating support, not tolerance. They further argued that tolerance judgments are part of a two-stage process. Citizens first identify potential target groups

whose ideas they dislike, and then they decide how much or how little to tolerate those groups. From this understanding, the authors developed the "least-liked group" approach to studying tolerance. First, respondents identify the group (or groups) they like the least. Then they indicate how far they are willing to extend ordinary rights and liberties to that group. We discuss this approach more fully in Chapter 7.

5. "Support for tolerance and civil liberties becomes still more remarkable when we consider how much social learning is needed before people will not only permit but also protect ideas and conduct they consider morally or socially unacceptable" (McClosky & Brill, 1983: p. 15). The authors emphasize how easy it is to be intolerant, and the difficult cognitive demands made by tolerance.

6. It is important to note, however, that about one-fourth of those giving the intolerant response suggested that the Klan, because of its ideology, did not deserve the basic civil liberties accorded to other groups. These responses suggest that they had already made a standing decision to be intolerant of the KKK because of its nature and ideology. Information about this particular situation or march did not affect their views. They were in favor of allowing other groups to demonstrate, but the particular qualities of the Klan led them to be intolerant.

3: THINKING AND MOOD

1. See Marcus (1991) for a review of how academic psychology has recently understood affect. Until recently, research in social cognition has largely ignored affect, or treated it as primarily derivative of cognitive processes (Fiske, 1981; Fiske & Pavelchak, 1985; Lazarus, 1982, 1984; Schachter & Singer, 1962).

2. In psychology, the term reinforcer is used to describe the effect of reward and nonpunishment, on the one hand, and nonreward and punishment on the other. Put more simply, positive reinforcers are good things (e.g., food) or signs related to good things (e.g., a meal bell that regularly accompanies the arrival of food). Negative reinforcers are those that disappoint (e.g., something good that was anticipated to arrive, but did not) or that punish (e.g., food that has spilled).

3. The fight/flight system modulates the emotions of rage and terror. It is a simple but powerful system. Direct sensory input of punishment or nonreward (but not secondary stimuli that signal punishment or nonreward) are the particular stimuli that trigger this system. In addition to generating rage or terror, the fight/flight system initiates specific behaviors of either unconditioned escape or defensive aggression. Terror is the affect associated with the first and rage is the affect associated with the second. For the most part, the determination of which behavioral response may occur is dependent upon whether the environment will allow escape. If it does, unconditioned escape is the response; if not, defensive aggression is the response. This system is engaged only in conditions of *direct*, painful, punishing experience.

4. To a psychologist, the first kind of threat, unpredictability, defines set-

tings of uncertainty – circumstances where the unfolding events cannot be anticipated – and the second kind of threat, danger, defines settings that are anticipated to be punishing or unrewarding.

5. Therefore the name, behavioral inhibition system (BIS). By using the term display, we mean to include not only a direct appearance of a threat but also any mediated signals that have come to represent a novel intrusion or threat.

6. And, we should add, this description applies to most normal individuals. Shifts in mood readily occur as new circumstances or new information warrant. There are psychiatric conditions, such as fear of being in an open space, in which people are not responsive to changing circumstances or in which they are overreactive (i.e., have a heightened anxiety to an undifferentiated and overly wide array of cues). Here, we ignore such clinical conditions.

7. The schematic portraits of the two limbic systems in Figure 3.1 and 3.2 simplify and therefore obscure two important aspects of neural systems. First, all neurological networks have feedback processes; i.e., information flows both ways, not in one way as depicted in these figures (Kossly & Koenig, 1992). Second, there are two pathways from the sensory inputs, not just the single pathway depicted. The second pathway goes to the neocortex for processing so there is a "top-down" as well as "bottom-up" pathway (Mishkin & Appenzeller, 1987). It is beyond the scope of our work to describe all the complex interconnections that a proper account of neural networks justifies. Here we intend to give a general and simplified account of how these two limbic systems process information and then influence conscious awareness and behavior. Further, we simplify the two outputs of each system by representing them as dichotomous and discrete states. This is a distortion. We should think of the two outputs as ends of a continuum rather than as discrete opposites.

8. Psychologists over the past decade have conducted many studies of mood. They have consistently found a two-dimensional pattern, a dense circle or circumplex, within which could be placed all the emotional responses people describe (Plutchik, 1980; Russell & Bullock, 1985; Watson & Tellegen, 1985). Comparative studies have consistently reported the same two-dimensional structure (Almagor & Ben-Porath, 1989; Russell, 1983; Russell, Lewicka, & Niit, 1989a; Watson, Clark, & Tellegen, 1984). Finally, considerable psychometric attention has been paid to the measurement of affect relying on the circumplex model (Plutchik & Kellerman, 1989; Russell, Weiss, & Mendelsohn, 1989b; Watson, 1988a, b; Watson, Clark, & Tellegen, 1988).

9. As we have noted, we do not mean to suggest that moods of anxiety are stimulated only by a physical appearance of a threat. As both the BAS and BIS are learning systems, they enable people to associate a variety of mediating stimuli with more directly rewarding or punishing stimuli. For example, we often become anxious when we see representations that we have come to associate with the appearance of threat. We learn from distant or mediated representations, such as news stories or reports from friends or neighbors, and these can be as threatening or reassuring as a physical appearance that is directly before us.

10. The fight/flight system is not central to our analysis.

4: TOLERANCE JUDGMENTS AND CONTEMPORARY INFORMATION

1. Covariates in an analysis of covariance model are continuous variables that are not manipulated in the experimental situation (i.e., they are not part of the experimental manipulation of contemporary influences).

2. Other predispositions and standing decisions will be discussed in subsequent chapters.

3. Scale reliability, as well as a full listing of this and all other items used in our survey-experiments, are provided in Appendix B.

4. The response options ranged from "strongly agree" to "strongly disagree." The highest democratically principled response was assigned a 5 and the lowest a 1.

5. While this paragraph does note that violence occurs, it does not depict the group as engaged in illegal actions or as the direct cause of the violence.

6. The normative violations manipulations for the other hypothetical groups were very similar. Only the group's name was changed in the reassuring paragraph, and in the threatening paragraph we varied what the group yelled at the rally and the group name. See Appendix A for these manipulation paragraphs.

7. In order to enhance credibility, we created two versions of this paragraph that would not be so implausible as to risk incredulity among the subjects. We ran one experiment to test how far we could push people's credulity by having them read one of three paragraphs: the low paragraph, the high paragraph, or an even higher-probability paragraph (not shown). We found that the mean tolerance score of those in the highest-paragraph condition was even higher than the low-probability condition. We therefore assume that subjects questioned the credibility of the group having as much power as the paragraph indicated. In an unpublished study by Professor Michal Shamir (1987) in Israel, a parallel experiment using a more powerful and believable "high" probability paragraph was used. In Israel, unlike the United States, some extreme groups have had significant success in elections (for example, the right-wing extremist group Kach and its former leader, the late Rabbi Meir Kahane). In Shamir's study, the low-probability paragraph had a hypothetical group gaining one to two seats in the Knesset; the high-probability paragraph had the group gaining 20–25% of Knesset seats. Given Israel's proportional representation system, this high-probability manipulation is realistic. Her results on the impact of the probability paragraphs, however, were identical to ours discussed below.

8. The probability of power paragraphs for the six hypothetical groups differed only in the name of the group, the regions of the country where the group was having electoral success, and the type of monitoring organization.

9. Previous work has shown that when subjects are given no instructions with respect to thoughts or feelings, they respond in the same way as if they had been given the affective instruction set (Kuklinski et al., 1987). For this reason, we did not add a control group to this already complex design. We placed the instruction set where we did because of our interest in mood accessibility. We did, however, conduct a study in which people received the instruction set before reading the scenario. The results are discussed in the appendix to this chapter.

10. Interested readers may contact the authors for a full analysis of each of the three data sets.

11. One of the five-way interactions is also significant (study by probability of power by normative violations by order by instruction set) but will not be discussed here.

12. Two hypothetical groups were more tolerated than the others: Christians in Politics and Americans Against the Military.

13. The idea of a baseline is not meant to abandon our earlier conception of attitude latitude. The baseline might itself be a range that has a "center of gravity."

APPENDIX 4A: THE BASIC EXPERIMENTS

1. It is becoming common practice in social and political psychology to conduct an internal analysis – called a manipulation check – to determine whether the treatment succeeded in producing the internal state that constituted the conceptual variable (Aronson, Ellsworth, Carlsmith, & Gonzales, 1990: pp. 213–216). We describe several manipulation-check studies in this appendix.

2. The questionnaire was administered before the Rodney King verdict was announced.

3. Almost 70% selected one of these groups as their least-liked.

4. We conducted a two-way analysis of variance, examining the effects on probability ratings of two factors: whether the respondent read the high- or the low-probability paragraph; and whether the respondent selected a racist or nonracist least-liked group. In each case, the paragraph had a significant effect, whereas the selection of a racist or nonracist least-liked group did not have a significant effect, nor were there any significant interaction effects.

5. As noted in Chapter 1, Millar and Tesser (1986) and Wilson et al. (1989) also found that people made very different decisions when told to think about their choices than when they were told to rely on their feelings.

6. We dropped socialists as an option and replaced it with homosexuals.

7. Affect is central to conducting a manipulation check on the thoughts/feelings instruction. Earlier in this appendix, we demonstrated that affective reactions to the WSF differed between those who selected a racist least-liked group and those who did not. As a result, we concluded that in this manipulation check, we had to revert to our earlier procedure of identifying respondents' least-liked groups and then returning with tailored scenarios. We reduced the complexity of the study by using only one left-wing (FGF) and one right-wing (WSF) target group in the tailored, hypothetical scenarios.

8. The intercoder agreement, between two coders, was 78%. The coders were unaware of which subjects were assigned to which manipulation.

5: THREAT AND POLITICAL TOLERANCE

1. Some have argued that these normative measures of threat are really just evaluations of the group – they all measure whether the respondent likes the group or thinks it is good or bad. The factor loadings (Sullivan, Piereson,

& Marcus, 1982) and correlations with tolerance (see Table 5.1 here) demonstrate that the normative measures capture more than just good/bad evaluations. They measure broader threat perceptions. In fact, four adjective pairs have higher factor loadings than good/bad. Note that predictable/unpredictable has the highest correlation with tolerance.

2. We treat personality, and Gray's account thereof, more fully in Chapter 8.

3. Green and Waxman (1987), however, made imaginative use of the 1972-through-1984 General Social Science surveys to conduct a quasi-experiment that found that the order in which salient target groups were presented to respondents influenced their tolerance judgments.

4. We focus in this chapter on threat as a predisposition and as a standing decision, and exclude other predispositions such as personality. This does not pose a problem of misspecification because the personality measures are not correlated with the measures of threat. We analyze personality predispositions in Chapter 8.

5. Recall that we define a predisposition as a *generalized* disposition that applies across a broad class of phenomena and that tends to be stable and enduring.

6. A standing threat decision is defined as a *specific* belief about a *particular* group or action that is stable, enduring, and has its antecedents in some earlier learning.

7. We measure threat as a contemporary assessment as we have before, by testing for reactions to the manipulations of probability and normative violations information.

8. Although we do not present the findings, we included study and scenario as treatments in order to ensure that their effects would not confound the analyses reported above and to follow. We discussed the impact of these effects in Chapter 4, so we will not present them in Table 5.2 or in the tables that follow. In addition, the two-way interaction between order and normative violations, discussed in Chapter 4, is also unchanged ($p = .04$).

9. In Chapter 7, where we explore the role of expertise, and in Chapter 8, where we explore the role of personality, we find as we do here that the standing decisions seem to encapsulate much, if not all, of the effects of predispositions. In this case, the antecedent threat measures remain influential after taking into account the effects of other standing decisions, but that influence is substantially reduced.

10. In yet another study, to be introduced in Chapter 7, we replicated this overall pattern: threat convictions shape contemporary judgments, although in that study, in part due to its different design, we found threat standing decisions to be more influential than the global threat predisposition. The encapsulation effect was also replicated in that study.

11. In general, we have attempted to divide the samples into unequal groups, with either the high or low segments containing approximately one-quarter of the subjects. In this way, we are comparing those who are very extreme in one direction with everyone else in the sample. We experimented with alternative cutting points and this general rule seemed to work best.

12. This interpretation of the interaction in Figure 5.3 is bolstered by the

fact that, when we contrast those extraordinarily low in threat predispositions with those medium or high, there are no significant interactions.

13. We can speculate that the results displayed in Figure 5.3 might offer some explanation for the conventional expectation that those who are most fearful are also most likely to "project" their fears "blindly" onto convenient targets – those who are more threat sensitive are less tolerant than those who are less threat sensitive. However, when we examine reactions to reassuring information about normative compliance, the threat sensitive subjects take that information into account and adjust their civil liberties decisions slightly more than do the less threat sensitive subjects.

6: DEMOCRATIC VALUES AS STANDING DECISIONS AND CONTEMPORARY INFORMATION

1. A more complete literature review is available in Chapter 2, especially in Figure 2.1.

2. The pretest and posttest tolerance had scale reliabilities of .76 and .80. The reliability of the democratic-norms scale was .73.

3. Recall that when the normative violations paragraph was placed last, the findings in the basic studies showed that the difference between conditions doubled over that shown in the main effect. When placed prior to the probability paragraph, the difference was not significant.

4. The finding that people who have strongly internalized democratic values are less responsive to contemporary information about how to apply these values may be indicative of a more general phenomenon. Utilizing the data from the three basic experiments (Chapter 4), we again divide the sample into those higher (N = 177) and those lower (N = 437) on pretest support for democratic principles. There also we found a significant interaction between antecedent support for democratic norms and the normative violations manipulation (respondents were not exposed to the democratic-norms manipulation in these studies). Those in the higher support group were unaffected by the normative violations information (means for both reassuring and threatening conditions = .67), while those in the lower support group were influenced (the mean for the reassuring condition = .54 and the mean for the threatening condition = .45). Thus, it may be that those stronger in their commitment to democratic principles are generally unresponsive to contemporary information when they make their tolerance judgments.

5. To test this idea, we created two subscales from the tolerance items. The direct tolerance scale focused on items mentioned in the scenario as important, such as freedom of speech, the right to hold a public rally, and the right of the group to exist (alpha = .80). The indirect tolerance scale focused on items that, while related to tolerance, were not specifically mentioned in the scenario, such as the government tapping phones, or members of the group running for public office or teaching in the public schools (alpha = .60). Both scales range from 3 to 15. No significant differences existed between the experimental effects when analyzed with these smaller scales. However, the main effect of democratic norms was slightly stronger on the direct measures of tolerance. This

may indicate that support for civil liberties is likely to increase when discussions
of democratic rights include the specific liberties under contention, rather than
abstractions about general rights.

7: THE TEXAS EXPERIMENT

1. The new scenario also placed the formation of the group at the beginning of the twenty-first century, rather than the end of the 1990s. Otherwise
the scenario was identical to that reported in Chapter 4.

2. The posttest was administered to students two weeks after the first survey,
as in our previous experiments.

3. Manipulation checks showed significant differences between subjects'
perceptions of the reassuring and threatening paragraphs. Subjects read either
the threatening or reassuring paragraph and then rated the group's threat –
its belligerence, treachery, dangerousness, dishonesty, and untrustworthiness.
Those who read the reassuring paragraph had an average threat score of .66,
while those who read the threatening paragraph had an average threat score
of .78 ($p < .05$). Comparing this manipulation check with that reported in
Appendix 4A shows that the new paragraphs were more effective.

4. Since the influence of threat antecedent considerations is substantively
modest, though statistically significant, we exclude them from the models presented in this chapter. The substantive results presented here are not affected
by this model specification.

5. But see Rahn et al. (1990), who argue that expert–novice differences in
the decisional processes that lead to presidential-vote choice should be minimal
because of the ease of information acquisition and the redundancy of information during such visible, salient media campaigns. Their data showed few
differences in the factors that influenced experts' and novices' presidential-vote
choice.

6. Table 7.2 includes a dummy variable for whether the respondent selected a robust least-liked group. As shown in the next section of this chapter,
there are significant differences in both tolerance and decision making processes between these two types of respondents. As a result, the racist group
dummy variable in Table 7.2 has a significant effect on tolerance judgments,
and there are two significant interactions between this dummy variable and
contemporary influences: the instruction set by racist group interaction is significant ($p = .06$) as is the normative violations by racist group interaction ($p
= .09$). Analyzing those who selected a racist group separately from those who
selected a nonracist group shows that the three-way interaction between normative violations, expertise, and the racist group dummy variable is insignificant
in both cases. We will discuss the significance of the interactions with the racist
group in the following section.

7. The one-to-eleven–point scale was transformed to zero-to-one with a
mean score of .79. Those below that point exhibited low animus and those
above it strong animus.

8. Levels of dislike and threat perceived from racist groups are the average
dislike and threat placed on a zero-to-one scale.

9. Of course, for the low-animus respondents, our conceptualization of tolerance would lead us to interpret this high score as evidence of support, not tolerance.

10. In fact, the low-animus respondents had a lower level of pretest support for democratic principles than the higher-animus respondents ($p < .01$). So their apparently higher level of "tolerance" does not reflect a general commitment to democratic norms. It just means that they do not object to racist groups and hence cannot be said to tolerate them.

8: INDIVIDUAL DIFFERENCES – PERSONALITY

1. Gray and Eysenck disagree about the exact form of each of these dimensions, though they are in general agreement. Currently there is a consensus forming around a "big five" typology of personality (Digman, 1989; John, 1990). The first three of these five, most often labeled social adaptability, emotional control, and conformity, are generally held to be roughly equivalent to Eysenck and Gray's three dimensions.

2. Thus, it seems similar to the extraversion dimension in that those low on this dimension, like the extraverts, are more assertive, confident, and wide-ranging.

3. Although Gray's third dimension is linked to the fight/flight system, Costa and McCrae (1985) call it openness to experience.

4. There is strong evidence of personality differences both in the internalization of democratic norms and in levels of political tolerance (McClosky & Brill, 1983; Sullivan et al., 1982).

5. The adult data set did not include the need-for-cognition scale so we postpone a discussion of its role until we present the next data set.

6. The relationship between extraversion and tolerance is also negative in the other two studies – the first Nebraska student sample and the Minnesota student sample. We mention this despite the problems with the personality scales in these samples because they make it unanimous. Extraversion seems to promote intolerance rather than tolerance.

7. The need-for-cognition scale was included in the first Nebraska student study, and in the Minnesota democratic norms study. As we mentioned earlier in this chapter, the other personality scales we used in those studies were not reliable and valid, so we changed to the Costa and McCrae scales in the studies reported in this chapter. However, the need-for-cognition scale worked satisfactorily in both the Nebraska and Minnesota student studies, and both showed the same result as Table 8.2. Need for cognition had a signficant relationship with political tolerance judgments before controls for standing decisions were added, but none afterward. In fact, in these two studies, the regression coefficients between need for cognition and political tolerance (before controlling for standing decisions) were even stronger than in the Texas study reported in Table 8.2. People who take a more intellectual approach to life in general have more tolerant standing decisions than those whose approach is more intuitive or instinctive, and who prefer not to think too much.

8. Throughout his book, Zaller (1992) argues that people with more

knowledge are more likely to be exposed to political information than people who are less knowledgeable. More-knowledgeable individuals are also, however, less likely to be influenced by the information they are exposed to because they have the contextual knowledge to relate the information to their predispositions (e.g., p. 44, axiom A2). In other words, they change less as a result of internalizing contemporary information.

9. We also trichotomized the need-for-cognition scales to see whether McGuire's and Zaller's more general argument about people in the middle of the scale being more responsive was true in this instance. The results were the same using a trichotomy and in both instances, there were no significant differences between the medium and low need-for-cognition groups, thus justifying our decision to collapse them into one group to be contrasted with the high group.

10. Since the need for cognition and expertise both had significant interactions with contemporary information in the Texas data set, we ran the analysis with both variables simultaneously. The interaction between expertise and normative violations, reported in Figure 7.2, remains significant ($p = .07$) when need for cognition is incorporated into the analysis; the interaction between need for cognition and instruction set reported in Figure 8.3 remains significant ($p < .01$) when expertise is incorporated into the analysis. These variables have independent effects.

11. We also explored whether other personality dimensions interacted with any of the treatment variables; there were no strong and consistent results.

9: INTENSITY, MOTIVATIONS, AND BEHAVIORAL INTENTIONS

1. We are making the argument here that attitudes can predict behaviors, but psychologists have also noted that behaviors can predict attitudes (see, e.g., Bem, 1970, 1972) and that behaviors can predict behaviors (see, e.g., Chaiken & Stangor, 1987). For example, we could study the effects on tolerance attitudes of a tolerant person joining an intolerant group and becoming involved in intolerant behaviors.

2. For minor exceptions to this general finding, see Barnum & Sullivan (1989); Duch & Gibson (1992); Fletcher (1988); Gibson & Duch (1991); Shamir (1991); Sniderman, Fletcher, Russell, Tetlock, and Gaines (1991b).

3. One could question whether we have accurately identified tolerant and intolerant behavioral intentions since we have made this determination based on only one of the six tolerance statements. In other words, subjects' tolerant or intolerant responses to the last statement may not reflect their overall tolerance level. To test for this, we ran a difference-of-means test using a scale created from the first five posttest tolerance statements for those who gave a tolerant response and those who gave an intolerant response to the last question. The mean difference in tolerance level for these two groups of subjects is striking: .30 for the intolerant group and .67 for the tolerant group ($p < .01$). We conclude, then, that relying on the single item adequately designates subjects as tolerant or intolerant.

4. This disparity in behavioral intentions between the tolerant and intol-

erant is further corroborated by data from a survey of British citizens. A nationwide survey of 1,266 respondents in England, Wales, and Scotland, conducted in 1986 by Market and Opinion Research International (London), included questions on tolerance and behavioral intentions. Among those who gave an intolerant response to the rally statement, 84% said they would take some kind of action against the judge's decision. Among those who gave a tolerant response, only 36% said they intended to act (Chi-square = 240.7; t = 17.9; $p < .01$). The intolerant British respondents were definitely more likely to indicate a willingness to take action against their least-liked group than were the tolerant British respondents likely to act to defend the group's rights.

5. We exclude the order of presentation of the normative violations and probability paragraphs because our focus is on the main effects in this analysis.

6. Another possible measure of dislike that may be related to behavioral intentions is the degree to which respondents dislike their least-liked group. On a scale that ranges from 0 to 1, the intolerant respondents had a mean dislike score of .98 and the tolerant a mean score of .97. It is obvious that both the tolerant and intolerant respondents disliked their least-liked group intensely. Given the lack of variance on this measure, it is not surprising that this specific dislike intensity measure is not significantly related to either tolerant or intolerant behavioral intentions ($r = -.07$ and $r = .09$, respectively).

7. Perhaps the intolerant are not just less intensely committed to democratic principles but actually are intensely antidemocratic. To test this possibility, we ran a difference-of-means test on support for democratic principles. There is a significant difference in means: .62 for the intolerant and .73 for the tolerant. The scale, however, ranges from 0 to 1, which puts the midpoint at .50. Both the tolerant and the intolerant respondents' means are on the prodemocratic principles side of the scale.

8. Sullivan et al. (1982) similarly found more intense intolerance than tolerance: "Those who are intolerant feel more intensely than those who would protect the norms of tolerance and civil liberties" (p. 84).

9. The current tolerance intensity scale was created in the same way as the standing decision intensity scale, using the posttest tolerance statements (coefficient alpha = .64).

10. We replicated these results using data from a survey of British citizens. Interested readers can contact the authors for this analysis.

10: HUMAN NATURE AND POLITICAL TOLERANCE

1. As pointed out in Chapter 1, how much responsibility citizens should have is hotly debated. At the normative level the issue is whether such responsibilities should be extensive or limited, and at an empirical level, the issue is whether the capacity for wise use of such authority is adequately displayed by the citizenry (Barber, 1984; Dahl, 1977; Mueller, 1992; Pateman, 1970; Sartori, 1987; Schumpeter, 1943).

2. Of course, once people display the capacity to participate, they may nonetheless make fallible choices.

3. We do not mean to suggest that only to the extent that a democratic

citizenry is politically tolerant can a democratic society protect the political rights of its citizens. There are many devices available to a regime to inculcate and protect certain rights. However, to the extent that a citizenry does not believe in political tolerance it is hard to see how a more extensive democratic society can be established or sustained.

4. Zaller notes that contextual information influences the "considerations" people bring to bear when they express an opinion. Thus, people can express a range of opinions depending on which considerations they focus on in a particular context.

5. Of course, depending on the specific character of the contemporary information, it will move some people toward the neutral position. Thus, for example, if a tolerant person felt the group to be violating norms of good behavior and most arguments counseled intolerance, then such a person, especially if not prompted to think through his or her judgment, might become more neutral.

6. The analysis in Chapter 7 reports on the influence of support for democratic principles. While pretest political tolerance had no impact on contemporary tolerance judgments, other antecedent considerations, as we note in Table 10.4, did affect their judgments. The coefficients presented in Table 10.4 are obtained from an analysis of covariance with only the covariates entered (and as none of the manipulations are significant [see Chapter 7], and are in any case randomized, this does not misspecify this analysis).

7. Here we are using the combined weighted data, using the subjects from all three studies described in Chapter 4.

8. The media also play a crucial agenda-setting role in conjunction with cue giving from political elites (Iyengar & Kinder, 1987; Krosnick & Kinder, 1990).

9. It seems to us that David Duke was mindful of the alienating consequences of hateful and violent actions, and so he carefully attempted to distance himself from his prior connection with the Klan. Of course, while many found this change to be successful, far more remained distrustful and skeptical.

10. This is not to suggest that everyone will display the same emotional faculties equally well. Indeed, research suggests that as rational faculties are distributed unevenly, so are affective faculties (Mayer, DiPaolo, & Salovey, 1990; Salovey & Mayer, 1990). As we noted in Chapter 3, the inability to experience emotional responses may be a hallmark of the asocial (Kling, 1986, 1987; Kling & Steklis, 1976).

References

Aboud, F. (1988). *Children and Prejudice.* Oxford: Basil Blackwell.

Achen, C. H. (1975). Mass Political Attitudes and the Survey Response. *American Political Science Review, 69,* 1218–1231.

Ajzen, I. (1988). *Attitudes, Personality, and Behavior.* Milton Keynes: Open University Press.

Ajzen, I., & Fishbein, M. (1969). The Prediction of Behavioral Intentions in a Choice Situation. *Journal of Experimental Social Psychology, 5,* 400–416.

    (1970). The Prediction of Behavior from Attitudinal and Normative Variables. *Journal of Experimental Social Psychology, 6,* 466–487.

    (1977). Attitude–Behavior Relations: A Theoretical Analysis and Review of Empirical Research. *Psychological Bulletin, 84,* 888–918.

    (1980). *Understanding Attitudes and Predicting Social Behavior.* Englewood Cliffs, NJ: Prentice-Hall.

Ajzen, I., & Madden, T. (1986). Prediction of Goal-Directed Behavior: Attitudes, Intentions and Perceived Behavioral Control. *Journal of Experimental Social Psychology, 22,* 453–474.

Allport, G. W. (1954). *The Nature of Prejudice.* Cambridge, MA: Addison-Wesley.

Almagor, M., & Ben-Porath, Y. S. (1989). The Two-Factor Model of Self-Reported Mood: A Cross-Cultural Replication. *Journal of Personality Assessment, 53*(1), 10–21.

Altemeyer, B. (1988). *Enemies of Freedom: Understanding Right-Wing Authoritarianism.* San Francisco: Jossey-Bass.

    (1994). Reducing Prejudice in Right-Wing Authoritarians. In M. P. Zanna & J. M. Olson (eds.), *The Psychology of Prejudice: The Ontario Symposium,* vol. 7 (chapter 6). Hillsdale, NJ: Erlbaum.

Aristotle (1954). *Rhetoric* (W. Rhys Roberts, trans.). New York: Modern Library.

Arkes, H. (1993). Can Emotion Supply the Place of Reason? In G. E. Marcus & R. L. Hanson (eds.), *Reconsidering the Democratic Public* (pp. 287–305). University Park: Pennsylvania State University Press.

Aronson, E., Ellsworth, P. C., Carlsmith, J. M., & Gonzales, M. H. (1990). *Methods of Research in Social Psychology* (2d ed.). New York: McGraw-Hill.

Arrow, K. (1982). Risk Perception in Psychology and Economics. *Economic Inquiry, 20*(1), 1–9.

Avery, P., Bird, K., Johnstone, S., Sullivan, J. L., & Thalhammer, K. (1992). Exploring Political Tolerance with Adolescents. *Theory and Research in Social Education, 20*(4), 386–420.

Bagozzi, R. (1981). Attitudes, Intentions, and Behavior: A Test of Some Key Hypotheses. *Journal of Personality and Social Psychology, 41,* 136–146.

Bandura, A. (1986). *Social Foundations of Thought and Action.* Englewood Cliffs, NJ: Prentice-Hall.

Barber, B. (1984). *Strong Democracy: Participatory Politics for a New Age.* Berkeley and Los Angeles: University of California Press.

Barber, J. D. (1985). *The Presidential Character: Predicting Performance in the White House* (3d ed.). Englewood Cliffs, NJ: Prentice-Hall.

Barnum, D. G., & Sullivan, J. L. (1989). Attitudinal Tolerance and Political Freedom in Britain. *British Journal of Political Science, 19,* 136–146.

   (1990). The Elusive Foundations of Political Freedom in Britain and the United States. *Journal of Politics, 52,* 719–739.

Belknap, G., & Campbell, A. (1951–52). Party Identification and Attitudes toward Foreign Policy. *Public Opinion Quarterly, 15,* 601–623.

Bellah, R. N., Madsen, R., Sullivan, W. M., Swidler, A., & Tipton, S. M. (1985). *Habits of the Heart.* Berkeley and Los Angeles: University of California Press.

Bem, D. (1970). *Beliefs, Attitudes, and Human Affairs.* Belmont, CA: Brooks, Cole.

   (1972). Self-Perception Theory. In L. Berkowitz (ed.), *Advances in Experimental Social Psychology* (pp. 2–62). New York: Academic.

Berelson, B. R., Lazarsfeld, P. F., & McPhee, W. N. (1954). *Voting: A Study of Opinion Formation in a Presidential Campaign.* University of Chicago Press.

Blaney, P. H. (1986). Affect and Memory: A Review. *Psychological Bulletin, 99,* 229–246.

Blight, J. G. (1990). *The Shattered Crystal Ball: Fear and Learning in the Cuban Missile Crisis.* Savage, MD: Rowman & Littlefield.

Boehnke, K., Macpherson, M., Meador, M., & Petri, H. (1989). How West German Adolescents Experience the Nuclear Threat. *Political Psychology, 10*(3), 419–443.

Bogardus, E. S. (1925). Measuring Social Distance. *Journal of Applied Sociology, 9,* 299–308.

Borch, K. H. (1968). *The Economics of Uncertainty.* Princeton, NJ: Princeton University Press.

Bornstein, R. F. (1989). Exposure and Affect: Overview and Meta-analysis of Research, 1968–1987. *Psychological Bulletin, 106,* 265–287.

Bower, G. H. (1981). Mood and Memory. *American Psychologist, 36,* 129–148.

Brady, H., & Sniderman, P. (1985). Attitude Attribution: A Group Basis for Political Reasoning. *American Political Science Review, 79,* 1061–1078.

Brody, R. A. (1991). *Assessing Presidential Character: The Media, Elite Opinion, and Public Support.* Stanford, CA: Stanford University Press.

   (1994). Secondary Education and Political Attitudes: Examining the Effects on Political Tolerance of the "We the People" Curriculum. Paper presented at the annual meeting of the Comparative and International Education Society, March, San Diego, CA.

Cacioppo, J. T., & Petty, R. W. (1982). The Need for Cognition. *Journal of Personality and Social Psychology, 42,* 116–131.

Campbell, A., Converse, P. E., Miller, W. E., & Stokes, D. E. (1960). *The American Voter.* New York: Wiley.

Carlson, M., Charlin, V., & Miller, N. (1988). Positive Mood and Helping Behavior: A Test of Six Hypotheses. *Journal of Personality and Social Psychology, 55*(2), 211–229.

Chaiken, S., & Stangor, C. (1987). Attitudes and Attitude Change. *Annual Review of Psychology, 38,* 575–630.

Chong, D. (1993). How People Think, Reason, and Feel about Rights and Liberties. *American Journal of Political Science, 37*(3), 867–899.

Cloninger, C. R. (1986). A Unified Biosocial Theory of Personality and its Role in the Development of Anxiety States. *Psychiatric Developments, 3,* 167–226.

   (1987). A Systematic Method for Clinical Description and Classification of Personality Variants. *Archives of General Psychiatry, 44* (June), 573–588.

Conover, P., & Feldman, S. (1986). Emotional Reactions to the Economy: I'm Mad as Hell and I'm Not Going to Take It Any More. *American Journal of Political Science, 30,* 30–78.

Converse, P. E. (1962). Information Flow and the Stability of Partisan Attitudes. *Public Opinion Quarterly, 26,* 578–599.

   (1964). The Nature of Belief Systems in Mass Publics. In D. Apter (ed.), *Ideology and Discontent.* New York: Free Press.

Costa, P. T. Jr., & McCrae, R. R. (1985). *The NEO Personality Inventory Manual: Form S and Form R.* Odessa, FL: Psychological Assessment Resources.

   (1992). *Revised NEO Personality Inventory (NEO-PI-R) and NEO Five Factor Inventory (NEO-FFI) Professional Manual.* Odessa, FL: Psychological Assessment Resources.

Dahl, R. (1977). On Removing Certain Impediments to Democracy in the United States. *Political Science Quarterly, 92,* 1–20.

Davidson, A., & Jaccard, J. (1975). Population Psychology: A New Look at an Old Problem. *Journal of Personality and Social Psychology, 31,* 1073–1082.

   (1979). Variables that Moderate the Attitude–Behavior Relation: Results of a Longitudinal Survey. *Journal of Personality and Social Psychology, 37,* 1364–1376.

Davidson, A. R., Yantis, S., Norwood, M., & Montano, D. E. (1985). Amount of Information about the Attitude Object and Attitude–Behavior Consistency. *Journal of Personality and Social Psychology, 49,* 1184–1198.

Davis, J. (1975) Communism, Conformity, Cohorts, Categories: American Tolerance in 1954 and 1972–73. *American Journal of Sociology, 81,* 491–513.

de Sousa, R. (1987). *The Rationality of Emotion.* Cambridge, MA: MIT Press.

Delli Carpini, M. X., & Keeter, S. (1993). Measuring Political Knowledge: Putting First Things First. *American Journal of Political Science, 37*(4), 1179–1206.

Devine, P. G. (1989). Stereotypes and Prejudice: Their Automatic and Controlled Components. *Journal of Personality and Social Psychology, 56*(1), 5–18.

Devine, P. G., Monteith, M. J., Zuwerink, J. R., & Elliot, A. J. (1991). Prejudice With and Without Compunction. *Journal of Personality and Social Psychology, 60*(6), 817–830.

Digman, J. M. (1989). Five Robust Trait Dimensions: Development, Stability and Utility. *Journal of Personality, 57*, 195–214.

Downs, A. (1957). *An Economic Theory of Democracy.* New York: Harper & Row.

Duch, R., & Gibson, J. (1992). "Putting Up With" Fascists in Western Europe: A Comparative, Cross-Level Analysis of Political Tolerance. *Western Political Quarterly, 45*, 237–273.

Duckitt, J. (1989). Authoritarianism and Group Identification: A New View of an Old Construct. *Political Psychology, 10*(1), 63–84.

Dunn, J. (1979). *Western Political Theory in the Face of the Future.* Cambridge University Press.

Eagly, A. H., & Wood, W. (1991). Explaining Sex Difference in Social Behavior: A Meta-analytic Perspective. *Personality and Social Psychology Bulletin, 17*(3), 306–315.

Edelman, M. (1964). *The Symbolic Uses of Politics.* Urbana: University of Illinois Press.

(1988). *Constructing the Political Spectacle.* University of Chicago Press.

Ehrlichman, H., & Halpern, J. N. (1988). Affect and Memory: Effects of Pleasant and Unpleasant Odors on Retrieval of Happy and Unhappy Memories. *Journal of Personality and Social Psychology, 55*(5), 769–779.

Ekman, P., Friesen, W. V., O'Sullivan, M., Chan, A., Diacoyanni-Tarlatzis, I., Heider, K., Krause, R., LeCompte, W. A., Pitcairn, T., Ricci-Bitti, P. E., Scherer, K., Tomita, M., & Tzavaras, A. (1987). Universals and Cultural Differences in the Judgments of Facial Expressions of Emotion. *Journal of Personality and Social Psychology, 53*(4), 712–717.

Enelow, J. M., & Hinich, M. J. (1984). *The Spatial Theory of Voting: An Introduction.* Cambridge University Press.

Fan, D. (1988). *Predictions of Public Opinion from the Mass Media.* New York: Greenwood.

Fazio, R. H., & Williams, C. J. (1986). Attitude Accessibility as a Moderator of the Attitude–Perception and Attitude–Behavior Relations: An Investigation of the 1984 Presidential Election. *Journal of Personality and Social Psychology, 51*(3), 505–514.

Fazio, R. H., & Zanna, M. (1981). Direct Experience and Attitude–Behavior Consistency. In L. Berkowitz (ed.), *Advances in Experimental Social Psychology* (pp. 161–202). New York: Academic.

Feldman, S., & Zaller, J. (1992). Political Culture of Ambivalence: Ideological Responses to the Welfare State. *American Journal of Political Science, 36*(1), 268–307.

Ferejohn, J. A., & Kuklinski, J. H. (eds.). (1990). *Information and Democratic Processes.* Urbana: University of Illinois Press.

Festinger, L. (1957). *A Theory of Cognitive Dissonance.* Stanford, CA: Stanford University Press.

Fishbein, M. (1980). A Theory of Reasoned Action: Some Applications and Implications. In H. Howe & M. Page (eds.), *Nebraska Symposium on Motivation,* 1979 (pp. 65–116). Lincoln: University of Nebraska Press.

Fishbein, M., & Ajzen, I. (1975). *Belief, Attitude, Intention and Behavior: An Introduction to Theory and Research.* Reading. MA: Addison-Wesley.

Fishbein, M., Ajzen, I., & Hinkle, R. (1980). Predicting and Understanding

Voting in American Elections: Effects of External Variables. In I. Ajzen & M. Fishbein (eds.), *Understanding Attitudes and Predicting Social Behavior*. Englewood Cliffs, NJ: Prentice-Hall.

Fishbein, M., & Coombs, F. (1974). Basis for Decision: An Attitudinal Analysis of Voting Behavior. *Journal of Applied Social Psychology, 4*, 95–124.

Fiske, S. T. (1981). Social Cognition and Affect. In J. Harvey (ed.), *Cognition, Social Behavior, and the Environment*. Hillsdale, NJ: Erlbaum.

Fiske, S. T., Kinder, D. R., & Larter, W. M. (1983). The Novice and the Expert: Knowledge-Based Strategies in Political Cognition. *Journal of Experimental Social Psychology, 19*, 381–400.

Fiske, S. T., Lau, R. R., & Smith, R. A. (1990). On the Varieties and Utilities of Political Expertise. *Social Cognition, 8*(1), 31–48.

Fiske, S., & Pavelchak, M. (1985). Category-based versus Piecemeal-based Affective Responses: Developments in Schema-triggered Affect. In R. Sorrentino & E. Higgins (eds.), *The Handbook of Motivation and Cognition: Foundations of Social Behavior*. New York: Guilford.

Fiske, S. T., & Taylor, S. E. (1991). *Social Cognition* (2d ed.). New York: McGraw-Hill.

Fletcher, J. (1988). Mass and Elite Attitudes about Wiretapping in Canada: Implications for Democratic Theory and Politics. *Public Opinion Quarterly, 53*, 225–245.

Forgas, J. P. (1992). On Mood and Peculiar People: Affect and Person Typicality in Impression Formation. *Journal of Personality and Social Psychology, 62*(5), 863–875.

Foster, C. B. (1984). The Performance of Rational Voter Models in Recent Presidential Elections. *American Political Science Review, 78*(3), 678–690.

Frank, R. (1988). *Passions With Reason*. New York: Norton.

Fried, R. M. (1990). *The McCarthy Era In Perspective*. New York: Oxford University Press.

Fujita, F., Diener, E., & Sandvik, E. (1991). Gender Differences in Negative Affect and Well-Being: The Case for Emotional Intensity. *Journal of Personality and Social Psychology, 61*(3), 427–434.

Galston, W. (1988). Liberal Virtues. *American Political Science Review, 82*(4), 1277–1290.

Geddes, B., & Zaller, J. (1989). Sources of Popular Support for Authoritarian Regimes. *American Journal of Political Science, 33*(2), 319–347.

Gibbard, A. (1990). *Wise Choices, Apt Feelings*. Cambridge, MA: Harvard University Press.

Gibson, J. L. (1987). Homosexuals and the Ku Klux Klan: A Contextual Analysis of Political Tolerance. *Western Political Quarterly, 40*, 427–448.

(1992). The Political Consequences of Intolerance: Cultural Conformity and Political Freedom. *American Political Science Review, 86*(2), 338–356.

Gibson, J. L., & Bingham, R. D. (1985). *Civil Liberties and Nazis: The Skokie Free-Speech Controversy*. New York: Praeger.

(1983). Elite Tolerance of Nazi Rights. *American Politics Quarterly, 11*, 403–42.

Gibson, J. L., & Duch, R. M. (1991). Elitist Theory and Political Tolerance in Western Europe. *Political Behavior, 13*(3), 191–212.

Goldberg, L. R. (1990). An Alternative "Description of Personality": The Big-

Five Factor Structure. *Journal of Personality and Social Psychology, 59*(6), 1216–1229.

Goldstein, R. J. (1987). The United States. In J. Donnelly & R. E. Howard (eds.), *International Handbook of Human Rights* (pp. 429–456). New York: Greenwood.

Granberg, D., & Holmberg, S. (1988). *The Political System Matters.* Cambridge University Press.

Gray, J. A. (1981). The Psychophysiology of Anxiety. In R. Lynn (ed.), *Dimensions of Personality: Papers in Honour of H. J. Eysenck.* New York: Pergamon.

(1984). The Hippocampus as an Interface between Cognition and Emotion. In M. L. Roitblar, T. G. Bever, & M. S. Terrace (eds.), *Animal Cognition.* Hillsdale, NJ: Erlbaum.

(1985). The Neuropsychology of Anxiety. In C. D. Spielberger (ed.), *Stress and Anxiety* (pp. 201–227). Washington, DC: Hemisphere.

(1987a). The Neuropsychology of Emotion and Personality. In S. M. Stahl, S. D. Iversen, & E. C. Goodman (eds.), *Cognitive Neurochemistry* (pp. 171–190). Oxford University Press.

(1987b). Perspectives on Anxiety and Impulsivity: A Commentary. *Journal of Research in Personality, 21*, 493–509.

(1987c). *The Psychology of Fear and Stress* (2d ed.). Cambridge University Press.

(1988). Anxiety and Personality. In M. Roth, R. Noyes Jr., & G. D. Burrows (eds.), *Handbook of Anxiety, vol. 1: Biological, Clinical and Cultural Perspectives* (pp. 231–257). New York: Elsevier.

(1990). Brain Systems that Mediate both Emotion and Cognition. *Cognition and Emotion, 4*(3), 269–288.

Green, D. P., & Waxman, L. M. (1987). Direct Threat and Political Tolerance: An Experimental Analysis of the Tolerance of Blacks Toward Racists. *Public Opinion Quarterly, 51*, 149–165.

Gutmann, A. (1987). *Democratic Education.* Princeton, NJ: Princeton University Press.

Hamilton, A. (1961). Federalist No. 11. In *The Federalist Papers.* Cleveland: World.

Haney, C., Banks, C., & Zimbardo, P. (1983). Interpersonal Dynamics in a Simulated Prison. *International Journal of Criminology and Penology, 1*, 69–97.

Hanson, R. L. (1989). Democracy. In T. Ball, J. Farr, & R. L. Hanson (eds.), *Political Innovation and Conceptual Change* (pp. 68–89). Cambridge University Press.

(1993). Deliberation, Tolerance and Democracy. In G. E. Marcus & R. L. Hanson (eds.), *Reconsidering the Democratic Public* (pp. 273–286). University Park : Pennsylvania State University Press.

Hastie, R. (1986). A Primer of Information-Processing Theory for the Political Scientist. In R. Lau & D. Sears (eds.), *Political Cognition.* Hillsdale, NJ: Erlbaum.

Herblein, T. A., & Black, J. S. (1976). Attitudinal Specificity and the Prediction of Behavior in a Field Setting. *Journal of Personality and Social Psychology, 33*, 474–479.

Higgins, T. E., & King, G. (1981). Accessibility of Social Constructs: Information-processing Consequences of Indvidual and Contextual Variation. In

N. Cantor & J. F. Kihklstrom (eds.), *Personality, Cognition, and Social Interaction* (pp. 69–121). Hillsdale, NJ: Erlbaum.

Hobbes, T. (1968). *Leviathan.* London: Penguin.

Hume, D. (1739–40). *A Treatise of Human Nature.* London: Penguin.

(1975). *Enquiries Concerning Human Understanding and Concerning the Principles of Morals* (3d ed.). Oxford University Press.

Huntington, S. P. (1981). *American Politics: The Promise of Disharmony.* Cambridge, MA: Harvard University Press.

Iyengar, S., & Kinder, D. (1987). *News That Matters: Television and American Public Opinion.* University of Chicago Press.

Jackman, M. R. (1978). General and Applied Tolerance: Does Education Increase Commitment to Racial Integration? *American Journal of Political Science, 22*(2), 302–324.

Jackman, R. (1972). Political Elites, Mass Publics, and Support for Democratic Principles. *Journal of Politics, 34,* 753–773.

Janis, I. L. (1982). *Groupthink* (2d ed.). Boston: Houghton Mifflin.

Janis, I. L., & Mann, L. (1977). *Decision Making.* New York: Free Press.

John, O. P. (1990). The "Big Five" Factor Taxonomy: Dimensions of Personality in the Natural Language and in Questionnaires. In L. A. Pervin (ed.), *Handbook of Personality Theory and Research* (pp. 66–100). New York: Guilford.

Jones, E. E., & Goethals, G. (1972). Order Effects in Impression Formation. In E. E. Jones, D. E. Kanouse, H. H. Kelley, R. E. Nisbett, S. Valins, & B. Weiner (eds.), *Attribution: Perceiving the Causes of Behavior.* Morristown, NJ: General Learning Press.

Judd, C. M., & Krosnick, J. A. (1989). The Structural Bases of Consistency Among Political Attitudes: Effects of Expertise and Attitude Importance. In A. R. Pratkanis, S. J. Breckler, & A. G. Greenwald (eds.), *Attitude Structure and Function* (pp. 99–128). Hillsdale, NJ: Erlbaum.

Kahneman, D., Slovic, P., & Tversky, A. (1982). *Judgment under Uncertainty: Heuristics and Biases.* Cambridge University Press.

Kallgren, C. A., & Wood, W. (1986). Access to Attitude-Relevant Information in Memory as a Determinant of Attitude–Behavior Consistency. *Journal of Experimental Social Psychology, 22,* 328–338.

Kant, I. (1970). Idea for a Universal History with a Cosmopolitan Purpose. In H. Reiss (ed.), *Kant's Political Writings* (pp. 41–53). Cambridge University Press.

(1977). *Prolegomena to Any Future Metaphysics* (Paul Carus, trans., revised by James W. Ellington, ed.). Indianapolis: Hackett.

Kelley, S., & Mirer, T. (1974). The Simple Act of Voting. *American Political Science Review, 68,* 572–591.

Kelman, H. (1974). Attitudes are Alive and Well and Gainfully Employed in the Sphere of Action. *American Psychologist, 29,* 310–324.

Kelman, H., & Hamilton, V. L. (1989). *Crimes of Obedience.* New Haven, CT: Yale University Press.

Key, V. O. Jr. (1961). *Public Opinion and American Democracy.* New York: Knopf.

Kiesler, C. A., Nisbett, R. E., & Zanna, M. (1969). On Inferring One's Beliefs from One's Behavior. *Journal of Personality and Social Psychology, 11,* 321–327.

Kinder, D. R., & Sears, D. (1981). Prejudice and Politics: Symbolic Racism Versus Racial Threat to the Good Life. *Journal of Personality and Social Psychology, 40,* 414–431.

(1985). Public Opinion and Political Action. In G. Lindzey & E. Aronson (eds.), *Handbook of Social Psychology* (pp. 659–742). New York: Random House.

King, G. (1986). How Not To Lie with Statistics: Avoiding Common Mistakes in Quantitative Political Science. *American Journal of Political Science, 30,* 666–687.

Kling, A. (1986). Neurological Correlates of Social Behavior. In M. Gruter & R. Masters (eds.), *Ostracism: A Social Biological Phenomenon* (pp. 27–38). New York: Elsevier.

(1987). Brain Mechanisms and Social/Affective Behavior. *Social Science Information, 26,* 375–384.

Kling, A., & Steklis, H. D. (1976). A Neural Substrate for Affiliative Behavior in Nonhuman Primates. *Brain, Behavior and Evolution, 13,* 216–238.

Kosslyn, S. M., & Koenig, O. (1992). *Wet Mind: The New Cognitive Neuroscience.* New York: Free Press.

Krosnick, J. (1989). Attitude Importance and Attitude Accessibility. *Journal of Personality and Social Psychology Bulletin, 15,* 297–308.

(1990). Government Policy and Citizen Passion. *Political Behavior, 12,* 59–92.

Krosnick, J. A., & Kinder, D. R. (1990). Altering the Foundations of Support for the President through Priming. *American Political Science Review, 84*(2), 497–512.

Kuklinski, J., Riggle, E., Ottati, V., Schwarz, N., & Wyer, R. (1987). Why the Slippage? Explaining Why People Support Abstract Principles More than the Application of Them. Paper presented at the annual meeting of the Midwest Political Science Association, Chicago.

(1991). The Cognitive and Affective Bases of Political Tolerance Judgments. *American Journal of Political Science, 35*(1), 1–27.

(1993). Thinking about Political Tolerance, More or Less, With More or Less Information. In G. E. Marcus & R. L. Hanson (eds.), *Reconsidering the Democratic Public.* University Park: Pennsylvania State University Press.

Lane, R., & Sears, D. (1964). *Public Opinion.* Englewood Cliffs, NJ: Prentice-Hall.

Lanzetta, J. T., & Englis, B. G. (1989). Expectations of Cooperation and Competition and Their Effects on Observers' Vicarious Emotional Responses. *Journal of Personality and Social Psychology, 56*(4), 543–554.

LaPiere, R. T. (1934). Attitudes vs. Actions. *Social Forces,* 13, 230–237.

Larsen, R. J., & Ketelaar, T. (1989). Extraversion, Neuroticism, and Susceptibility to Positive and Negative Mood Induction Procedures. *Personality and Individual Differences, 10,* 1221–1228.

(1991). Personality and Susceptibility to Positive and Negative Emotional States. *Journal of Personality and Social Psychology, 61*(1), 132–140.

Larson, D. W. (1985). *The Origins of Containment: A Psychological Explanation.* Princeton, NJ: Princeton University Press.

Lavine, H., Thomsen, C. J., & Gonzales, M. H. (1994). Political Expertise and

Value–Attitude Relations: The Value-based Mediation of Political Attitude Consistency. Unpublished manuscript.

Lawrence, D. (1976). Procedural Norms and Tolerance: A Reassessment. *American Political Science Review, 70*(1), 70–80.

Lazarsfeld, P. F., Berelson, B., & Gaudet, H. (1944). *The People's Choice*. New York: Duell, Sloan, & Pearce.

Lazarus, R. (1982). Thoughts on the Relations of Emotion and Cognition. *American Psychologist, 37*, 1019–1024.

(1984). On the Primacy of Cognition. *American Psychologist, 39*, 124–129.

Leventhal, H. (1970). Findings and Theory in the Study of Fear Communications. In L. Berkowitz (ed.), *Advances in Experimental Social Psychology*. New York: Academic.

LeVine, R. A., & Campbell, D. T. (1972). *Ethnocentrism: Theories of Conflict, Ethnic Attitudes and Group Behavior*. New York: Wiley.

Lewicki, P. (1986). *Nonconscious Social Information Processing*. New York: Academic.

Linville, P. W., & Jones, E. E. (1980). Polarized Appraisals of Out-Group Members. *Journal of Personality and Social Psychology, 38*(5), 689–703.

Luskin, R. C. (1990). Explaining Political Sophistication. *Political Behavior, 12*(4), 331–361.

(1991). Abusus non tollit usum: Standardized Coefficients, Correlations, and R^2. *American Journal of Political Science, 31*, 1032–1046.

Lyons, W., & Scheb, J. M. (1992). Ideology and Candidate Evaluation in the 1984 and 1988 Presidential Elections. *Journal of Politics, 54*, 573–584.

MacLeod, C., & Mathews, A. (1988). Anxiety and the Allocation of Attention to Threat. *Quarterly Journal of Experimental Psychology, 40A*(4), 653–670.

Madison, J., Hamilton, A., & Jay, J. (1961). *The Federalist Papers*. Cleveland: World.

Mansbridge, J. J. (1980). *Beyond Adversary Democracy*. New York: Basic.

Marcus, G. E. (1988a). Democratic Theories and the Study of Public Opinion. *Polity, 21*(1), 25–44.

(1988b). The Structure of Emotional Response: 1984 Presidential Candidates. *American Political Science Review, 82*(3), 735–761.

(1991). Emotions and Politics: Hot Cognitions and the Rediscovery of Passion. *Social Science Information, 30*(2), 195–232.

Marcus, G. E., & Hanson, R. (eds.). (1993). *Reconsidering the Democratic Public*. University Park: Pennsylvania State University Press.

Marcus, G. E., & MacKuen, M. (1993). Anxiety, Enthusiasm and the Vote: The Emotional Underpinnings of Learning and Involvement during Presidential Campaigns. *American Political Science Review, 87*(3), 688–701.

Masters, R., & Sullivan, D. (1993). Nonverbal Behavior and Leadership: Emotion and Cognition in Political Attitudes. In S. Iyengar & W. McGuire (eds.), *Explorations in Political Psychology*. Durham, NC: Duke University Press.

Masters, R. D., Frey, S., & Bente, G. (1991). Dominance & Attention: Images of Leaders in German, French, & American TV News. *Polity, 23*(4), 373–394.

Mauro, R., Sato, K., & Tucker, J. (1992). The Role of Appraisal in Human

Emotions: A Cross-Cultural Study. *Journal of Personality and Social Psychology*, 62(2), 301–317.

Mayer, J. D., DiPaolo, M., & Salovey, P. (1990). Perceiving Affective Content in Ambiguous Visual Stimuli: A Component of Emotional Intelligence. *Journal of Personality Assessment*, 54, 772–781.

McClosky, H. (1964). Consensus and Ideology in American Politics. *American Political Science Review*, 58, 361–382.

McClosky, H., & Brill, A. (1983). *Dimensions of Tolerance*. New York: Sage.

McClosky, H., & Zaller, J. (1984). *The American Ethos: Public Attitudes toward Capitalism and Democracy*. Cambridge, MA: Harvard University Press.

McGraw, K. M., & Pinney, N. (1990). The Effects of General and Domain-Specific Expertise on Political Memory and Judgment. *Social Cognition*, 8(1), 9–30.

McGuire, W. J. (1985). Attitudes and Attitude Change. In G. Lindzey & E. Aronson (eds.), *Handbook of Social Psychology* (pp. 243–346). New York: Holt, Rinehart, & Winston.

(1993). The Poly-Psy Relationship: Three Phases of a Long Affair. In S. Iyengar & W. J. McGuire (eds.), *Explorations in Political Psychology* (pp. 9–35). Durham, NC: Duke University Press.

Mendus, S. (1989). *Toleration and the Limits of Liberalism*. London: MacMillan.

Mill, J. S. (1956 [1861]). *On Liberty*. Indianapolis: Bobbs-Merrill.

Millar, M. G., & Tesser, A. (1986). Effects of Affective and Cognitive Focus on the Attitude–Behavior Relation. *Journal of Personality and Social Psychology*, 51(2), 270–276.

(1989). The Effects of Affective–Cognitive Consistency and Thought on the Attitude–Behavior Relationship. *Journal of Experimental Social Psychology*, 25, 189–202.

Mishkin, M., & Appenzeller, T. (1987). The Anatomy of Memory. *Scientific American*, 256, 80–89.

Mogg, K., Mathews, A., Bird, C., & Macgregor-Morris, R. (1990). Effects of Stress and Anxiety on the Processing of Threat Stimuli. *Journal of Personality and Social Psychology*, 59(6), 1230–1237.

Mueller, J. (1992). Democracy and Ralph's Pretty Good Grocery: Elections, Equality, and the Minimal Human Being. *American Journal of Political Science*, 36(4), 983–1003.

Neuman, R. (1986). *The Paradox of Mass Politics: Knowledge and Opinion in the American Electorate*. Cambridge, MA: Harvard University Press.

Nunn, C. Z., Crockett, H. J., & Williams, J. A. (1978). *Tolerance for Nonconformity*. San Francisco: Jossey-Bass.

Okin, S. (1989). Reason and Feelings in Thinking about Justice. *Ethics*, 99 (January), 229–249.

Ordeshook, P. (1986). *Game Theory and Political Theory*. Cambridge University Press.

Ottati, V. C., Riggle, E. J., Wyer, R. S., Schwarz, N., & Kuklinski, J. (1989). Cognitive and Affective Bases of Opinion Survey Responses. *Journal of Personality and Social Psychology*, 57(3), 404–415.

Page, B. I., & Shapiro, R. Y. (1992). *The Rational Public*. University of Chicago Press.

Paine, T. (1973). *The Rights of Man.* Garden City, NY: Anchor.

Pateman, C. (1970). *Participation and Democratic Theory.* Cambridge University Press.

Petty, R. T., & Cacioppo, J. E. (1986). *Communications and Persuasion.* New York: Springer-Verlag.

Piazza, T., Sniderman, P., & Tetlock, P. (1989). Analysis of the Dynamics of Political Reasoning: A General Purpose Computer-Assisted Methodology. In J. Stimson (ed.), *Political Analysis* (pp. 99–119). Ann Arbor: University of Michigan Press.

Pierce, J. C., & Rose, D. D. (1974). Nonattitudes and American Public Opinion: The Examination of a Thesis. *American Political Science Review, 68,* 626–649.

Pierce, P. A. (1993). Political Sophistication and the Use of Candidate Traits. *Political Psychology, 14*(1), 21–35.

Plutchik, R. (1980). *Emotion: A Psychoevolutionary Synthesis.* New York: Harper.

Plutchik, R., & Kellerman, H. (eds.). (1989). *Emotion Theory, Research, and Experience, vol. 4: The Measurement of Emotions.* San Diego: Academic.

Pratto, F., & John, O. P. (1991). Automatic Vigilance: The Attention-Grabbing Power of Negative Social Information. *Journal of Personality and Social Psychology, 61*(3), 380–391.

Prothro, J. W., & Grigg, C. W. (1960). Fundamental Principles of Democracy: Bases of Agreement and Disagreement. *Journal of Politics, 22,* 276–294.

Rabinowitz, G., & MacDonald, S. E. (1989). A Directional Theory of Issue Voting. *American Political Science Review, 83*(1), 93–121.

Rabow, J., Hernandez, A. C. R., & Newcomb, M. D. (1990). Nuclear Fears and Concerns Among College Students: A Cross-National Study of Attitudes. *Political Psychology, 11*(4), 681–698.

Rahn, W. M., Aldrich, J. H., Borgida, E., & Sullivan, J. L. (1990). A Social–Cognitive Model of Candidate Appraisal. In J. Ferejohn & J. Kuklinski (eds.), *Information and Democratic Processes* (pp. 136–159). Urbana-Champaign: University of Illinois Press.

Rahn, W. M., Krosnick, J. A., & Breuning, M. (1992). Rationalization and Derivation Processes in Political Candidate Evaluation. Paper presented at the annual meeting of the Midwest Political Science Association, Chicago.

Rawls, J. (1971). *A Theory of Justice.* Cambridge, MA: Harvard University Press.

Rhine, R., & Severance, L. (1970). Ego Involvment, Discrepancy, Source Credibility and Attitude Change. *Journal of Personality and Social Psychology, 16,* 175–190.

Robinson, J. H. (1937). *The Human Comedy as Devised and Directed by Mankind Itself* (2d ed.). New York: Harper.

Rogers, R. W. (1983). Cognitive and Physiological Processes in Fear Appeals and Attitude Change: A Revised Theory of Protection Motivation. In J. T. Cacioppo & R. E. Petty (eds.), *Social Psychophysiology: A Source Book.* New York: Guildford.

Russell, J. A. (1980). A Circumplex Model of Affect. *Journal of Personality and Social Psychology, 39,* 1161–1178.

(1983). Pancultural Aspects of Human Conceptual Organization of Emotions. *Journal of Personality and Social Psychology, 45*(6), 1281–1288.

Russell, J. A., & Bullock, M. (1985). Multidimensional Scaling of Facial Expressions: Similarity From Preschoolers to Adults. *Journal of Personality and Social Psychology, 48*(5), 1290–1298.

Russell, J. A., Lewicka, M., & Niit, T. (1989). A Cross-Cultural Study of a Circumplex Model of Affect. *Journal of Personality and Social Psychology, 57*(5), 848–856.

Russell, J. A., Weiss, A., & Mendelsohn, G. A. (1989). Affect Grid: A Single-Item Scale of Pleasure and Arousal. *Journal of Personality and Social Psychology, 57*(3), 493–502.

Sacks, C. H., & Bugental, D. B. (1987). Attributions as Moderators of Affective and Behavioral Responses to Social Failure. *Journal of Personality and Social Psychology, 53*(5), 939–947.

Salovey, P., & Mayer, J. D. (1990). Emotional Intelligence. *Imagination, Cognition, and Personality, 9*, 185–211.

Saltzer, E. (1981). Cognitive Moderators of the Relationship between Behavioral Intentions and Behavior. *Journal of Personality and Social Psychology, 41*, 260–271.

Sartori, G. (1987). *The Theory of Democracy Revisited.* Chatham, NJ: Chatham House.

Scarman, L. (1987). Toleration and the Law. In S. Mendus & D. Edwards (eds.), *On Toleration.* Oxford University Press.

Schachter, S., & Singer, J. E. (1962). Cognitive, Social, and Physiological Determinants of Emotional State. *Psychological Review, 69*(5), 379–399.

Schatz, R. T., & Fiske, S. T. (1992). International Reactions to the Threat of Nuclear War: The Rise and Fall of Concern in the Eighties. *Political Psychology, 13*(1), 1–29.

Schumpeter, J. A. (1943). *Capitalism, Socialism and Democracy.* London: Allen & Unwin.

Schwartz, S. H. (1978). Temporal Instability as a Moderator of the Attitude–Behavior Relationship. *Journal of Personality and Social Psychology, 36,* 715–724.

Sears, D. O. (1990). Symbolic Politics: A Socio-Psychological Analysis. Paper presented at the annual scientific meetings of the International Society of Political Psychology, Washington, DC.
    (1993). Symbolic Politics: A Socio-Psychological Theory. In S. Iyengar & W. J. McGuire (eds.), *Explorations in Political Psychology* (pp. 113–149). Durham, NC: Duke University Press.

Sears, D. O., Hensler, C., & Speer, L. (1979). Whites' Opposition to "Busing": Self-interest or Symbolic Politics? *American Political Science Review, 73,* 369–385.

Sears, D. O., Lau, R. R., Tyler, T. R., & Allen, H. M. Jr. (1980). Self-Interest vs. Symbolic Politics in Policy Attitudes and Presidential Voting. *American Political Science Review, 74*(3), 670–684.

Seligman, M. (1975). *Helplessness: On Depression, Development and Death.* San Francisco: Freeman.

Shamir, M. (1987). Personal communication.
    (1991). Political Intolerance Among Masses and Elites in Israel: A Reevaluation of the Elitist Theory of Democracy. *Journal of Politics, 53,* 1018–1043.

Sherif, C. W. (1980). Social Values, Attitudes and the Involvement of the Self. In M. M. Page (ed.), *Nebraska Symposium on Motivation, 1979: Beliefs, Attitudes and Values* (pp. 1–64). Lincoln: University of Nebraska Press.

Sherif, C. W., Sherif, M., & Nebergall, R. (1965). *Attitude and Attitude Change.* Philadelphia: Saunders.

Sherif, M., & Cantril, H. (1947). *The Psychology of Ego-Involvements.* New York: Wiley.

Sherif, M., & Hovland, C. (1961). *Social Judgment.* New Haven, CT: Yale University Press.

Sivacek, J., & Crano, W. D. (1982). Vested Interest as a Moderator of Attitude–Behavior Consistency. *Journal of Personality and Social Psychology, 43,* 210–221.

Smith, E. R. A. N. (1989). *The Unchanging American Voter.* Berkeley and Los Angeles: University of California Press.

Smith, M. B., Bruner, J., & White, R. (1956). *Opinions and Personality.* New York: Wiley.

Sniderman, P. M. (1975). *Personality and Democratic Politics.* Berkeley and Los Angeles: University of California Press.

Sniderman, P. M., Brody, R. A., & Tetlock, P. E. (1991a). *Reasoning and Choice: Explorations in Political Psychology.* Cambridge University Press.

Sniderman, P. M., Fletcher, J. F., Russell, P. H., Tetlock, P. E., & Gaines, B. J. (1991b). The Fallacy of Democratic Elitism: Elite Competition and Commitment to Civil Liberties. *British Journal of Political Science, 21*(3), 349–370.

Sniderman, P. M., & Piazza, T. (1993). *The Scar of Race.* Cambridge, MA: Harvard University Press.

Sniderman, P. M., Tetlock, P., Glaser, J., Green, D. P., & Hout, M. (1989). Principled Tolerance and the American Mass Public. *British Journal of Political Science, 19,* 25–45.

Staub, E. (1989). *The Roots of Evil: The Origins of Genocide and Other Group Violence.* Cambridge University Press.

Stinson, L., & Ickes, W. (1992). Empathic Accuracy in the Interaction of Male Friends Versus Male Strangers. *Journal of Personality and Social Psychology, 62*(5), 787–797.

Stouffer, S. (1955). *Communism, Conformity and Civil Liberties.* New York: Doubleday.

Sullivan, D., & Masters, R. (1988). "Happy Warriors": Leaders' Facial Displays, Viewers Emotions, and Political Support. *American Journal of Political Science, 32*(2), 345–368.

Sullivan, J. L., Piereson, J., & Marcus, G. E. (1982). Political Tolerance and *American Democracy.* University of Chicago Press.

Sullivan, J. L., Shamir, M., Walsh, P., & Roberts, N. S. (1985). *Political Tolerance in Context.* Boulder, CO: Westview.

Sullivan, J. L., Walsh, P., Shamir, M., Barnum, D. G., & Gibson, J. L. (1993). Why Are Politicians More Tolerant? Selective Recruitment and Socialization Among Political Elites in New Zealand, Israel, Britain, and the United States. *British Journal of Political Science, 23*(1), 51–76.

Taylor, C. (1989). *Sources of the Self.* Cambridge, MA: Harvard University Press.

Tellegen, A. (1982). A Brief Manual for the Differential Personality Questionnaire. Unpublished manuscript.

Tesser, A., & Clary, G. (1978). Affect Control: Process Constraints versus Catharsis. *Cognitive Therapy and Research, 2,* 265–274.

Thompson, D. (1970). *The Democratic Citizen: Social Science and Democratic Theory in the Twentieth Century.* Cambridge University Press.

Tocqueville, A. (1974 [1835]). *Democracy in America.* New York: Schocken.

Usala, P. D., & Hertzog, C. (1991). Evidence of Differential Stability of State and Trait Anxiety in Adults. *Journal of Personality and Social Psychology, 60*(3), 471–479.

Volkan, V. D. (1988). *The Need to Have Enemies and Allies.* Northvale, NJ: Aronson.

Warshaw, P., & Davis, F. (1985). Disentangling Behavioral Intentions and Behavioral Expectations. *Journal of Experimental Social Psychology, 21,* 213–228.

Watson, D. (1988a). Intraindividual and Interindividual Analyses of Positive and Negative Affect: Their Relation to Health Complaints, Perceived Stress, and Daily Activities. *Journal of Personality and Social Psychology, 54*(6), 1020–1030.

(1988b). The Vicissitudes of Mood Measurement: Effects of Varying Descriptors, Time Frames, and Response Formats on Measures of Positive and Negative Affect. *Journal of Personality and Social Psychology, 55*(1), 128–141.

Watson, D., Clark, L. A., & Tellegen, A. (1984). Cross-Cultural Convergence in the Structure of Mood: A Japanese Replication and a Comparison with U.S. Findings. *Journal of Personality and Social Psychology, 47*(1), 127–144.

(1988). Development and Validation of Brief Measures of Positive and Negative Affect: The PANAS Scales. *Journal of Personality and Social Psychology, 54*(6), 1063–1070.

Watson, D., & Tellegen, A. (1985). Toward a Consensual Structure of Mood. *Psychological Bulletin, 98,* 219–235.

Weigel, R. H., & Newman, L. S. (1976). Increasing Attitude–Behavior Correspondence by Broadening the Scope of the Behavioral Measure. *Journal of Personality and Social Psychology, 33,* 793–802.

Wicker, A. W. (1969). Attitudes versus Actions: The Relationship of Verbal and Overt Behavioral Responses to Attitude Objects. *Journal of Social Issues, 25,* 41–78.

Williams, D. G. (1990). Effects of Psychoticism, Extraversion, and Neuroticism in Current Mood: A Statistical Review of Six Studies. *Personality and Individual Differences, 11*(6), 615–630.

Wilson, T. D., Dunn, D. S., Bybee, J. A., Hyman, D. B., & Rotondo, J. A. (1984). Effects of Analyzing Reasons on Attitude–Behavior Consistency. *Journal of Personality and Social Psychology, 47*(1), 5–16.

Wilson, T. D., Dunn, D. S., Kraft, D., & Lisle, D. J. (1989). Introspection, Attitude Change, and Attitude–Behavior Consistency: The Disruptive Effects of Explaining Why We Feel the Way We Do. *Advances in Experimental Social Psychology, 22,* 287–343.

Wilson, T. D., Laser, P., & Stone, J. I. (1982). Judging the Predictors of One's Own Mood: Accuracy and the Use of Shared Theories. *Journal of Experimental Social Psychology, 18,* 537–556.

Wilson, T. D., & Schooler, J. W. (1991). Thinking Too Much: Introspection

Can Reduce the Quality of Preferences and Decisions. *Journal of Personality and Social Psychology, 60*(2), 181–192.

Wrightsman, L. S. (1969). Wallace Supporters and Adherence to "Law and Order." *Journal of Personality and Social Psychology, 13*, 17–22.

Young, J., Borgida, E., Sullivan, J. L., & Aldrich, J. (1987). Personal Agendas and the Relationship between Self-Interest and Voting Behavior. *Social Psychology Quarterly, 50*, 64–71.

Zajonc, R. B. (1980). Feeling and Thinking: Preferences Need No Inferences. *American Psychologist, 39*, 151–175.

Zaller, J. R. (1987). Diffusion of Political Attitudes. *Journal of Personality and Social Psychoglogy, 53*(5), 821–833.

(1992). *The Nature and Origins of Mass Opinion.* Cambridge University Press.

Zaller, J., & Feldman, S. (1992). A Simple Theory of the Survey Response: Answering Questions versus Revealing Preferences. *American Journal of Political Science, 36*(3), 579–616.

Zuckerman, M. (1991). *Psychobiology of Personality.* Cambridge University Press.

Index

affect, 105, 126, 163, 168, 202, 221–3, 258n.1, 261n.7

affective attitudes, 63, 96, 122–5, 215–16

Ajzen, I., 188–9, 257n.3

Altemeyer, B., 103, 155, 156, 166

American Civil Liberties Union, 188

American Nazis. *See* National Socialist Party of America

antecedent considerations: and behavioral intentions, 192, 194–5, 200; and civil liberties, 210; and contemporary information, 19–22, 24, 25, 111–12; gender as, 65; influence of, on tolerance levels, 76, 78, 137; threat perception as, 105–13; in tolerance literature, 25–33; and the tolerance model, 58–9. *See also* predispositions

anxiety, 10, 42–4, 62, 87–9, 91, 259n.9

Arkes, H., 227

attitude-behavior relationship, 184–5, 193, 219–20, 224

authoritarianism, 103, 166

Barber, J. D., 16

behavioral approach system (BAS), 41, 44–7, 50–1, 162, 163, 185–6, 223–4

behavioral consequences, 183, 184–5

behavioral intentions, 188–91, 266nn.3, 4, 6; and antecedent considerations, 192, 194–5, 200; and intensity, 191–205, 206; and tolerance, 191–4

behavioral inhibition system (BIS), 41–4, 48–9, 61–2, 80, 111, 147, 162, 163

Bingham, R. D., 183, 187

Bower, G. H., 64

Bradley, Thomas, 104

Brady, H., 156

Brill, A., 3, 28, 35, 59, 79, 116–19, 182, 222

Brody, R. H., 18

Cacioppo, J. T., 137, 166, 167, 170, 172, 212

capitalism, 4

civil liberties, 7, 117–20, 126, 210–12, 217–18

Civil Liberties Study, 117–18

Clark, L. A., 168

cognition, 17, 19, 166–7, 170, 172–5, 212, 265n.7, 266n.10

cognitive attitudes, 63, 94–5, 122–6, 220–4

cohort replacement, 34

Common Cause, 188

284

cal tolerance, 168–72; as predisposition, 16, 166, 169, 171; and
threat perception, 37; and tolerance, 164–8; treated in tolerance
literature, 26; typology of, 265n.1.
See also extraversion; openness; neuroticism; cognition
persuasion, 129–30, 132
Petty, R. W., 137, 166, 167, 170, 172,
212
Piazza, T., 57
Piereson, J., 26, 27, 119, 187, 257n.4
pluralism, 6
political activism, 186–8, 192, 206–7,
226–7
political ideology, 16, 18
political knowledge, 18, 140, 142,
222. *See also* expertise, political
political participation, 213
political socialization, 187
predispositions, 13; and civil liberties,
210, 211–12; and contemporary information, 33; of experts, 141–2;
shaped by group identification, 5;
and survey-experiments, 176; and
standing decisions, 20–2, 27–9; of
threat, 107–8, 109, 111, 113, 200,
202; and tolerance judgments, 9,
76, 216–17; treated in tolerance literature, 25–7. *See also* antecedent
considerations; education; expertise; gender; global threat; party
identification; personality; political
ideology; prejudice
prejudice, 4, 16, 104–5, 112–13, 148–
57
probability of power, 60–2, 65, 73–5,
78–80, 82–7, 90, 98, 104, 122, 136,
192, 200, 202, 215, 260n.7. *See also*
group malice; threat
protection motivation theory, 60–1
Prothro, J. W., 26, 27–8, 115, 116,
182, 186

R.A.V. v. *the City of St. Paul,* 121
racism. *See* prejudice
Rahn, W. M., 264n.5
rational-actor models, 60

rational choice theory, 17
reason, 10–12
reinforcers, 258n.2
responsibility, 267n.1
right wing, 156
Robinson, J. H., 11
Rogers, R. W., 73–4, 79

Scarman, L., 205–6
Sears, D. O., 16, 105, 210
Shamir, Michal, 260n.7
Shapiro, R. Y., 18
Smith, R. A., 142
Sniderman, P., 18, 57, 156
social learning, 119, 258n.5
socialization, 15, 16
source credibility, 23, 134, 137, 139
standing decisions, 65; and behavioral
intentions, 192; and current information, 35, 214–17; and decision
making, 176; and democratic principles, 59, 114–21, 126–7; of experts, 141–2; importance of, 125;
and personality, 164; and predispositions, 20–2, 27–9; and threat,
103, 106–9, 112, 113, 199–200,
202, 262nn.6, 7; and tolerance, 59,
76–7, 131, 147, 212–17
state of mind, 62–5
status, 140
Staub, E., 181
stereotypes, 4, 5
Stouffer, S., 26–7, 33–4, 36–7, 62,
187
strangers, 41–2
Sullivan, J. L., 26, 27, 119, 187, 198,
257n.4
survey-experiment, 56–8
symbolic politics literature, 15–16
symbols, 16

Taylor, S. E., 172–3
Tellegen, A., 168
Tesser, A., 278
Tetlock, P., 57
Thomsen, C. J., 141
threat: and contemporary informa-
tion, 9, 36–8, 51, 59–61, 101–4,